Heroes of the Nations

EDITED BY

Evelyn Abbott, M.A.

FELLOW OF BALLIOL COLLEGE, OXFORD

FACTA DUCIS VIVENT, OPEROSAQUE
GLORIA RERUM.—OVID, IN LIVIAM, 265.

THE HERO'S DEEDS AND HARD-WON
FAME SHALL LIVE.

LOUIS XIV.

LVDOVICVS XIIII DEI GRATIA FRANCIAE
ET NAVARRAE REX CHRISTIANISSIMVS.

LOUIS XIV. IN 1661.
(From an illustration, based on an old print, in Philippson's
Das Zeitalter Ludwigs XIV.)

LOUIS XIV

AND THE ZENITH OF THE FRENCH MONARCHY

BY

ARTHUR HASSALL, M.A.

STUDENT OF CHRIST CHURCH,
OXFORD

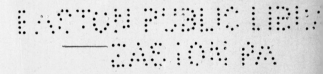

G. P. PUTNAM'S SONS

NEW YORK
27 WEST TWENTY-THIRD STREET

LONDON
24 BEDFORD STREET, STRAND

The Knickerbocker Press

1895

The Knickerbocker Press, New York

CONTENTS.

CHAPTER X.

CHAPTER XI.

CHAPTER XIV.

CHAPTER XV.

ILLUSTRATIONS.

The medals at the heads of chapters are from *Les Médailles sur les Principaux Événements du Regne Entier de Louis*, Paris, 1723.

[1] From Philippson's *Zeitalter Ludwigs des Vierzehnten*, Grote, Berlin.

[2] Smith, Elder, & Co.

[1] From Erdmannsdörfer's *Deutsche Geschichte von 1648-1740*,
Grote, Berlin.

[2] From Philippson's *Zeitalter Ludwigs des Vierzehnten*, Grote,
Berlin.

[3] From Courcy's *Coalition of 1701.*

NOTE ON THE AUTHORITIES OF THE
REIGN OF LOUIS XIV.

F EW periods of European history offer such unrivalled opportunities for investigation as that known as the Age of Louis XIV.

In the *Bibliographie de l'Histoire de France* by G. Monod, will be found an admirable list of the works dealing with the history of France in the 17th century. The contemporary sources of information are numerous. Of these the memoirs of Saint-Simon and those of Mme. de Motteville are the best known and the most valuable, and with the letters of Mme. de Maintenon, of Mme. de Sévigné, and of Charlotte Elizabeth, Duchesse d'Orléans, the memoirs of Villars, Retz, Choisy, Le Fare, and Torcy, the journal of Dangeau, and the memoirs of Louis XIV., *Pour l'Instruction du Dauphin*, enable the reader to appreciate the true character of the times. These and many other sources of information have been carefully sifted by the great historians of this particular period, of whom Martin, Ranke, Mignet, and Chéruel are the most distinguished.

The histories of France by Martin and Ranke, the *History of England, Principally in the 17th Century*, by Ranke, Mignet's *Négociations Relatives à la Succession d'Espagne sous Louis XIV.*, Chéruel's *Histoire de la France pendant la Minorité de Louis XIV. et sous le Ministère de Mazarin*, will continue to be consulted by all who make a serious study of French history in Louis XIV.'s reign.

Valuable supplementary works are the Duc d'Aumale's *Histoire des Princes de Condé*, Lair's *Nicolas Fouquet*, Clément's *Colbert*, Rousset's *Histoire de Louvois*, Lefevre-Pontalis' *John de Witt*, Legrelle's *La Diplomatie Française et la Succession d'Espagne*, Courcy's *Coalition de 1701*, Baudrillart's *Philip V. et la Cour de France*, and Parkman's volumes—*The Old Régime in Canada* and *Count Frontenac and New France under Louis XIV.* Equally important is the excellent series of *Instructions aux Ambassadeurs et Ministres de France* now in course of publication.

It is impossible to enumerate all the monographs and essays written to elucidate various episodes of Louis' reign.

Lavallée's *Histoire de la Maison Royale de Saint-Cyr ;* Lair's *Louise de la Vallière et la Jeunesse de Louis XIV. ;* Legrelle's *Louis XIV. et Strasbourg ;* Lanier's *Étude Historique sur les Rélations de la France et du Royaume de Siam ;* Reynald's *Louis XIV. et Guillaume III. ;* Dr. Döllinger's *Lectures on Louis XIV. and Mme. de Maintenon ;* Mr. Armstrong's *Elizabeth Farnese ;* Rocquains' *L'Esprit Révolutionaire avant la Révolution ;* are but a few instances of the wealth of material ready to the hand of the student.

In my attempt to write, with the aid of the knowledge gained from a study of some of the memoirs and histories of the time, a *Life of Louis XIV.* I have received very considerable assistance from Mr. Evelyn Abbott, Editor of this series. To him and to Mr. Charles E. Thompson, whose courteous help to me when choosing the portraits for the volume has been most valuable, I wish to tender my best thanks.

H.

OXFORD, February, 1895.

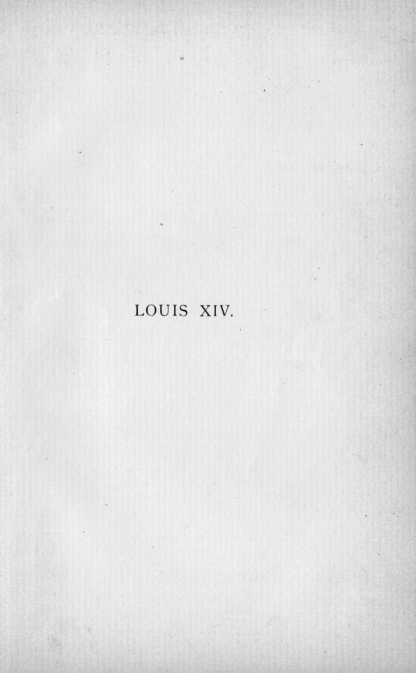

LOUIS XIV.

LOUIS XIV.

PROLOGUE.

HE character and position of Louis XIV. are peculiarly difficult to estimate, partly on account of the attitude taken towards him during his lifetime by his own subjects, partly owing to the entire misapprehension under which foreign nations laboured as to his real aims. The French people during more than two-thirds of his long reign made him into a god and worshipped him, while at the time of the Spanish Succession war a generation had grown up in England which, says Mr. Wyon in his *History of Great Britain during the Reign of Queen Anne*, regarded "Louis XIV. as a monster of ambition with a mission from the devil to make

slaves and Papists of the whole human race, a per-
fidious tyrant with whom it was useless to think of
entering into a compact, whom it was absolutely
necessary to bind with chains of iron."

Again at the present day, modern historical writers,
for the greater part hailing from France, are well-
nigh unanimous in wholesale condemnation of the
age of Louis XIV. on the ground that it was essentially the cause of the French Revolution. Even
allowing that it be strictly historical to say that
Louis' reign made the Revolution inevitable, it remains none the less true that the blame, if there be
any, must be shared by the people with the King.
The French nation made Louis, and Louis was the
epitome of the French nation. It is easy to sympa-
thise with the many hostile criticisms levelled at the
King by German historians, who cannot forgive the
devastation of the Palatinate or forget the loss of
Strasburg. But it is peculiarly ungracious, ungrate-
ful, and unhistorical for French writers who are well
acquainted with the history of their own country,
to allow themselves to be so carried away by feeble
republican predilections, as to pour virulent abuse
upon the most brilliant period of their history, and
their most hardworking, painstaking, and on the
whole successful ruler.

Louis has certainly as great a claim as Napoleon
to be considered a Hero. He, at any rate, left his
country holding a powerful position in Europe, and
when he died he could boast that his foes had never
entered Paris. In spite of his mistakes he succeeded
in placing Philip on the Spanish throne.

The French Revolution undoubtedly tended for a long time to damage Louis' reputation and to blind men to the real character of his work. And yet the Revolutionists only developed Louis' system of internal administration, and continued with vigour and success his foreign policy. To credit Louis with the evils under which France suffered during the eighteenth century is to ignore the history of the reigns of Louis XV. and Louis XVI. These monarchs, it is true, found themselves handicapped through the position of the nobles and the weight of taxation. But had they been energetic and enlightened administrators, had they adapted themselves to the needs of the day, France might by securing timely reforms have escaped from the horrors of revolution.

As it was, when Louis established a bureaucracy dependent on an absolutism, he gave the French government the shape which it preserved unchanged till 1789. His administrative reforms were admirably suited to the France of his own day. It was the fault of his successors that the bureaucratic system became an impassable barrier between the people and their rulers.

There is no doubt whatever that with the majority of his countrymen the rule of Louis XIV. was in the seventeenth century extremely popular. It was admirably calculated to arouse the enthusiasm of his subjects. The French, more than any other European nation, have always been most easily affected by the love of military glory. They have of all nations ever been sensitive of their prestige, and appreciative of a brilliant foreign policy.

Louis' reign was, as far as military glory was concerned, the most glorious in the annals of French history, and never did the prestige of the French arms stand higher. Even at the end of the Spanish Succession war, that prestige was nobly maintained by Villars. At no period in French history was the foreign policy of France conducted with greater ability or with more conspicuous success. In the clearness of his views on foreign policy, Louis was always essentially a Frenchman, while in his dogged perseverance, his close attention to details, his careful grasp of facts, and his recognition of the necessity of withdrawing from untenable positions, he showed that he possessed characteristics rarely found among Latin nations. Unlike George III., who never rose to a higher level than that of most of his subjects, Louis was in many respects head and shoulders above the majority of the Frenchmen of his day. And he was really great when dealing with questions bearing on the future welfare of France as a European Power. His foreign and colonial policy is superior to that of any of his predecessors or successors and should be keenly appreciated by his countrymen of the present day.

An unerring instinct told him that Belgium should be in French hands. He was equally bent upon securing Lorraine, Luxemburg, and Savoy. His attempts to make the Mediterranean a French lake showed consummate statesmanship, while if his colonial, Indian, and Siamese projects had been continued and wisely developed by his successors, France would have very practical reasons for looking back on his reign with gratitude and respect.

Whether he was revoking the Edict of Nantes, or was avenging an insult offered to his ambassador, or was appealing to the patriotism of the people against the impolitic demands of the insatiable allies after Oudenarde, Louis was always in touch with the majority of his subjects. He set a great value on himself as the holder of the kingly office and the nation accepted his estimate of its importance. In spite of the many faults of his rule, France was ably administered during his reign. The noble class, who hitherto had influenced the government of the country, were unfit to take any share in the administration. Like the Parisians of all time, they were wanting in balance, they had no principles, they were carried away by every passing impulse. The conduct both of the nobles and the Parisians during the Fronde troubles amply justified the establishment of a strong centralised monarchy. Accepted by the French nation as the only form of government possible after the years of anarchy, it soon became thoroughly popular.

In spite of the criticisms offered by Madame de Sévigné, Gui Patin, Bussy-Rabutin, and Ormesson, royalty came to be regarded by a large majority of the nation as the glorious personification of the unity and power of France. And with his natural acuteness of observation, his decision, and his grand manner, Louis satisfied the aspirations of his people. For more than fifty years he had the most brilliant Court in the world, and he directed the affairs of France and Europe with a magnificence which the reverses at the end of his reign could not efface. The history of the world presents few epochs on which civilisation and literature have thrown greater *éclat* than that of Louis XIV.

Louis was thus pre-eminently a Frenchman in the unique sympathy that existed between him and the nation—a sympathy seen in their aims, in love and in hate, in taste and in prejudice. As a man he may not have been great, but a great King he certainly was, and the age in which he lived and which bears his name was a great age. Whatever claim he may bear to the title of Hero must be based upon the determination and courage shown during the last fourteen years of his reign. In spite of the calamities which the war brought upon his country, in spite of the domestic afflictions which wellnigh overwhelmed him, Louis' skill and ability and courage succeeded, with honour and with comparatively small territorial loss, in extracting France from a death grapple with Europe. Few periods in the reign of any European monarch present more striking examples of real patriotism and heroism than will be found in the history of the great King of France during the years from 1707 to 1713.

CHAPTER I.

OUIS XIV. was born on the 5th of September, 1638, at Saint-Germain, in the Château Neuf. The news of this event was received with great rejoicings. The birth of the Dauphin in the pavilion of Henry IV. coincided with successes abroad, which must have recalled to men's minds the deeds of the King of Navarre.

The year 1638 brought with it the capture of Alsace by the French armies; it saw also French ascendancy established in the Mediterranean waters. The terrible Thirty Years' War was then at its height and till this year, in spite of the victorious career of Gustavus Adolphus, men were still doubtful as to the issue. Under the great Cardinal Richelieu,

France had plunged into the war; and the year 1638 proved to be the "turning-point of the struggle between France and the House of Austria."

The birth of Louis XIV. upset all the plans of the Court party, and strengthened the hands of Richelieu at home. The hopes of the opponents of the Minister had been founded entirely on the expectation that Gaston of Orleans, the brother of Louis XIII., would succeed to the throne, and destroy at one blow the work of Richelieu. These hopes were now scattered to the winds and in spite of the spasmodic resistance of the nobles during the Fronde, the birth of Louis XIV. decided the momentous question for France that the administrative reforms of Richelieu should be adhered to and developed. Aristocratic tyranny and selfishness were to yield to an irresistible despotism.

A year later Louis XIII. had another son, Philip, destined to become celebrated as the husband of the ill-fated Henrietta, daughter of Charles I. of England.

At the close of 1642 Richelieu died and with the beginning of the next year it became apparent that the reign of Louis XIII. was drawing to a rapid close. In April the King moved to the new Palace of Saint-Germain, where the air was purer than in Paris. Feeling his end was at hand, he devoted himself to religious exercises and to the settlement of all matters affecting the government of France. On the 25th of April he declared his wishes with regard to the future. In the event of his death his wife Anne of Austria was to be Regent, his brother Orleans to be Lieutenant-General. The real power, however, was to lie with the Council of Regency, a body composed of Mazarin, the Chancellor Seguier, Condé, and others. The members were to be irremovable and the Queen and Orleans were to refer to them all questions of importance. The appointment of such a Council was, as Mazarin said, an affront to the Queen.

On April 21st, the Dauphin was christened, Mazarin and the Princess of Condé being his sponsors, and after the ceremony, though only four and a half years old, he told his dying father that he had received the name Louis XIV. "Not yet, not yet," answered the sick monarch.

Within a month, on May 14th, Louis XIII. died, leaving his country in a far more prominent position than when he succeeded to the throne. France was now recognised "as the champion of the true rights of nations against the domination of an arrogant House and the Catholic reaction in its worst aspect." German Protestantism was by the combined efforts of France and Sweden practically secure. At home feudalism had received its death blow; lawless disorder and selfish tyranny were crushed. While Germany was torn in pieces through religious divisions, in France the Huguenots had become loyal subjects. The monarchy was steadily growing and already was beginning to symbolise the unity and the grandeur of France. This improvement in the position of France was due to Richelieu. Though his name is not associated with the treaties of Westphalia and of the Pyrenees or with the final overthrow of the great nobles in the

Fronde, he had prepared the way. Under her able minister France was supreme in diplomacy, in arms, and in letters.

France was left by Richelieu in a strong position. She held Alsace, Artois, Roussillon, and part of Catalonia. Victorious on the Rhine, she occupied Brisach and the Forest Towns. Sweden and the United Provinces were her trusted allies, the House of Savoy leant on her for protection. The capture of Arras laid open the road into the heart of the Spanish Netherlands.

Within France the policy of the great Cardinal seemed equally successful. The kingdom was peaceful and flourishing. Time to complete and consolidate his work was alone required. And there is little doubt that had Richelieu lived a few more years he would have established his system on so firm a basis that no Fronde would have been possible. For Richelieu, though intensely monarchical, in many points resembled the enlightened despots of the eighteenth century. He was keenly alive to the necessity of conciliating public opinion ; he often studied the *cahiers* of the States-General of 1614 to discover the popular needs. In 1626 he had summoned an Assembly of Notables and had laid before it his policy.

So loyally had this Assembly—composed of magistrates, financial officials, and merchants—supported his plans for the repression of the political designs of the Huguenots, for the creation of a navy and for the development of commerce, that just before his death he had resolved to call another such Assembly to strengthen his hands in the probable event of Louis XIII.'s death.

Unfortunately for his country Richelieu died before his great work was thoroughly consolidated, and France had in consequence to pass through upwards of ten years of confusion till his successor Mazarin was strong enough to complete the overthrow of the discordant elements within the kingdom and to place the monarchy at the head of an obedient and united France.

- No sooner was Louis dead than the *Parlement* of Paris—that close corporation of lawyers, that body of hereditary magistrates which had bought or inherited judicial places and which aspired to take the place of the States-General—at once asserted itself. In 1641 Richelieu had dealt what seemed a decisive blow at its political pretensions. He had forbidden it to take any part in or cognisance of state affairs. On financial matters they could remonstrate, but henceforward these turbulent magistrates were not to regard themselves as a political assembly. The minority of Louis XIV. was, however, an opportunity too good to be lost. Just as during the minority of Louis XV. so now the *Parlement* asserted its authority, and attempted to regain its former position.

Louis XIII. had appointed a Council to control the Queen Regent. On May 18th, four days after Louis XIII.'s death, the *Parlement* abolished this Council and placed the whole power in the hands of Anne of Austria. At the meeting of the *Parlement* the young King was present. On May 15th, the day after his father's death, Louis XIV. had left the ancient château of Saint-Germain and had made a solemn entry into Paris, amid the greatest enthusiasm. "The Queen," says Gui Patin, " arrived in Paris at four o'clock in the afternoon attended by ten thousand men, without reckoning the cavaliers and volunteers, who swarmed out of Paris to meet the little King." The Venetian ambassador was favourably impressed by the appearance of the youthful monarch, and anticipated an era of prosperity for France as soon as this prince " of noble aspect, with his air of greatness" had attained his majority.

On May 18th at 8 A.M. a *Lit-de-Justice* was held— a solemn assembly to which not only the *Parlement* but also the Dukes and Peers of France and the great officers of the Crown were summoned. The importance of the assembly lay in the attitude assumed by the *Parlement*. Over this *Lit-de-Justice* the young King in a violet dress presided. On the right of the throne stood his mother, on the left Madame de Lansac, his governess. Assisted by the latter Louis stood up and said the few words necessary to open the proceedings. The *Parlement*, filled with hopes of regaining their political influence, invested Anne with absolute power during the King's minority, and appointed the Duke of Orleans Lieutenant-General of the kingdom and President of the King's Council. The only symptom of future trouble was to be found in the words of Barillon one of the Presidents of the *Chambre des Enquêtes*, who asserted that the *Parlement* should have the power

Françoise, d. of Réné, Duke of Vendôme = Charles, Duke of Alençon (1495-1557)

Antony = Jeanne d'Albret, (1557-1562) Queen of Navarre

Charles, Cardinal of Bourbon

Margaret = Francis, Duke of Nevers

Henry IV. of France = Margaret, d. of Henry II. (1589-1610) = (2) Marie de' Medici

Louis, Prince of Condé
Henry, † 1588
Henry, † 1646
Louis II., The Great Condé

Henrietta = Charles I. of England
Maria

Gaston, Duke of Orleans = Marie, Heiress of Montpensier
La Grande Mademoiselle

Louis XIII. = Anne, d. of Philip III. (1610-1643) of Spain

Elizabeth = Philip IV. of Spain

Christina = Victor Amadeus I. of Savoy

Henrietta = (1) Philip, Duke of Orleans = (2) Charlotte Elizabeth, d. of Charles Louis, Elector Palatine

Anne Marie = Victor Amadeus II. of Savoy

Marie Louise = Charles II. of Spain

Elizabeth Charlotte = (2) Leopold Joseph, Duke of Lorraine

Louis XIV. (1643-1715) = Maria Theresa, d. of Philip IV. of Spain
(Louise de la Vallière)
(Madame de Montespan)

Philip, Duke of Orleans

Françoise of Bourbon = Philip, 'The Regent' (1715-1723)

Louise of Bourbon

Louise Elizabeth = Louis I. of Spain (1724-1725)

Louis, † 1752
Louis Philippe, † 1785
Louis Philippe (Égalité), executed 1793
Louis Philippe, King of France (1830-1848) = Maria Amelia, d. of Ferdinand I. of the Two Sicilies

Louis, the Dauphin, † 1711 = Maria Anna, d. of Ferdinand, Elector of Bavaria

The Count of Vermandois
Mlle. de Blois
The Duke of Maine
The Count of Toulouse

Charles, Duke of Berry † 1714 = Marie Louise

Louis, Duke of Burgundy, † 1712 = Marie Adelaide of Savoy

Philip, Duke of Anjou (Philip V. of Spain)

The Duke of Brittany, † 1712
Louis XV. (1715-1774)
Louis XVI. (1774-1793)

César, Duke of Vendôme = Françoise, Heiress of Mercoeur (1598-1665)

Louis (1665-1669)

Louis Joseph, General of Louis XIV. (1669-1712)

of urging measures for the reforms of the state. But his words received little support, so satisfied was the majority of the *Parlement* with the prospects of the reign. The work of Richelieu would be undone, the intendants would be dismissed, the Chancellor Pierre Seguier, one of Richelieu's ministers, would be replaced perhaps by Bailleul a member of the *Parlement*, perhaps by Châteauneuf, a noble who had suffered during the late reign. The policy of Richelieu would, in a word, be entirely reversed and Mazarin would at once return to Italy.

On the very evening of the 18th of May the *Parlement* knew the worst. The Queen had confirmed Mazarin as First Minister. The pupil and confidant of Richelieu, an Italian adventurer, a low-born ecclesiastic who could hardly speak the French language, had been deliberately chosen to continue Richelieu's work, the humbling of the Austro-Spanish House and the consolidation of the French monarchy. After the first surprise had worn off, men of the mental calibre of the Duke of Beaufort consoled themselves with the hope that the Queen would simply employ Mazarin temporarily, till she had learnt how to govern the kingdom. Mazarin's position had hardly been confirmed before the news of the battle of Rocroi came to strengthen and shed lustre upon the new government. The death of Richelieu had raised fresh hopes in the minds of the Spaniards and Imperialists. The time had, it seemed to them, come for striking a decisive blow at the heart of France—a blow that should have a telling effect upon the negotiations for peace, which had

already begun. But the youthful Enghien proved
equal to the task of defending France. Aided by
the rare gifts of the veteran Captain Gassion,
Enghien won a brilliant victory at Rocroi. France
was saved from all danger of invasion, Thionville
shortly afterwards fell before the victorious French
troops, and the way into Germany and the Low
Countries lay open for attack from the side of
France. The victory of Rocroi and the capture of
Thionville came most opportunely to the aid of the
government of Anne of Austria and Mazarin. For
the moment these successes silenced the voices of
intrigue and faction. They proved, moreover, to the
world that though Richelieu was dead, his spirit still
guided the foreign policy of France, and that the
Spanish leanings of Anne of Austria were completely
subordinated to her feelings of patriotism and affection for her son. These successes then reassured
the allies of France, disheartened her enemies, and
helped to establish the government on a firm basis
at home. Still the difficulties of Mazarin were
enormous. Though France was safe from fear of
invasion, though her armies were preparing if possible to advance into the heart of Germany and
dictate peace at the gates of Vienna, the attitude
of the enemies of the government was most threatening.

The Condé family were opposed to and jealous of
Mazarin; Madame de Chevreuse, who returned to
France in July was bitterly hostile to him; the Duke
of Beaufort, grandson of Henry IV. and Gabrielle
d'Estrées, headed a faction mainly composed of the

ANNE OF AUSTRIA.

lower *noblesse*, and was prepared to compass his
overthrow. Uncertain as to the future policy of the
government, the Huguenots were becoming unquiet,
and some of the provinces, owing to the heavy taxation, were discontented and ready to take advantage
of any weakness shown by those in authority. It
was difficult too to prevent Anne of Austria from
showering favours on the most unworthy objects.
With the indolent Orleans as Lieutenant-General,
the avaricious Henry of Condé in the Council, the
weak and good-natured Anne as Queen Regent, the
docile Pierre Seguier as Chancellor, and the ever
watchful and active Mazarin as Chief Minister, the
situation was well summed up in the lines:

> " La reine donne tout,
> Monsieur joue tout,
> M. le prince prend tout,
> Le cardinal fait tout,
> Le chancelier scelle tout."

But perhaps the most serious danger to the monarchy was to be found in the claims of Orleans and
the House of Condé to some of the most important
governorships in France. Already Henry of Condé
held Burgundy; his son-in-law, the Duke of Longueville, Normandy; while Provence was under the
Count of Alais, a relation of the Condé family. The
ambitious Henry of Condé now demanded Languedoc for himself, proposing to transfer Burgundy to
Enghien. Orleans was at the same time pressing
his claims for Champagne. It seemed that Richelieu's work was in imminent danger of being undone,
and that France would again suffer all the evils of

provincial governments under a feudal aristocracy which, humiliated by Richelieu, still preserved the memory of its former independence. The whole provincial question bristled with danger to the centralised system lately established by the great Cardinal.

By the end of 1643, however, Mazarin had by dint of patience, tact, fertility of resource, and tenacity of purpose triumphed over all the dangers which threatened, during the early days of the minority, the authority of the infant King. By appealing to Anne's maternal instinct he checked her over-liberality and induced her to adopt a more dignified and a firmer attitude towards the factions which surrounded her. He quieted the Huguenots by assuring them that the toleration of their religion should not be interfered with. He conciliated Orleans by allowing him the semblance of power, and he successfully undermined the influence of the dangerous Henry of Condé with the Queen. But with the handsome Beaufort and his faction, *Les Importants* as they were termed, owing to their ridiculous pretensions, he could make no terms. Reinforced by the returning exiles and especially by the clever and dangerous Duchess of Chevreuse, they threatened to become even dangerous.

The Duchess, whose exile by Louis XIII. should have been made perpetual, on her return in July at once attacked Mazarin indirectly. Having failed to secure for the Condé family Brittany, she attempted again unsuccessfully, to introduce her own friends into the Council. Defeated on this point she en-

2

FRANCOIS DE VENDOSME, Duc de Beaufort, Pair de France, s'est rendu signalé dans les guerres d'Italie, et des Pais Bas, mais principalement dans les troubles de Paris, ayant esté affectionné de tous les bons Francois, tant pour sa piete que pour les seruices qu'il a rendus a sa Ma.te en combatant valeureusem.t en plusieurs rencontres, pour la conseruation de l'Estat, et Monarchie Francoise.

A Paris chez B. Moncornet   Auec priuilege du Roy

BEAUFORT.

(From a print in the library of Christ Church, Oxford.)

deavoured to revolutionise the foreign policy of France and to bring about a Spanish alliance. Foiled by Anne's patriotism and defeated on all points she relinquished her policy of assailing Mazarin indirectly, and resolved by allying with Beaufort and the *Importants* to make a direct attack on the Minister's power. The exile of Madame de Montbazon, one of Beaufort's allies, owing to a quarrel with Madame de Longueville, determined Beaufort to assassinate Mazarin. But courage failed the conspirators, and Beaufort—*le roi des Halles*, as he was popularly termed—was arrested on September 2nd and the party of the *Importants* dispersed. The suddenness of the blow and the completeness of the overthrow of the *Importants* recalled the energetic measures of Richelieu. The latter lived again in the prompt and decisive action of his successor. The following lines composed at this time show the popular feeling on the subject :

" Il n'est pas mort ; il n'a que changé d'âge,
Ce Cardinal, dont chacun en enrage ;
Mais sa maison en a grand passetems ;
Maints Chevaliers n'en sont pas trop contens,
Ains l'ont voulu mettre en pauvre équipage
Sous sa faveur renait son parentage
Par le même art qu'il mettoit en usage,
Et, par ma foi, c'est encore leur tems ;
          Il n'est pas mort.

" Or nous taisons de peur d'entrer en cage ;
Il est en cour, l'éminent personage,
Et pour durer encor plus de vingt ans
Demandez-leur à tous ces Importans ;
Ils vous diront d'un moult piteux langage,
          Il n'est pas mort."

Mazarin was now firmly established in power. A guard of three hundred gentlemen accompanied him whenever he went out. In the Council he was supreme. The Secretaries of State, Le Tellier, Brienne, Guénégaud, and La Vrillière, were merely his agents and the Duke of Orleans was perfectly docile. Supported by the Queen, Mazarin decided all important matters without consulting anybody. The minister's position was immensely strengthened by the overthrow of Beaufort and his friends. He was now strong enough to deal with the serious question of the provincial governments. Champagne owing to its proximity to Lorraine could not be taken out of the hands of the central administration, so he offered and gave the government of Languedoc to Orleans with the ulterior design of stirring up enmity between him and Henry of Condé, who had set his heart on securing Languedoc for himself. All agitation in the provinces subsided early in 1644 and the government of the Regency seemed to have triumphed over its enemies both within and without the kingdom. Throughout this trying period Mazarin had acted with great discretion. The Queen was surrounded by men and women devoted to herself but hostile to Mazarin. To conciliate these enemies of Richelieu's home policy Mazarin reversed many of the late Cardinal's appointments. Madame de Senecey took the place of Madame de Bressac as maid-of-honour to Anne; Claude Le Bouthilier, the Superintendent of the Finances made way on June 5th for Bailleul and the Count of Avaux, Madame de Vaucelas succeeded Madame de Lansac as the

young King's governess. Léon Le Bouthilier, Count
of Chavigny, refused to remain in the Council after his
father's fall and his Secretaryship of State was given
to Henri de Lomenie de Brienne. The adoption of
these well-timed measures rendered Mazarin's position still more secure. At the end of 1643, too, another
change took place which affected the young King.
The headquarters of the royal family were moved
from the Louvre to the Palais Royal which Richelieu
had bequeathed to Louis XIV. In the apartments
of Richelieu the young monarch, then five years old,
was installed, while Mazarin also occupied rooms in
the palace. Under the care of his female attendants
Louis remained till his seventh year, though Villeroi,
Dumont, Péréfixe, and Laporte were respectively
nominated his governor, sub-governor, preceptor, and
first *Valet-de-Chambre*. His tastes were warlike and
consequently all his amusements had a military character. A troop of the noblest children in France was
organized, was subjected to military discipline, and
with the King was drilled each day. Louis delighted
in his young soldiers and was very fond of marching
at their head, up and down the long gallery of the
Louvre. "The King's amusements were all warlike" wrote the Count of Brienne, who was one
of the young soldiers; "as soon as his little hands
could grasp a stick the Queen had a large drum prepared upon which he played continually." His
principal companions were his brother the Duke of
Anjou, the young Count of Guiche, and Louis Henri
de Lomenie.

But these early years of Louis were not spent in

comfort. Whether through the avarice of the Cardinal or through the difficulty of getting sufficient
supplies, there is no doubt that the condition of the
Court was often that of extreme penury and discom-
fort. It is at any rate certain that the finances of
France were in a most desperate state. The good-
nature of Anne, the rapacity of the courtiers, the
large bribes which had to be paid to Orleans and
Henry Condé, the unscrupulousness of the farmers
of the taxes, the exorbitant rate of interest paid on
loans, the enormous expenses of the war—all these
explain the expenditure which in 1642 had been
ninety-nine millions, and by 1644 had increased to
one hundred and twenty-four millions.

The very method of collecting taxes gave opportunity for unlimited embezzlement, and Emery, the
Controller-General of Finance, was known to take
every advantage of a pernicious and oppressive system to enrich himself and the bankers who provided
the loans. To raise more money the *Taille* was
severely enforced, numerous fresh offices were created and sold, new taxes were levied. And when
these methods did not prove adequate a tax called
the *Toisé* was invented—a fine on all houses built
outside Paris since 1548, followed by a forced loan
on the richer classes.

These measures, however, not only failed in their
object, but caused popular revolts in the provinces
and provoked a strenuous resistance on the part of
the *Parlement* of Paris. In fact, the attitude taken
by the opponents of the policy of the government
was so threatening that Mazarin's position, if not

actually shaken, tended rapidly to become one of considerable danger.

Fortunately another brilliant success abroad came to his aid and gave a temporary prestige to the government. The year 1644 had witnessed the defeat of Rantzau by Mercy at Duttlingen, followed by the three desperate battles of Fribourg and the occupation of the Rhine valley by the French armies. The year 1645 saw the famous attempt of Turenne to arrange with the Swedes a concerted attack on Vienna. In March, 1645, the latter had won the battle of Jankowitz, and Mazarin had arranged that George Ragotsky of Transylvania should send an army to aid Torstenson while Turenne should enter Suabia and march on Vienna. The Emperor was saved by the want of a proper understanding among his enemies, by the illness of Torstenson, and by the defeat of Turenne at Mergentheim on May 5th. The French were checked for the time, but reinforced by Enghien and eight thousand men, Turenne aided his brilliant colleague to win the great battle of Nördlingen on August 3d, when Mercy was killed and the road to Vienna lay open. Though the weakness of the French army after the battle, the illness of Enghien, the retreat of Torstenson into Thuringia, and the retirement of Ragotsky rendered an advance on Vienna for the moment hopeless, the victory of Nördlingen had important effects. The death of Mercy was worth many successes to the French, but above all the brilliant victory of Nördlingen enabled Mazarin to deal firmly with his foes at home. The check at Mergentheim had encouraged the resistance to the government, and had impressed Mazarin with the necessity of being more than usually circumspect. All through his ministry the influence exercised by the course of events outside France upon the home policy of the government was immense, and Mazarin at once took advantage of the victory of Nördlingen to strike a blow at the growing opposition to his rule.

A *Lit-de-Justice* was held on September 7th, presided over by the young King. At this solemn assembly the Queen took a very firm attitude. The *Parlement* made no opposition to her demands, and the government withdrew the most unpopular of the taxes, the *Toisé* and the *Taxe des aisés*. To raise money numerous new offices were created, taxes were laid on various trades, and other expedients adopted for increasing the revenue.

Two days before the *Lit-de-Justice* Louis XIV. had attained his seventh year, and had arrived at the age when kings were accustomed to pass from the care of women into the hands of men. The Queen, anxious to give Mazarin the supervision of Louis' education, created him *Superintendent of the Education of the King*, and letters-patent were published announcing to the world the elevation of the Cardinal to this dignity. Until the King was much older Mazarin seems to have taken little active participation in Louis's education, which he left in charge of Villeroi his governor, Péréfixe his teacher, and La Porte his principal *Valet-de-Chambre*. Villeroi, whose principal claim to fame lies in the fact of his being the father of the Marshal Villeroi, so

prominent in the Spanish Succession war, was bound
to accompany Louis everywhere, to watch over his
safety, and generally to direct his actions. He
was a born courtier, and taught Louis at an early
age the usages of the Court. His son, the young
Villeroi, became one of the young King's companions and favourites. Péréfixe, his tutor, was a Doctor of the Sorbonne, who became later Archbishop
of Paris, and who was the author of a history of
Henry IV. composed for the benefit of Louis.

The young King, Madame de Motteville tells us,
" was taught to translate the *Commentaries of Cæsar* ;
he learnt to dance, to draw, and to ride, and he was
very skilful at all athletic exercises." He became
also greatly interested in history, and especially delighted in the wars of Charles the Great, St. Louis,
and Francis I. La Porte, the King's chief *Valet-de-
Chambre*, the author of some memoirs on the early
years of Louis XIV., served him faithfully, though he
apparently disliked Mazarin, who always ranked him
amongst his enemies. It is La Porte who asserts
that Mazarin cared nothing about Louis' education,
and was merely anxious to surround him with his
own friends and relations. On the contrary, it
seems certain that Mazarin was fully alive to the
necessity of carefully educating Louis, but during his
early years left the direction of it to his governors.
In 1647, when Louis was in his tenth year, he told
his mother at a ball at Fontainebleau that he wished
to take the government into his own hands. It was
discovered that one of Louis' attendants had suggested the thought, and Mazarin took the opportu-

nity of reprimanding Villeroi for the bad education which he was giving Louis. The Cardinal was always keenly alive to the danger of letting the King be surrounded by flatterers. "These perpetual flatteries are most prejudicial," wrote Mazarin, "and make the King dislike those who tell him the truth." The Cardinal was at that period too much occupied in the absorbing political movements of the time to be able to superintend closely the King's education. But in the later years of his own life it is well known how carefully and successfully he instilled into Louis the necessity of cultivating habits of order, of regular work, of perseverance, of firmness, and of taking into his own hands the supreme direction of affairs. It is probable that Louis disliked the Cardinal just as any child is apt to dislike his schoolmaster. There seems no doubt that he was encouraged in this dislike by several of those round him, who hoped in some way to profit by sowing discord between the King and the Minister. The numerous stories bearing on Louis' aversion to the Minister as shown on various occasions at Compiègne, at Fontainebleau, or at the Palais Royal, though doubtless in the main true, have no historical importance.

At this period, however, Louis was having forced upon him, by stern experience, convictions of immense importance to France.

Though the *Importants* had been crushed, and though the young Louis had successfully presided at the *Lit-de-Justice*, where the complaisance of the *Parlement* seemed to prove that absolutism in France rested on a secure basis, in reality the position of the government was most precarious. The political and social condition of France at the beginning of 1646 was full of danger, and at any moment the throne of the Bourbons might be shaken, if not overthrown. Though France was victorious abroad, and apparently tranquil at home, she was in truth on the verge of bankruptcy. The expedients of Mazarin to avert the inevitable crisis only tended to alienate every class. The discontent was universal, but for the moment the brilliant victories of the French armies postponed an outbreak in Paris.

Successful abroad and supreme at home, the government of the Regency seemed in 1646 to be in an almost enviable position. Anne of Austria presided over a brilliant circle, and the "happy hours" of Compiègne, Fontainebleau, and the Louvre were often looked back upon with regret by many who witnessed the glories of Versailles.

In this frivolous and yet magnificent, noble and yet vicious society, Enghien was the most striking figure. He was the hero of Rocroi and Nördlingen, and by these victories he had inaugurated the ascendancy of the arms of France, which continued till the battle of Blenheim. In spite of his treasonable conduct during the latter years of the conflict between France and Spain, he deserves to be placed with Richelieu and Turenne, as having aided in raising the monarchy to the highest point of splendour. On his return to the capital, he was welcomed by Mazarin and Anne of Austria, and even the little King was taught to praise his "Cousin." He was the favourite of Paris, and his father, the President of the

Council of State, demanded for him provinces and governments. But Enghien, though an admirable representative of the frivolity, the licentiousness, the lawlessness, and the magnificence of the society of which he had become the idol, had sterner work on hand, and was not content to remain in Paris while French armies were busy on the frontiers.

In the Low Countries, the Spanish forces had been successful, and Mardyck, Bergues, and Cassel had been retaken. It was necessary at once to recommence the war, and to resume active operations. The Court proceeded as far as Amiens, and in 1646 Gaston of Orleans and Enghien, at the head of the French armies, turned the tables on their enemies. Though Orleans's adhesion to the old routine of a campaign, which regarded long sieges as the height of military skill, checked the achievement of any brilliant successes in the field, Enghien's presence made itself felt, and the capture of Dunkirk at the end of the campaign was one of his greatest triumphs. His return to the capital was followed by the death of his father, and by his appointment to the civil and military command in Spain. On arriving at Barcelona in the spring of 1647, he found the influence of France almost destroyed in Catalonia, and the small French army in a very perilous condition. His well known failure before Lerida was his only reverse when leading a French army, and he was no doubt perfectly right in raising the siege of that strong fortress. Condé's check, however, unfortunately coincided with disasters and misfortunes to the French arms in other parts of Europe, and with an increasing deficit in the treasury and a deepening discontent at home.

The year 1647 seemed indeed fraught with disaster and even danger to the French monarchy. The failure of the French at Lerida had shaken its reputation in Catalonia, the revolt of the Weimarian troops and the quarrel of Gassion and Rantzau had for the moment not only destroyed Mazarin's hopes of securing the Spanish Netherlands, but, combined with the success of the Archduke Leopold in taking Landrecies, had even imperilled the French conquests from Courtrai to Dunkirk; even in Italy the French cause had suffered reverses. " Mazarin has grown pale," wrote the Venetian ambassador in August, 1647, "and his hair has turned white." Disaster abroad was accompanied by anxieties at home. In September of the same year the young Duke of Anjou fell dangerously ill; in November the King himself was attacked by small-pox, and the Queen, worn out, was seized with fever. The friends of Orleans actually looked forward to the reign of Gaston I., the *Importants* once more raised their heads, epigrams became numerous, certain members of the *Parlement* began to make preparations for asserting their rights on the first opportunity, and Paris, already seething with discontent, began to stir uneasily.

The recovery of the Queen and her sons destroyed the ambitious schemes of Orleans and the *Parlement*; the appointment of Condé to the command of the army of Flanders seemed to augur well for the future success of the French arms. But for a time bad

luck dogged all Mazarin's efforts, and his efforts to
make peace with the Empire seemed destined to
come to nothing. The Elector of Bavaria, who had
in 1647 signed the treaty of Ulm with France, now
early in 1648 broke the treaty and returned to his
allegiance to the Emperor. This defection seemed
to destroy all chance of an early peace with the Empire. But what was even a more serious blow to the
foreign policy of Mazarin was the conclusion of a
treaty (of Münster) between the United Provinces
and Spain, in January, 1648. Ever since the capture
of Dunkirk by the French, the Dutch had become
uneasy, lest the French should within the near
future secure the Belgian Provinces. This uneasiness was accentuated by the discovery that Mazarin
was endeavouring early in 1646 to arrange a peace
with Spain—the latter to yield the Spanish Netherlands to France, which country would on her part,
abandon all Catalonia and Portugal to the Spaniards.
To extend the French frontiers to the Scheldt was
always one of Mazarin's favourite schemes, and the
year 1646 seemed unusually favourable for the execution of this design. England occupied with her
Civil war could not interfere; Spain had had ample
opportunity of recognising not only the difficulty of
defending her distant and often disloyal Belgian
Provinces against the attacks of French and Dutch,
but also the vast importance of thoroughly conquering Catalonia, and if possible Portugal.

The Dutch opposition to this scheme soon showed
itself. It was feared in Holland that Antwerp in
French hands would not only rival Amsterdam and

so endanger the Dutch trade, but that the presence of a powerful neighbour, such as France, would be a constant menace to the liberties and independence of the Republic. Aided by these fears on the part of the Dutch, the work of Spanish diplomacy was easy. The ancient alliance between the French and the United Provinces was broken, and in January, 1648, the treaty between the Dutch and Spanish governments destroyed all chance of the French frontiers being pushed to the Scheldt.

But though the year 1648 opened so gloomily for the French foreign policy, four events revolutionised the condition of affairs in Europe and compelled the Emperor to agree to make peace. The victory of Turenne over the Bavarian troops at Zusmarshausen (May 17th) rendered Bavaria, now occupied by the troops of Turenne and Wrangel, useless as a check upon a march on Vienna ; the capture of Tortosa (July 13th) laid Spain open to a French invasion ; the success of the Swede Koenigsmarck in occupying Little Prague was a strong argument in the mouths of the Duke of Bavaria and the other German Princes who pressed the Emperor to make peace ; Condé's splendid and decisive victory at Lens on August 20th, after a long campaign at the head of a very inferior force, finally decided the Emperor to conclude the peace of Westphalia.

As far as foreign policy was concerned the minority of Louis XIV. had seen France achieve brilliant successes. She had not extended her frontier to the Scheldt, but she had by securing Alsace advanced her boundaries wellnigh to the Rhine. Her rival Austria, moreover, was permanently weakened by the changes effected in the Germanic constitution. The independence of each German state and the introduction of Sweden into the north of Germany were in themselves a considerable check on the power of the Emperor. The Empire was paralysed and the Rhine was no longer a German river. The French were established almost throughout all Alsace, and the Imperial dignity was enormously lessened. The smaller German Princes had learned to look upon France as their protector, and Louis XIV. was to reap later the benefits of Mazarin's skilful advocacy of the rights of these petty states.

The Austro-Spanish House had indeed suffered a severe fall in the Thirty Years' War. A balance of power was established in Europe under the guarantee of France which could not easily be overthrown. In spite of her internal troubles the French monarchy had gained immensely in the consideration of Europe; France remained the leading power in Europe and was regarded by the secondary states as their ally and protector.

The year 1648 was disastrous to the cause of royalty. Charles I. fell into the hands of his foes and early in the following year ended his life on the scaffold, in Naples a republic was proclaimed and the arms of Spain defied, in Germany the Emperor's power had been for ever weakened by the recognition of the federal character of the Empire, even in Russia an aristocratic movement hostile to the royal power took place.

France was no exception to the general rule. There the murmuring *Parlement* of the early years of Louis XIV.'s reign became the mutinous and rebellious *Parlement* of the period of the Fronde. "The constellations were terribly against Kings," wrote Madame de Motteville. For some five years the Fronde filling France with the turmoil and misery of a civil war compromised the conquests and the glory gained by the French armies during the years 1643–48. Dominated at one time by the *Parlement*, at another by the Princes, at another by a union of both, the period of the Fronde is marked by intrigue, by selfishness, and by an entire absence of patriotism.

There is probably no period in later French history which afforded more justification for absolutism. The ready acceptance by the French people of the establishment of Louis XIV.'s despotic power was in great measure due to the factious character of the Fronde movement.

It was during these years 1648–54 that Louis learnt some of his first lessons in the art of government. It was during these years that he gained his earliest political experiences. Opposed on all sides by a curious medley of princes like Beaufort, of generals like Turenne and Condé, of ecclesiastics like Paul de Gondi, of ambitious intriguers like Madame de Chevreuse and Madame de Longueville, it was not to be wondered at that Louis' early experiences taught him the necessity of crushing all opposition.

The failure of the Fronde movement to secure any constitutional concessions or any tangible

reforms was due to two causes. In the first place
the *Parlement* of Paris—a mere corporation of
magistrates holding their power from the King—
had no right to take the place of the States-General
and to pose as the representatives of the nation.
This official aristocracy, indignant at Mazarin's
attempt to deprive them of the hereditary rights
which belonged to their offices, now proved as hostile
to the minister as the feudal aristocracy had been
to Richelieu. Though these lawyers spoke brave
words about individual liberty, they were far more
anxious about the extension of their own privileges
and the threatened loss of the " paulette " than
about the advancement of the liberties of the
nation at large. It is indeed true that the first
or Parliamentary Fronde (1648–49) did certainly
number among its ranks men who, like Molé, the
President of the *Parlement* and a real patriot, were
honest citizens and anxious for the welfare of their
country. And undeniably this movement is worthy
of a certain amount of respect in that it did attack
a most wasteful administration, and a ruinous
system of taxation. But the *Parlement* was incapable, from its very constitution, of carrying through
a scheme of reform in face of the insuperable
difficulties which beset its path.

The second cause of the failure of the Fronde
movement is to be found in the fact that the New or
second Fronde (1649–1653) had no title whatever to
any respect.

The constitutional leanings of a certain portion of
the members of the first Fronde had been to a great

MESIRÉ, MATHIEV MOLLE CON⸱ᴱᴿ DV ROY
en ses conseils premier president au parlement de paris.
et garde des sceaux s de frnce du 3 Auril. 1651.
Monsrnit ex

MOLÉ.
(From a print in the library of Christ Church, Oxford.)

extent overshadowed by their exaggerated and unreasoning hatred of a First Minister—in the person of Mazarin. In the second Fronde the object of the new Frondeurs was simply to secure for themselves appointments, governments, pensions. They aimed, in a word, at the overthrow of Mazarin and the establishment of the government of the aristocracy. Had the first Fronde triumphed and officialism as represented by the members of the *Parlement* of Paris divided the government with the King, or had the nobles in the second Fronde triumphed, the country would have suffered far more evils than attended the establishment of the absolute monarchy.

Both Frondes had an object in common, viz. the overthrow of Mazarin and with him of the idea of an irresponsible Prime Minister bequeathed to France by Richelieu. Ostensibly both Frondes struggled to shake royalty free from the check imposed by the creation of a Prime Minister, but in reality, though struggling nominally for the King, the Frondeurs, whether as hereditary magistrates or as frivolous nobles, were mainly fighting for their own selfish interests. There is no doubt whatever that the triumph of the *Parlement* or of the nobles would have been equally disastrous to the interests of France.

And this is very clearly seen in the attitude taken by the thirty-two delegates from the *Parlement* and the sovereign Courts which met in the Chamber of St. Louis and there formed themselves into what practically amounted to a permanent political body for dealing with all existing grievances.

On June 30th, 1648 they demanded the abolition of Richelieu's *intendants*, whose extended powers often encroached upon the jurisdiction of the *Parlement*. Apart from their other demands, some of which were admirable, the attempt of the delegates to upset at one blow Richelieu's administrative system illustrates the folly and blindness of this self-constituted committee. The abolition of the unity of the French administration meant a return to feudal anarchy and local misgovernment. For the time being Mazarin found it advisable to persuade the Queen, who was herself determined to maintain intact her son's authority, to yield to the pressure of the *Parlement*, which had received with favour the propositions of the Chamber of St. Louis. Not only was Emery dismissed and his place given to a soldier, the Marshal de la Meilleraye, but all the intendants were removed except those in the Lyonnais, Champagne, and Picardy. These concessions not satisfying the *Parlement*, and the Chamber of St. Louis continuing its sittings, Mazarin waited till August, when on the 20th the battle of Lens seemed to come most opportunely to the aid of the Court. "At last," wrote Mazarin, "heaven has declared in our favour." The Queen's policy of maintaining intact the royal authority at all hazards was to be immediately tried.

The victory of Lens was to have a double effect. It was to hasten the conclusion of a general peace, it was to assure the triumph of the royal cause over that of the *Parlement*. It was reported that on hearing of the victory of Condé, Louis himself had

said : " The *Parlement* will be very sorry." The royal
Council, in which sat with the Queen, Mazarin, Orleans, Longueville, Seguier, La Meilleraye, and Chavigny, decided that the three most prominent members of the *Parlement*, Broussel, Blancmesnil, and
Charton, should be arrested on the very day when at
Notre Dame a Te Deum was being chanted in honour of Lens. Of the three Charton escaped, but the
other two were seized, Blancmesnil being taken to
Vincennes, while Broussel was imprisoned at Sedan.

The effect was as serious for France as had been
the attempted arrest of the five members by Charles
I. in England.

The Revolution had begun. In a frenzy of excitement barricades were thrown up, and the mob refused to lay down their arms till the prisoners were
released. The Palais Royal itself was in no little
danger. It was not till the Court had given way to
the demands of the *Parlement* and Broussel had
arrived and been escorted in triumph to Notre Dame
that the barricades were removed and tranquillity
reigned again in Paris. But it was evident that a
rupture with the *Parlement* was bound to take place.
The moderate section in the *Parlement* itself was
incapable of controlling the younger members who
were determined to carry through their projects of
reform and to exercise a powerful if not a permanent
influence on the government. Paul de Gondi, known
as the Cardinal de Retz, a born conspirator, whose
object in life was to be a successful party leader, had
taken up a position of bitter hostility to the Queen
and Mazarin. Instigating the younger and more

fiery members of the *Parlement*, he entered upon a course of definite hostility to Mazarin, which he expected would place him in a commanding position among the leaders of the factions of the day.

The rest of the picturesque history of the first or Parliamentary Fronde can be told in a few words. The war which seemed likely to break out upon the retirement of the Court to Rueil in September, and later to Saint-Germain, followed by some forcible measures of Mazarin, was temporarily averted by a conference at Saint-Germain, which lasted from September 25th to October 4th, and resulted in the declaration of October 22d, perhaps the most important act of the Parliamentary Fronde, a sort of charter in which a large number of the claims made by the Chamber of St. Louis were conceded. For a time the Court returned to Paris, where the *Parlement* was far too intent on securing the fulfilment of the promises made by the Declaration to appreciate the fact that on October 24th the memorable Treaties of Westphalia were signed—a signal tribute to the skill and success of Mazarin's foreign policy. Only by means of extensive bribery and by working on Condé's contempt for the *noblesse* of the gown had Mazarin succeeded in keeping Orleans and Condé faithful to the cause of the Court. But the intrigues of De Retz and the violent and aggressive policy of the younger members of the *Parlement* rendered war inevitable unless the Queen was prepared to consent to a considerable curtailment of the royal power. But Anne had no intention whatever of allowing her son's heritage to be shorn of any portion of its rights.

She had only agreed to the Declaration of October
22d on the assurance of Mazarin that she could violate it whenever she chose. Alarmed now at the appearance of numerous *Mazarinades*—personal attacks on the minister, which, as he pointed out, resembled those which preceded the fall of Strafford,
—she allowed herself to be persuaded by Orleans and
Mazarin, and agreed to leave Paris secretly and to
prepare for open hostilities. Condé, with the eye of
a great captain, had wished to keep the King and
the Court in Paris, and had devised a plan worthy of
the great Napoleon for destroying the barricades and
clearing the streets by means of artillery. But the
counsels of those who advocated the reduction of the
city by famine prevailed, and flight was decided upon.

The young Louis, now ten years old, was to have
a practical illustration of the inconvenience resulting
from the rebellious conduct of the *Parlement*. On
January 5, 1649, the flight from the Palais Royal
took place. Berringhen, the King's first Equerry,
had prepared the carriage, which stood ready at the
Palais Royal garden. With Louis and his brother
the Duke of Anjou, and accompanied by Villeroi,
Villequier, Guitaut, Comminges, and one lady-in-
waiting, Anne escaped at 3 A. M. on a winter morning to Saint-Germain. Arrived there the hardships
began. The *Château Vieux* had little or no furniture; there were no beds. For five days the Parisians
refused to allow the royal luggage to leave the city.
At the *Château Neuf*, where Monsieur had his apartments, matters were almost worse, and "Mademoiselle" has left an amusing account of the hardships

which she experienced. The inconveniences incident to this condition of affairs in midwinter, in an unfurnished house, made an impression on the mind of the youthful King which was never eradicated.

For three months, from January 6 to April 1, 1649, the civil war continued. That it lasted so long was due to the treachery of many of the Princes, who joined the *Parlement*, to troubles in Normandy, and to the treason of Turenne, who threatened to advance to the aid of Paris at the head of his large army. Condé, too, found that a force of 15,000 was insufficient to invest Paris, while the determination of the citizens to defend the ramparts was an unexpected obstacle to success. Eventually divisions among the Frondeurs, scarcity of food in Paris, the failure of the Fronde forces, dislike of the intrigues of Spain, and the death of Charles I—an event which shocked the moderate party in the *Parlement*, —and general weariness of the war felt by Court, *Parlement*, and *Bourgeoisie*, led to the treaty of Rueil, April 1st. The treaty of Rueil, received with enthusiasm by the *Bourgeoisie* in Paris, where a solemn Te Deum was chanted and a display of fireworks took place, proved to be only a truce.

The restrictions on the royal power were so excessive that it was impossible for the Court party to regard the terms of the treaty as valid for any length of time. And, moreover, a large number of the Frondeurs never ceased insulting the Queen and Mazarin in their pamphlets. These attacks redoubled in vigour after the failure of the French arms to capture Cambrai in July.

For many months the return of the Court to Paris was postponed, the Queen preferring the quiet of Compiègne to the insults of the Frondeurs. At last on August 18, 1649, the Court definitely returned to the capital. In the entry to Paris the young King played a considerable part. The royal carriage was received with great pomp by the municipal authorities half way between Paris and Saint-Denis, and there, on bended knee, the city dignitaries asserted their loyalty to the King. Then they escorted Louis on horseback to the Palais Royal, the plain of Saint-Denis being covered with triumphal arches, and the people stirred up to great enthusiasm. Some days later, on August 25th, the King went with considerable pomp to celebrate the festival of Saint-Denis at the principal Jesuit Church. This time the *cortège* surrounding the King included the *élite* of the nobility with their horses magnificently caparisoned. All along the route the King was received with extravagant demonstrations of popular rejoicing.

But in the midst of these manifestations of the popular joy there were signs of the approach of a storm, which assumed proportions far more serious than those of the late movement. Known as the New Fronde, this fresh development of hostility to the government was distinguished by its contempt for all reform, its insolence towards the *bourgeois* magistracy and the open selfishness of its aims. This New Fronde illustrated well the influence of women in politics in France; it amply demonstrated the political incapacity of the nobles; it justified the policy of Richelieu and Mazarin. Moreover, the conduct of the nobles during the New Fronde made an ineffaceable impression upon the mind of Louis, and led to the adoption by him of a policy justifiable at the time, but fatal to the nobles as a class, a policy destined to make still wider that cleavage between classes which more than any other single circumstance was answerable for the French Revolution.

Between August 18, 1649, and the declaration of his majority in September, 1651, the young King passed through a stormy period of his career. Both Paris and the provinces rebelled, and a general rising all over the country was with difficulty prevented. This internal commotion was disastrous to the conduct of the war against Spain, and the Spaniards eagerly seized the opportunity of taking the offensive and invading France. The first sign of trouble came from Condé. He was very powerful, being supported by the nobles and princes of the Fronde; he was very jealous of Mazarin; he was exceedingly ambitious. But his cruelty, his pride, and his arrogance had destroyed that popularity which Rocroi and Lens had brought him. Dissatisfied with the recognition of his services, Condé determined to seize the reins of government, and to break with Mazarin. The position of the Court was most unenviable. Mazarin, universally unpopular, was daily subject, at the hands of Condé, to insults which reflected on the royal authority. The treasury was empty, some of the Court jewels were in pawn, and the royal table was but ill supplied with provisions.

But Condé played into the hands of Mazarin. He quarrelled with the *noblesse*, he was insolent to the Queen, and by the end of the year he had so alienated all sections in Paris that Mazarin felt strong enough to strike a blow at the once popular general. On January 18, 1650, Condé was suddenly arrested and imprisoned at Vincennes. With him were seized Conti and Longueville. " They have taken," said the Duke of Orleans, " the lion, the monkey, and the fox."

Paris made no movement in favour of the prisoners, but in the provinces Condé's influence was great. The danger from Normandy, Burgundy, and Guienne was peculiarly pressing, and it must always be remembered that at this time Turenne, committing the one great fault of his life, had decided, at the instigation of the Duchess of Longueville, to oppose the Court, and held Stenai—a fortress in a most important position—for Spain. But Mazarin's *coup d' état* was at first attended with conspicuous success.

To Normandy the young King was taken by the cardinal in the hope that the royal presence there might do something to counteract the intrigues of such women as Madame de Longueville and Madame de Chevreuse, who could in his own words overthrow ten states. Successful in securing the submission of Normandy, the Court proceeded to Burgundy in March, and the siege of Bellegarde was undertaken. The presence of Louis aroused the greatest enthusiasm among both the besiegers and besieged, and the place capitulated on April 11th. But though Normandy and Burgundy had been quieted, Guienne

remained a serious danger, and in July it was found
necessary to take the King to Bordeaux. The royal
presence in the south, however, had not the effect desired. Bordeaux, already the focus of a widespread rebellion, refused to admit Louis and declared strongly
for Condé. On September 5th the royal forces under
La Meilleraye definitely began the siege of the town,
and at the end of the month an agreement was come
to, the inhabitants receiving a fresh amnesty. Mazarin's moderation was caused by his increasing difficulties in the north-east. The Spaniards in alliance
with Turenne had invaded France and at the end of
August had advanced within ten leagues of Paris.
The doubtful attitude of Orleans and the continual
intrigues of De Retz aided in making the position of
the Court very insecure. To allay the political discontent the three Princes were removed on November 16th from Paris to Havre, and on December 13th
the courage and dash of the royal troops defeated
Turenne at the battle of Rethel, and the New Fronde
was overthrown.

But this victory did not strengthen the position of
Mazarin. The east of France remained in the hands
of the foe; the Minister could not possibly stand unless he was supported by Condé or Orleans, for his
many enemies were reunited to secure his ruin.
Directly after Rethel he was vigorously attacked by
De Retz and the *Parlement*, aided and abetted by the
powerful Anne of Gonzaga, the Princess Palatine, and
the other partisans of Condé; and Orleans after much
wavering threw himself into the opposition. The
alliance of Orleans with the Frondeurs marked a new

combination of the two Frondes and determined Mazarin, who was probably taken by surprise, to retire into voluntary exile. He recognised that the demand for his overthrow united all parties. The coalition against him would during his absence break up into its former discordant elements. On February 4th, 1651, he left Paris for Saint-Germain, and on the 9th the *Parlement* of Paris decreed that within fifteen days he must leave the kingdom.

The Queen-Mother and the young King were in a helpless and isolated position. The city was under arms and a close watch was set on the movements of the Court.

On Mazarin's retirement from Paris the Queen-Mother, like Louis XVI., determined to escape with the King. Rumours of this intention got about and at once a scene was enacted which resembles some of the incidents of the French Revolution. De Retz sounded the alarm and De Souches was sent to the Palais Royal. He forced his way into the King's bedroom and found Louis in bed. He was in fact a prisoner, and on February the 10th the Queen-Mother signed an order for the release of the Princes. On February 13th Mazarin himself set free the Princes, who were received three days later in Paris with the utmost enthusiasm. Excited by the fall of Mazarin the populace forgot that thirteen months earlier they had been equally pleased at Condé's imprisonment.

But though the plotters were apparently successful and had imposed their terms on the Queen, their position was far from strong. Henceforward Louis hated Condé with a vindictive hatred. Already

master of himself he had indeed " caressed Monsieur
le Prince " on his first appearance at Court after his
imprisonment. For the moment Condé was all powerful. But as Mazarin then at Brühl had foreseen,
discord soon arose among the parties who composed
the Fronde and within six months Condé was at war
with the men who now supported him. A certain
number of the nobles desired the summoning of the
States-General. The *Parlement* of Paris, anxious to
secure political power for itself, was strongly opposed
to such a proposal. Though Anne consented that
the States-General should meet on September the
8th, the day after the attainment of the King's majority, Condé soon ceased to care about the States-
General and attempted to make a close alliance with
Anne.

But his arrogance and rashness destroyed his
chance. He was most insolent to Louis ; he was the
dupe of unworthy counsellors. He intrigued against
Beaufort ; he quarrelled with De Retz. His relations
with Orleans became strained.

Intrigues and general discord thus filled the first
half of 1651, the Queen quietly waiting for the cele-
bration of the King's majority. By August feeling
strong enough to definitely oppose Condé, she boldly
appealed to Retz to aid her. Amid scenes of turbulence the month of August closed, all moderate men
looking forward to the restoration of order, even
under the once hated Mazarin.

CHAPTER II.

FIRST EXPERIENCES OF WAR AND POLITICS.

1651–1661.

AT nine o'clock on the morning of September 7th the procession left the Palais Royal, and met with a magnificent reception from the crowd which thronged the streets. Every window was occupied; among the spectators of the brilliant scene being Henrietta of England, then a hapless exile in France; while the immense concourse of people were with difficulty restrained by the troops who lined the whole of the route from the Palais Royal to Notre Dame. The appearance of Louis XIV. was the signal for a great ovation. His youth, his manly looks, and his courtesy made an excellent impression, and the multitude to whom the King was the personification of the unity and the power of France testified by

45

their shouts of joy the hope that the days of civil disorder had passed away. After hearing Mass at the Sainte Chapelle, Louis proceeded to the Grande Chambre where his majority was formally declared with the accustomed ceremonies. The King signified his intention of governing himself ; the Chancellor made a long harangue on the policy about to be pursued by Louis ; and after a discourse by the First President of the *Parlement*, Anne of Austria, in a few simple words, resigned the powers which she had wielded for nine years. The King, after thanking her, received homage from all present. Omer Talon then delivered a long oration which wearied his hearers, and shortly afterwards the ceremony came to an end, and the procession returned to the Palais Royal. Fireworks and a general illumination, concluded the day's proceedings. The self-possession of Louis and his dignified behaviour during the ceremony had created a most favourable impression. He behaved, it was said, like a man of four and twenty. That he already possessed considerable firmness was shown the next day, when he constituted a new ministry in direct opposition to the wishes of the Duke of Orleans. Louis also began to hold his court at the Palais Royal, as he did for some fifty years, with that regularity and dignity which so strongly marks all that he did. The words attributed to Mazarin, that the King had in him the making of many kings and of one honest man, seemed on the day when he attained his majority fully justified. Already he had shown a knowledge of men very unusual in one so young. For Louis, who had experienced the drawbacks of imprisonment in his own palace, and who had been exposed to frequent insults at the hands of the ambitious Princes during the Fronde period, had been taught the lesson of discernment in the bitter school of adversity. Moreover during the ensuing two years, the King's experience of the character of the French nobility was to be further strengthened. His responsibilities may be said to date from the proclamation of his majority. For Condé still hoping to overthrow the Ministry threw himself into rebellion.

The struggle which ensued, though serious enough, differed in many points from the earlier Fronde movement. All opposition to the government had now become rebellion against the King's person. In this new civil war the ministers had the advantage of using the royal authority as a lever against the rebels. It was, however, a critical period in the history of France. Spain, not yet sank into decrepitude, was almost openly supported by the Emperor, while Lorraine was a constant danger to the French government. The outbreak of hostilities gave the Spaniards an opportunity of making inroads into France, and Cromwell an admirable excuse for hampering a Court which he had every reason to suppose, would support the young Charles II. Had the ministers been freed from the Spanish War, and from all fear of English intervention, Condé's rebellion would have been easily and quickly crushed. As it was, one army had to be sent to oppose the Spaniards in Champagne, while another under Harcourt opposed the far-reaching schemes of Condé, who had been received in almost regal state in Bordeaux and generally with enthusiasm throughout Guienne. Thus occupied with defending France against open foes, the government were unable to deal with the internal divisions of the country. Mazarin was almost universally hated, the party of the great nobles anxious for civil war was ready for open rebellion under Condé and Orleans. Many towns were disaffected, and the ladies of the Fronde were using all their influence on the side of faction.

But though Mazarin was still in exile the government proved successful. Harcourt defeated Condé in the south, and Cromwell refused to support an obviously lost cause ; even the Duke of Lorraine held his hand.

In January, 1652, Mazarin, in deference to an express order from Louis, joined the Court at Poitiers, and Turenne, disliking the lawless selfishness of Condé and his supporters, at the same time threw in his lot with the royal cause. The next six months proved to be the critical period in the civil war, and Turenne's admirable generalship proved decisive in the crisis. He saved the King from certain capture by his victory at Jargeau (March, 1652), while his prudence and presence of mind and tactical skill prevented Condé from gathering any advantage from a slight success secured at Bleneau in April. In May Turenne cut to pieces at Etampes an army of Spanish mercenaries introduced into France by Condé, and by skilfully averting a junction between the Prince and the Duke of Lorraine, he undoubtedly saved the Court from extreme peril ; a week later he occupied Saint

Denis. Paris in the meantime had been in a state of anarchy and chaos. The *Parlement* had shown itself utterly incapable of preserving order, and was deservedly despised ; the nobles were denounced, and the citizens saw in the triumph of the royal cause the only hope for peace and good government.

The dregs of the populace on whom Condé and the Princes relied became each day more violent, and by their conduct ensured the success of the King. Insurrections in June were followed by the flight of the Presidents of the *Parlement*, and Mazarin and Turenne then decided to strike a blow at the failing cause of the Prince. On July the 2nd Condé was defeated in the Faubourg Saint-Antoine and only saved from immediate overthrow by the cannon of the Bastille. Turenne had been unwilling to begin the contest till the royal artillery had arrived. But against his right judgment he was persuaded, by the Court and Louis impatiently anxious to witness the destruction of Condé, to adopt a wrong line of action. At the critical moment when the royal artillery had come up, and all was ready for the decisive effort, Mademoiselle had the gates of Paris opened, and Condé and his forces being safe, she turned the guns of the Bastille on the royal army. Louis XIV. never forgave her for this insult. Thus the Battle of Saint-Antoine was virtually a defeat of the King, and for a few months more Paris was to remain in the hands of the party of anarchy and treason.

But the end of the Fronde movement was at hand. No sooner had Turenne retired than the mob, incited by the Princes and by a large number of dis-

guised soldiers, set fire to the Hôtel de Ville, where
the city Assembly sat, and killed several of the
councillors. This massacre of the Hôtel de Ville
was the death-blow to the cause of the Princes.
Condé had no army, no moral authority ; he was in
alliance with the mob, and he was opposed by all
moderate men.

His violent acts only strengthened the royal cause.
The *Parlement* was summoned to Pontoise and presided over by Molé ; it secured the adhesion of more
of its members each day. Though it demanded and
obtained the retirement of Mazarin to Bouillon, the
support of the *Parlement* far outweighed the inconveniences caused to the royal party by the temporary
exile of Mazarin. The conciliatory policy of the
Court soon made itself felt. The reaction in Paris
grew stronger day by day, and in September the
royal party among the *bourgeoisie* and clergy in Paris,
taking advantage of Condé's illness, and fully alive
to the disasters brought upon France by the civil
war, sent a deputation headed by Retz to Compiègne and begged Louis to return to Paris. The
conduct of the Princes had become so unsupportable
to men of all classes, whether clergy, lawyers, merchants, or artisans, that the declaration of the King
dated September 17th, in which the citizens of Paris
were exhorted " to arm and deliver themselves from
this odious tyranny," was received with acclamation.
Chavigny died on October 4th ; Condé fled from
Paris on the 13th, and was made General-in-chief of
the forces of Spain. It was arranged that Louis,
who was at Saint-Germain, should enter Paris on

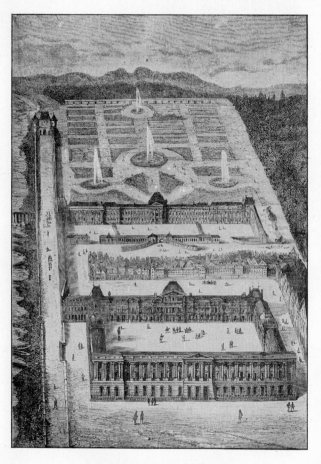

THE LOUVRE AND THE TUILERIES.
(From an old print, and reproduced in Philippson's
Das Zeitalter Ludwigs XIV.)

October 21st, that he should reside at the Louvre, his
brother at the Tuileries, and Henrietta Maria, Queen
of England, at the Palais Royal. About mid-day on
the 21st the King escorted by a small army under
Turenne, set out from Saint-Germain. All along
his route he was received with the wildest enthusiasm. In the young King men saw the personification
of order, peace, and prosperity. Never had a monarch
such a reception. Already an imposing figure, he
entered Paris on horseback by the light of torches
and accompanied by Charles II. and many Princes,
Dukes, and Marshals. When he reached the Rue
Saint-Honoré the excitement reached its height.
Not only the streets and the windows, but even the
roofs were crowded with enthusiastic spectators, and
so amid the extravagant joy of the Parisians the
King passed on to the Louvre which he had chosen
as his future residence on the ground, says Madame
de Motteville, that ordinary houses without any defences were not suitable in such times. But Paris
caused Louis little further anxiety. Orleans with
Beaufort and Chabot-Rohan retired quietly into
the country; Châteauneuf soon followed them;
Mademoiselle of Orleans, together with the Duch-
esses of Montbazon and Chatillon, was compelled
to leave Paris. And in December Retz was arrested
and imprisoned in Vincennes.

One of Louis' first acts had been to check all
possible opposition from the *Parlement*. The day
after his arrival in Paris a *Lit-de-Justice* was held at
the Louvre, and the *Parlement* was forbidden to take
any part in the affairs of state, or to interfere with

the public finances. It was to have no political influence in the future, but was to confine itself to its
legal functions. To impress upon the lawyers the
determination which underlay these edicts, Broussel
and nine other members of the *Parlement* shared the
fate of Beaufort and Rohan and were banished.

On the 26th of October, Louis sent a letter to
Mazarin pointing out that there was no reason why
he should be any longer deprived of the wise counsels of his minister, and expressing a hope that
Mazarin would at once return to the capital. It
was not, however, till the beginning of the next year
that Mazarin actually set out to resume his duties as
the King's Prime Minister. During the interval the
administration had enough on its hands in quelling
the last efforts of the adherents of the Fronde in the
provinces, and in making head against the Spaniards.
The year 1652 was a disastrous one for the French
arms. Picardy and all the country round Paris
were ravaged, and Gravelines was taken in May. In
September a severe blow was inflicted on France,
for Dunkirk was compelled to surrender to the
Spanish troops. In Italy and Catalonia the French
suffered similar reverses. Casale, so famous for its
capture by Richelieu, was lost in October, and in the
same month the whole of Catalonia had become
again an integral portion of the Spanish monarchy.
To remedy these losses, Mazarin, with the aid of
Turenne, had already begun to act on the defensive
on the eastern frontier, and it was arranged to begin
the new year with vigorous measures. In order to
obtain the necessary supplies, Louis, on December

31st, held another *Lit-de-Justice* and compelled the unwilling *Parlement* to agree to his demands.

In the part he played in carrying out what amounted to a revolution, Louis showed an amount of presence of mind, imperturbability, and indeed discrimination, which astonished his contemporaries. Mazarin is supposed to have taught the King the precept that he who cannot practise dissimulation, does not know how to govern. In the history of the arrest of Retz, Louis showed that he had mastered that lesson. When Retz visited the Louvre on December 19th, he was received with affability by the King, who at once renewed the orders for his arrest and retired to hear Mass with the utmost calmness.

At the beginning of 1653 the Fronde movement was over except in Provence, Burgundy, Saintonge, and especially in Guienne, where it still smouldered on. Condé was endeavouring to revive Huguenot disloyalty in La Rochelle, and encouraged the citizens to aim at securing republican institutions. Bordeaux was, however, the centre of disaffection, and though the party of order had been strengthened by the pacification of Paris, Bordeaux still occasioned the government some uneasiness owing to the rise of a radical party, known as the *Ormée*, among the lower orders. Like the Jacobins of later days its leaders numbered among their ranks a lawyer and a butcher; it hung out the red flag and perpetrated numerous atrocities. Unlike the Jacobins the insurrectionists appealed to England for aid. Deserted by Condé, failing to get any help from Cromwell, and divided in its own

ranks, the *Ormée* could not hope to make a successful resistance to the royal forces under the Dukes of
Vendôme and Candale. On July 31st the terms of
peace were accepted by the citizens of Bordeaux,
and the Fronde was finally over.

In this work of stamping out the last embers of
disaffection in the provinces, Mazarin had played a
leading part. On February 3d he had returned, being met some distance from Paris by the King and a
number of the courtiers. Till his death he governed
France with the full concurrence of the young King,
and to the great advantage of the country. A firm
and wise hand was indeed required. Order had to
be restored and the finances reorganised; the war
with Spain demanded vigorous treatment and careful supervision. It was of the utmost importance
to secure the alliance of England. In all these
matters he showed promptness and resource. La
Vieuville, the Superintendent of the Finances had
died on January 2nd. On February 7th Mazarin
appointed Servien and Nicholas Fouquet, who had
been useful in contributing to the overthrow of
the Fronde in Paris, to hold the post jointly.
Mazarin had appreciated the value of the latter's
services and his enterprising schemes; he also had
gauged his character, and knew his love of intrigue,
and perhaps his untrustworthiness. In 1653 Mazarin had put an end to the Fronde in the provinces,
and dispersed the remaining discontented Princes.
For the next six years his efforts were directed to
expelling the Spaniards from Champagne, and to
checking their influence in Italy and Catalonia.

MAZARIN.

(From an old engraving.)

Further he aimed at recovering the maritime places lost to Spain during the late internal troubles, and finally he hoped to impose on the Spanish King rigorous terms of peace and so to complete the work of Richelieu. It was not till 1659 that his policy was in great part carried out. No sooner had the troubles in the south of France been appeased than he definitely began to combat Spain. In 1654 Turenne, aided by the skilful diplomacy of the Cardinal, drove the Spaniards out of Champagne, and in 1655 invaded Hainault and encamped within the enemy's territory.

These years, important as they are in the history of France, are of great interest in the biography of the King. For it was in 1653 that he had his first real experience of warfare. Up to this period he had never passed more than a few days in camp. But now he was nearly fifteen years old, and in view of the dangerous crisis through which France was passing, Mazarin rightly thought that not only would Louis derive considerable advantage from seeing military operations conducted by Turenne, but that the presence of the King in camp would have a most beneficial effect upon the troops. In fact from 1653 Mazarin himself took the greatest pains with Louis' education. He pointed out the importance of a close application to business, and impressed on him the necessity of ruling by himself, while using the advice of his generals and ministers. From Mazarin, too, Louis learnt the art of choosing good instruments; he learnt also the advisability, when once his plans had been carefully thought out, of prudently choosing favourable occasions for boldly executing them. Perseverance combined with a certain elasticity in his methods was, he was taught, the true way to arrive at the end in view.

Louis remained throughout his life ignorant so far as the ordinary knowledge of letters was concerned. His judgment of men was, as a rule, sound. His intellectual development never proceeded far ; but in his acquaintance with those matters which were necessary at that time for a successful king, Louis soon became proficient.

The campaign of 1653 was one of the highest interest. Spain and her allies were superior to France in fighting strength, and Condé had resolved to march on Paris. But Turenne, by a series of brilliant operations, and aided by the discord among the allies, baffled Condé and saved Paris. In July, 1653, Louis joined Turenne's army. He was received with enthusiasm by the troops, saw some fighting, was present at councils of war, and remained in camp for about ten days. In the autumn Mazarin, hearing of conspiracies emanating from the north-east frontier, took the King with him to Amiens, and placed the government of that important town in the hands of the well tried Guy de Bar, whose devotion to the royal cause had been thoroughly tested. From Amiens he and the King proceeded to Soissons and then to Laon, where it was resolved, in spite of the custom of retiring into winter quarters in October, to besiege Sainte-Menehould. It was not till November 27th after the besiegers had suffered much from the rain, snow, and frost, that Louis took possession of the town. Though the tide of Spanish success was checked at the close of 1653, the position of France in Europe was still most critical. She was far from having recovered the position which she enjoyed at the time of the peace of Westphalia.

The Emperor Ferdinand III. had secured the election of his son Ferdinand as King of the Romans, and a strong coalition between Austria, Spain, the Duke of Lorraine and Condé seemed likely to come about, followed by a determined effort to conquer Alsace, Brisach, and Phillipsbourg. Good fortune and the mistakes of her foes came, however, to the assistance of France. The Spaniards in occupying the Bishopric of Liège which belonged to Cologne gave Mazarin an opportunity of interfering on behalf of Fürstenburg the Archbishop, and the prestige of the French name in Germany was restored to such an extent that when the young Ferdinand died in 1654 Mazarin thought of bringing forward the name of Louis XIV. as a candidate for the Imperial throne.

The good fortune of 1653 did not fail the minister in 1654. Early in the year the Spaniards arrested the Duke of Lorraine and sent him to Spain; in May, by clever intrigues, Mazarin circumvented Harcourt the traitorous governor of Alsace, and by the Treaty of Bâle secured Brisach, Alsace, and Phillipsbourg. So firmly was the royal power established in France and with it Mazarin's own position, that not only " all the great nobles were eager to marry the Cardinal's nieces," but it was considered practicable

to have Louis crowned at Rheims. The coronation
ceremony, which took place on June 7, 1654, bore
many traces of its origin in the days of Charles the
Great and was performed with all the necessary
adjuncts. No sooner was the coronation over than
Louis joined the army besieging Stenai in Lorraine,
while Condé and the Archduke Leopold were besieging the great fortress of Arras, the ancient capital
of Burgundian Artois, defended by Jean de Schu-
lemberg, Comte de Montdejeu. Extraordinary
efforts were made by the Spaniards to capture what
had been one of the gems of the monarchy, and
thousands of peasants aided their already considerable army. Mazarin no doubt acted wisely in again
introducing Louis to military life. His presence in-
spirited the troops, and, moreover, the experience of
warfare gave him manly tastes, though it may have
tended to produce later a somewhat dangerous love
of military glory. Success again attended the King
in this campaign, Stenai was captured by Hocquin-
court, Arras was relieved in spite of Condé's brilliant
efforts to drive back Turenne's force, and the northern frontier was safe. Turenne finished the year by
taking Quesnoi and Binche, and after a conference
in October with Mazarin and the King at Guise it
was resolved to send the Marshal de la Ferté to besiege Clermont, which fell on November 22nd. The
relief of Arras was a serious blow to Spain and may
be regarded as the turning-point in the war. From
this time the power of France began to revive with
extraordinary rapidity. The armies of Spain soon
ceased to be a match for those of France. Spain

was a declining, France a rising power. Louis was now really a King and was looked upon as the embodiment of an ancient, powerful monarchy.

During the winter of 1654–5, the Court was the scene of festivities. The King loved dancing and took a leading part in the ballets which were then very popular. Fêtes and carnivals made men forget the miseries of the Fronde period. But the financial difficulties remained a dreary heritage of the civil wars, and Mazarin again found that it required all the authority associated with the person of the King to overcome the resistance of the *Parlement* to edicts enforcing new taxation. A *Lit-de-Justice* was held on March 20, 1655, at which Louis was present surrounded with all the trappings of royalty. In spite of a speech from the lawyer Bignon testifying to the misery of the people, the Chancellor Seguier got the edict registered. But the next day the members of the *Chambres des Enquêtes*, which consisted mostly of the younger and more turbulent spirits among the *Parlement*, in contravention to the royal order of October 22nd, 1652, forbidding all interference on the part of the *Parlement* in political matters and in the administration of the finance, criticised the edicts and resolved to continue to do so. The situation recalled the early days of the Fronde. It seemed not improbable that the scenes of 1648 would be repeated. The crisis was serious. Louis XIV., however, showed himself capable of dealing with the Parliamentary opposition. He was at the time hunting in the woods round Vincennes. A very pretty legend has grown up in which Louis is

represented as arriving before the united *Parlement*
cane in hand and in hunting costume, and making
use of the famous expression, *"L'État, c'est moi."*
The truth is that, realising early in April the seriousness of the situation, Louis on April 13th, in his
every-day dress, suddenly burst in upon the astonished *Parlement* and upbraided the members for
their conduct. " Each of you," he said, " knows
how your assemblies stirred up troubles in my state.
I have learnt that you intend to continue these
meetings. . . . I am come here expressly to
forbid the continuation of them." On the completion of his short address the King, without hearing
a word in reply, went to the Louvre and thence to
Vincennes. Though the *Parlement* protested, Mazarin, by the aid of Turenne, by clever management,
and by bribery, averted any outbreak.

The King's determination astonished all who knew
him—a determination which he continued to show
during the campaign of 1655. The French took
Landrecies, and marched through part of the Spanish
Netherlands. "The King," wrote Mazarin on July
31st, " is indefatigable, and he has marched all along
with the army . . . after having been fifteen
hours on horseback, he is not tired." During this
campaign provisions ran short, but Louis bore all
his privations most good-humouredly. The capture
of Stenai the previous year had developed in him a
love of siege warfare, which increased as he grew
older. He was now delighted at invading the enemy's country, and in anticipation of future invasions
was very desirous of pushing on to Brussels. This

military promenade across the Belgian provinces made undoubtedly a great impression on the young King's mind, while it proved the superiority of the French arms over those of their Spanish rivals. It was only after long argument that Mazarin was able to persuade Louis—burning to remain with the army and to witness fresh successes—to stay behind with him at Quesnoi, while the French marshals pushed on. But Mazarin was well aware of the excellent effect produced on the army by Louis' arrival at the frontier. At Quesnoi then the King remained for a time, his presence there being keenly appreciated by his marshals and their men. After the town of Condé had been taken it was thought that the King could safely join the army then besieging Saint-Guillain. On August 22nd, to the great delight of Louis, Turenne arrived with three thousand horse, and escorted the King to the camp, which was, according to Turenne's usual custom, very carefully defended. On August 26th, Louis had the satisfaction of seeing the capitulation of Saint-Guillain, and after riding well-nigh up to Mons, he retired on August 27th from the camp, and joined his mother and the Court at La Fère, whence they all moved to Chantilly and later to Paris. The return of the King from the army was a matter of great satisfaction to the Court, who were bored to distraction by the quiet life at La Fère. At Paris all the festivities of the previous winter were repeated, and a grand ball was given— notable from the attentions paid by Louis to Olympe Mancini, one of Mazarin's nieces who married later the Comte de Soissons. There seems little doubt that the ambitious Countess hoped through her influence over Louis to govern France. But Mazarin's system of education saved Louis from an effeminate life. He had acquired a taste for martial exercises, he had thoroughly realised the dignity of his position, and he had acquired a certain elevation of soul, which enabled him at this time to steer safely through the shoals of Court life.

The last five years of his minority were not without their special dangers to the young King. In the first place, Louis ran some risk from his infatuation for Olympe Mancini in 1655, and for her sister, Marie Mancini, in 1659. During these years he had two more or less serious illnesses in 1655 and in 1658. In October, 1655, while Mazarin was busy fortifying the towns lately taken on the frontier, Louis fell ill at Fontainebleau. After à month's sickness, which gave Mazarin some uneasiness, Louis recovered, and in December visited Peronne and Ham, and by his presence strengthened the royal authority in these towns. The year 1655 was in many ways important.

The Lorraine army declared for France, the campaign in Flanders had been successful, and though in Catalonia and Italy success and failure were equally balanced, Mazarin's preparations, diplomatic, military, and naval, augured success in the near future. The year 1655, too, marked an epoch in the history of charitable institutions in Paris. Vincent de Paul brought into notice the condition of the Parisian poor, and by state aid the General Hospital was founded. Important religious developments

were taking place, Port Royal was becoming celebrated, and in 1656 Bossuet began to deliver his
famous sermons. The end of the Fronde had been
followed by a religious re-awakening. But France
could not turn to internal development as long as
she was burdened with a foreign war, as long as her
north-eastern frontier was not safe. It was necessary to bring the war to an immediate conclusion.

The Spaniards had been driven from Champagne
in 1654, and in 1655 French troops had entered
Hainault, and encamped in the enemy's territory.
It was now absolutely necessary to retake Gravelines, Mardyck, and Dunkirk. To effect the capture
of these maritime towns the assistance of the Dutch
or English fleet was necessary. The death of the
Stadtholder in 1650 destroyed any chance of assistance from the Dutch, and from 1651 Mazarin endeavoured to secure an English alliance. At the
end of 1652 the English Republic was officially
recognised by the French Government, and Antoine
de Bordeaux was sent to London as the French
representative, and in 1654 received the title of
French Ambassador.

But three years passed before Mazarin succeeded.
Cromwell wished to be head of all the Protestants
of Europe. Mazarin's objects were entirely political.
A commercial treaty—the treaty of Westminster—
which was at last agreed to in November, 1655,
paved the way to the more important political alliance. The treaty of Westminster was, however, received with enthusiasm in France. Its conclusion
was made the occasion for fêtes in which the King

took a prominent part—though all the supporters of the exiled Stuarts were furious with Mazarin for allying with Cromwell. After a vain attempt to negotiate a peace with Spain hostilities were resumed. In June Turenne with La Ferté laid siege to Valenciennes. It was to the south-east at the highest point of the rising ground that years later "Louis XIV., in front of William III., and on horseback at the head of his troops under arms halted, held a council of war, and finally gave up the hope of victory, not owing to personal fear, but that the King was not to be exposed to the risk of a defeat. And beyond, towards the west . . . is Denain . . . where Villars, turning to account with admirable readiness the mistake of a great captain, pierced the lines of Prince Eugène and saved France when exhausted."

Don John of Austria and Condé, however, routed La Ferté's division, and Turenne made a masterly retreat to Quesnoi. The progress of the French arms was for the moment checked, and the Spaniards gained several successes, retaking Condé and Saint-Guillain. As usual at the outbreak of hostilities Louis was very anxious to join Turenne and the army, but Mazarin, who expected a pitched battle, with difficulty prevailed on him to remain with the Court for a time until Turenne had inflicted a serious blow on the enemy by the capture of La Capelle, one of the strong places of Picardy, in September, 1656. Then neither Mazarin nor the generals could keep Louis away from the army, and with Turenne's troops Louis repeated the promenade of 1655 and advanced into the Spanish Netherlands. But such promenades availed little. The refusal of the Spaniards to negotiate a treaty, followed by their successes on the frontier, had encouraged the Emperor to draw closer his relations with Spain and to openly break the treaty of Westphalia by sending assistance to the Spaniards. A close alliance with England was more than ever necessary, and at length, after long negotiations and the exercise of much diplomacy on the part of Mazarin, the treaty of Paris was made March 23, 1657. Cromwell was to aid the French with six thousand soldiers. Dunkirk, Mardyck, and Gravelines were to be captured, and the two former were to be handed over to England. In May the English troops arrived, and Louis proceeded to Montreuil to review them. His position was each day becoming stronger. In August of the previous year Gaston of Orleans had been allowed to visit him, and their reconciliation had done much to destroy the hopes of the discontented. Madame Montpensier had followed her father's example early in 1657, and even Beaufort was reconciled with Mazarin. Condé and De Retz alone remained hostile. The winter of 1656–7 had as usual brought in its train numerous fêtes and balls, varied with hunting expeditions from Vincennes. It saw the marriage of Olympe Mancini to the Count of Soissons, the son of Prince Savoy, and witnessed the strange conduct of Christina, ex-Queen of Sweden, who spent a portion of the year 1656–7 in France. In spite of the death of Mazarin's sister, Madame Mancini, and that of his niece, the Duchess of Mercœur, the

5

Court gaieties proceeded with little interruption. In these festivities the King took the lead, danced in the ballet entitled *L'Amour Malade*, conceived a deep affection for one of the maids-of-honour, Mademoiselle de la Motte d'Argencour, and seemed likely to be influenced by a cabal of young men who called themselves *Les Endormis*. Mazarin, ever watchful, descended suddenly on *Les Endormis*. They and their leader Marsillac, son of the Duke de la Rochefoucauld, were scattered, and Mademoiselle de la Motte d'Argencour was sent away from the Court. Mazarin could not allow his influence over the King to be impaired or even endangered. These Court intrigues were broken in upon by the Treaty of Paris with Cromwell and by Louis' wish to review the English troops. He was astonished and pleased with the appearance and excellent discipline of the Ironsides. He was present later at the siege of Montmedi, in Luxemburg, where the young French nobles excited by the presence of the King performed prodigies of valour, and the place fell on August 4th. So far the campaign had not been very successful. The Spaniards had seized Saint-Guillain in March, and Condé by a brilliant feat of arms had compelled Turenne, who was taken by surprise, to raise the siege of Cambrai in June. With the fall of Montmedi fortune began to smile on the French cause. Turenne took in rapid succession Saint Venant in Artois, and La Motte-aux-Bois, a neighbouring stronghold, and on September 30th, in conjunction with the English, the siege of the maritime towns was seriously begun. Mardyck fell in October and was handed over to England, and preparations were made for the siege of Dunkirk in the following year. Louis himself was not present at the siege of Mardyck. The greater part of September and October had been spent by him and Mazarin at Metz. The Emperor Ferdinand III. had died on April 1st, after aiding the Spaniards against the French in contravention of the Treaty of Westphalia. To hamper the power of the Imperial House while the struggle continued between France and Spain became, therefore, one of the principal objects of Mazarin's policy. He incited Cromwell and Charles against the Court of Vienna, he sent an embassy into Germany to oppose the candidature of Leopold, Ferdinand's son, and he and Louis proceeded to Metz to influence and support the German Electors. It was an admirable opportunity for the Minister to give Louis a lesson in foreign policy and Mazarin did not let the occasion slip. He laid before him the general state of Europe and explained the objects of the foreign policy of each Power, and their several relations to France. Though Louis was put forward as a candidate for the Imperial throne his candidature was not considered as serious.

In July, 1658, Leopold was elected Emperor, but through Mazarin's influence his hands were so tied that he could not use the Spaniards against the French, and, moreover, in August the League of the Rhine was definitely formed, and France concluded defensive alliances for the preservation of the treaty of Westphalia. Sweden, Bavaria, the Rhine Electors, and Brunswick sided with the French King, who

thus, by isolating the Netherlands, had struck a
blow not only at the power of the Emperor, but also
at the Spanish monarchy. As under Richelieu and
Mazarin, so now under Louis XIV., France posed
as the defender of the independence of the German
Princes, menaced by the House of Austria. It was
only when Louis in later years, leaving this policy of
moderation, wished not only to extend the influence
but also the possessions of France in the direction
of Germany and began his Reunion policy, that the
Empire swung round and supported the Emperor
against the French monarchy.

While the League of the Rhine paralysed the
efforts of the Court of Vienna to aid Spain, the
renewal of the English alliance, followed by the
battle of the Dunes and the capture of Dunkirk,
destroyed all chance of any Spanish success and
compelled Philip to demand peace.

On March 28, 1658, the alliance with England was
formally renewed and the siege of Dunkirk began.
Louis was as anxious as ever to take part in warlike
operations, and wished to be present at the siege.
The Court moved to Calais, but Mazarin and the
Queen would only permit him to go as far as Mardyck. Mazarin, indeed, was strongly opposed even to
this step. He told the King plainly that provisions
were scarce, and that the Court only rendered the
lot of the soldier harder. Mazarin was right. The
water at Mardyck was bad, the heat was excessive,
and the dead of the preceding year had often been
only half buried. But Louis cared nothing for these
considerations. He was on horseback all day, seeing

everything, giving orders for putting Mardyck in a thoroughly defensible position, and generally showing great intelligence as well as activity.

On June 14th the Spaniards fought and lost the famous battle of the Dunes—a decisive battle as it turned out. The King and Queen were overjoyed, and the former was only with considerable difficulty prevented from visiting the camp if only for a day. On June 23d Dunkirk capitulated, and on the 25th Louis, after having witnessed the garrison marching out, entered the town accompanied by his guards, his principal officers, and all the Court. In accordance with the terms of the treaty, Dunkirk was to be handed over to the English. But Louis could not conceal his chagrin at seeing a French town in the hands of his hereditary foes. He refused to accept the hospitality of Lockhart, and declined to stay a night in the town. Cruel necessity had inflicted a hard blow on French patriotism, and one of Louis' first acts after the death of Mazarin was to recover Dunkirk. Personally he paid dearly for his energy during the summer of 1658. He was twenty years old, his constitution was good. But he had gone beyond the limits of prudence. His health suffered through over-fatigue during the great heat of June. He was so anxious to witness the capture of Bergues and to accompany the army to Furnes, that for several days he concealed his indisposition. At length on June 30th he confessed to Mazarin that he felt unwell, but insisted on staying at Mardyck. It was only when Mazarin threatened to send for his mother that Louis unwillingly agreed to return to

Calais. "You cannot imagine," wrote Mazarin, "the difficulty I have had to make him go."

It was evident at the beginning of July that Louis was suffering from a severe attack of fever. On July 7th two doctors arrived from Paris in addition to the four already in attendance. On July 8th the King's life was in danger, but from that day he gradually became better. On July 22d he was well enough to be moved from Calais, and July 26th he arrived at Compiègne. During his illness hostilities continued, and on August 27th Gravelines was taken and Turenne continued his conquests in Flanders. Success, too, attended the French army in Italy, and Mazarin's hopes of a speedy peace seemed likely of fulfilment. The Spaniards, defeated in Flanders and in danger in Italy, had just been defeated by the Portuguese near Elvas.

Mazarin was determined to force Philip to demand peace and to offer the Infanta in marriage to Louis. He therefore arranged an interview at Lyons with the Duchess of Savoy in order to negotiate a marriage between her daughter, Margaret of Savoy, and Louis XIV.

On October 26th the Court left for Lyons and arrived there on November 24th. It was on this journey that Louis' attachment for Marie Mancini was first noticed. Her grief during the King's illness was most demonstrative, and Louis was deeply touched by it. From that time dates his affection for Marie which caused Mazarin so much anxiety. The journey to Lyons had the result anticipated by that minister. Though the Duchess of Savoy and her daughter were received by Louis and the Court with great ceremony, the proceedings had no reality about them. Philip IV. had determined to demand peace and to offer the hand of the Infanta. The marriage of Louis XIV. to Margaret of Savoy or to Marie Mancini would have been a fatal blow to the hopes of Anne of Austria and to the policy of Mazarin. For years past the Queen-Mother had looked forward to the re-establishment of harmonious relations between her native country and France. Even during the darkest period of the war she had never lost hope. As early as 1651, according to Madame de Motteville, she had in her own mind fixed on the Infanta as the future bride of Louis XIV. That Marie Thérèse eventually became Queen of France was due in great measure to the unceasing efforts of Anne of Austria.

In Lionne, who had been sent to Spain in 1656 to try and arrange the basis of a treaty, she found an active supporter of her views, and to Lionne must belong no little of the credit of bringing about the celebrated marriage alliance. But for a time such an event seemed out of the question. The close connection existing between the Courts of Spain and Austria rendered it unlikely that the presumptive heiress of the Spanish Empire would be allowed to take her magnificent prospects to the House of Bourbon, especially as long as the Spaniards had any chance of coming out of the war as victors.

But towards the end of 1658 the situation was greatly modified. The alliance between Mazarin and Cromwell had had instantaneous effects and the

Spanish cause had suffered check after check. The
League of the Rhine had been formed under the
auspices of France and a fresh blow inflicted upon
the influence of the Emperor in Germany. Moreover
there was apparently no chance of any fresh Fronde
troubles which might again form a useful diversion.
The birth of a brother on November 28, 1657, and
the expected birth of another infant, rendered
Marie Thérèse's chances of ever securing the Spanish Empire improbable. Her marriage therefore
with Louis XIV. did not in 1658 seem likely to have
the dangerous results anticipated in 1656.

In order to force the hand of the Spaniards and to
bring Philip to a decision, Mazarin had opened the
negotiations for the marriage of Louis to the Princess
of Savoy. Anne of Austria was in despair, though
she pretended to be resigned to the prospect of
having a Savoyard daughter-in-law. But the policy
of Mazarin was successful. A Spanish envoy,
Pimental, met the French Court at Lyons, with
offers for peace and a marriage alliance. The Duchess of Savoy and her daughter went home in December and serious conferences were opened at Montargis
and Paris between Mazarin and Pimental in February, 1659. A suspension of arms was agreed
upon in May, 1659, and the final negotiations took
place later in the year. During the autumn the
passion of Louis for Marie Mancini reached its
height. And the episode has attracted more attention perhaps than it was worth owing to the demonstrative conduct of the young Italian girl and the
obstinacy of the King. Marie had worked herself

up into a state of fury at the idea of Louis marrying "a woman as ugly as Margaret of Savoy." After the negotiations with Savoy had been broken off, she undoubtedly hoped to bring to a similar conclusion the negotiation for Louis' marriage with the Infanta. Mazarin was as strongly opposed to the idea of a marriage between the King and his niece as was the Queen-Mother herself. The King was resolved, it is said, to marry Marie. Mademoiselle de Montpensier relates how he threw himself on his knees before Mazarin and his mother and begged to be allowed to do as he wished. Without the least hesitation Mazarin determined to remove the object of Louis' affections, and Marie on June 21st had to depart to Brouage. He then set out for Saint-Jean-de-Luz, where he arrived on July 28th. On the journey he wrote to Louis urging him not to allow himself to be mastered by every passion, but to be a great King, and in a later letter he conjured him in the name of glory, honour, and God's service to act wisely in this matter. For some weeks, however, Louis, backed up by a small Court clique, persisted in carrying on his suit and in corresponding with Marie. Mazarin therefore wrote several more letters to the King and the Queen-Mother, in all of which insisting vehemently on the damage which a marriage with Marie would inflict on France.

On August 13th Louis saw her, but from that time his passion calmed, and he entered with interest into the negotiation for his marriage with the Infanta. It was not till November 7th that the peace of the Pyrenees was finally signed and Mazarin's life-work

was completed. France gained all Artois, except Aire
and St. Omer, Roussillon and Cerdagne, Gravelines,
with several places in Flanders, and portions of Hainault and Luxemburg. Though the Duke of Lorraine was to be reinstated, the fortifications of
Nancy were to be destroyed. Several places were
to be ceded to France and French troops were
to be permitted to march through the duchy. This
treaty not only insured the preponderance of France
in Europe, but it prepared the way for her domination in Europe under Louis XIV. But the peace of
the Pyrenees was only part of the general pacification of Europe. A great northern war had been
raging for some years, intensified by the ambition
and conquests of Charles X. of Sweden. In February, 1658, the mediation of France and England
had brought about the treaty of Roskild between
Sweden and Denmark, but war broke out again the
same year, and Charles X. spoke of annihilating Denmark and even of pillaging Rome. During the negotiations which led to the treaty of the Pyrenees,
Mazarin discussed the affairs of the north, and as
soon as the treaty was signed intervened energetically. It is difficult to see how the northern war
would have ended, had not the death of Charles X.
in February, 1660, simplified the situation. In
March, 1660, under the mediation of England,
France, and the United Provinces, the treaty of
Copenhagen was signed between Sweden and Denmark, and in May of the same year the influence of
Mazarin was again conspicuously shown in bringing
about the conclusion of the treaty of Oliva between

Poland and Brandenburg. In the pacification of the North the traditions of French policy were preserved. Sweden, the ally of France, continued to hold her ancient superiority in the Baltic, and Mazarin had the glory of having done much to secure the peace of Europe in both the North and the South.

From Saint-Jean-de-Luz Mazarin proceeded to Toulouse to join the Court (November 21st). The early months of 1660 were spent in a tour through Languedoc and Provence. It was desirable that Louis should be acquainted with the south of France; his presence there was also imperatively demanded for political reasons.

Provence had never thoroughly shaken itself free from its Fronde leanings, and the old municipal spirit of independence was strong in the cities. Toulon had with difficulty been brought to obedience; Marseilles still was in a disturbed state. The presence of the King would do much to pacify the turbulent province. For many years, too, the French navy had been neglected, and one of the principal objects of Louis' visit to Toulon was to superintend measures for the improvement of the navy, for the overthrow of the pirates who swarmed in the Mediterranean, and for the encouragement of commerce in the Levant.

Louis arrived at Aix on January 17, 1660. There the Prince of Condé visited him and was reconciled. It was at Aix too that Louis received the ratification of the treaty of the Pyrenees—an event celebrated on February 3d by a solemn Te Deum. After visiting many interesting places in Provence, Louis

proceeded to Toulon, and his visit undoubtedly
gave a considerable impetus to the revival of the
French marine. During the King's stay at Toulon,
Marseilles was punished by the Duke of Mercœur,
and a citadel built to keep the population in order.
After the return of the Court to Aix on March
8th, Orange, which belonged to the House of Orange-
Nassau, was compelled to recognise the royal
suzerainty.

Having pacified the southern provinces, Louis
proceeded to Saint-Jean-de-Luz, passing through
Avignon and Montpellier, Narbonne, Perpignan,
Toulouse, to Bayonne, where he arrived on May 1st.
After numerous conferences the marriage of Louis
with the Infanta took place, the marriage ceremony
being performed by the Bishop of Pampeluna on
June 7th and the Bishop of Bayonne on June 9th.
The Court then returned slowly to Paris, the royal
entry not taking place till August 26th, and then
being celebrated in a most magnificent manner with
all the pomp which the capital and Court could
command. It was from the balcony of the Hôtel
d'Aumont that Madame Scarron "in company with
the Queen Dowager, the Queen of England, Princess
Henrietta, and Cardinal Mazarin" witnessed this
triumphal entry into Paris of Louis and his Queen
Marie Thérèse, and both Racine and La Fontaine
marked the occasion by respective productions, the
former writing an ode entitled *La Nymphe de la
Seine*. The procession lasted through the long hours
of a beautiful summer's day, and Madame Scarron,
who, twenty-four years later, was to be Marie Thé-

rèse's successor, declared in a letter to a friend that "nothing I or any one could say could give you an idea of the magnificent spectacle; nothing could surpass it."

The minority of Louis XIV. is a very important period in his long reign. It is impossible to understand the policy of the great King without carefully appreciating the atmosphere in which he passed his early years, and the varied circumstances of his long minority. Brought up amid the turbulent scenes of the Fronde he learnt to estimate at its true value not only the fidelity of the fickle populace of Paris, but also the loyalty of a large portion of the unstable nobility. The influence of the Fronde struggle upon Louis' policy in later years was not wholly beneficial. Much of his impatience of any opposition, much of his intolerance towards those who held religious or political views different from his own, may be traced to the events of the years 1648–1653. Somewhat naturally those events impressed him with a keen sense of the importance of unity. France divided against itself had seemed at one time likely to be the prey of the Spanish soldiery. As late as 1659 revolts in Normandy and Anjou, Poitou and Sologne, came to justify Mazarin's wisdom in making the treaty of the Pyrenees; while in 1660 it was thought advisable that Louis should make a progress through Provence to allay the discontent and curb the independent spirit of the south of France.

If there was one lesson more likely than another to be engrained upon the mind of a young ruler in France in 1660 it was the necessity of unity. The nobles were discredited, the *Parlement* of Paris had been unable to shake itself free from its narrow surroundings, the country was groaning under heavy taxation.

The only hope for France seemed to be in the establishment of a paternal despotism which should enforce peace on the warring factions within the country, and ensure the return of prosperity by a firm foreign and a well regulated home policy.

To repeat the common remark that Mazarin neglected Louis' education is simply to repeat what is absolutely untrue. That Louis was not well read, that he had no literary tastes, that as far as literary accomplishments went he was ignorant, is perfectly true. But was it no education to be from the year 1653 constantly with the most astute statesman in Europe, and continually to hear fall from his lips remarks teeming with political wisdom?

From his intercourse with Mazarin Louis learnt the advisability, while profiting by the advice of his able ministers and generals, of keeping the direction of affairs in his own hands. The necessity of prudence in making plans, and of perseverance and tact in carrying them out, was impressed upon Louis during his minority with great assiduity by the minister. No little of Louis' skill in managing men in later years was due to the principles inculcated by Mazarin. For France as she then was Mazarin could not have done better than to teach the King to love an active and energetic life, to be his own master, and to govern with dignity and firmness.

The Venetian ambassador in 1660 professed surprise at the dignity, grace, and affability of the young King; but if Louis's firm treatment of the *Parlement* of Paris at the Bed of Justice in April, 1655, is borne in mind there is no need for surprise when we find that he was quite prepared at the time of Mazarin's death to take up the *métier* of a king.

The turbulence, want of patriotism, and general disorder which characterised a large portion of his early years had by 1661 stamped firmly upon Louis' mind the advantages of government by one.

It is doubtful, however, if these conceptions of government, impressed upon him as they were, not only by his own experience, but also by Mazarin himself, would have been thoroughly put into execution had his character not developed in the right direction owing to the exigencies of the war with Spain. Louis was naturally susceptible to the temptations of a Court. He was always liable to be drawn by "the silken thread" of pleasure. During those important years of a man's life when boyhood gives place to manhood, the enervating atmosphere of the Court and its surroundings was constantly being replaced by the bracing atmosphere of the camp. Ever since 1649 Louis had lived more or less among his troops, and the enthusiasm created by his presence justified Mazarin's policy. The victory of Rethel in 1650 was in part due to that enthusiasm.

The influence of the war with Spain upon Louis' character was thus highly beneficial. Saved from effeminacy, he never yielded, to any serious extent, to the allurements and fascinations of Court life.

Blessed with a good physique, he boylike threw himself with the utmost readiness into military life.
Mazarin encouraged this taste, and, as we have seen,
had the greatest difficulty in checking Louis in his
constant wish to be at the front.   As it was, he saw
real warfare as practised by Turenne, and he took
part in sieges as well as in military progresses through
the Spanish Netherlands.   It was his over-exertions
during the campaign against the maritime towns that
brought on the one dangerous illness of his youthful days.

The effect upon the army, and indeed upon a
nation as susceptible as the French to military glory
of having among them a young King anxious to
take the lead in warlike enterprises, cannot be overestimated.   His military experiences during these
years not only gave him a powerful hold upon his
subjects, but aided him in conducting the numerous
wars in which France played so leading a part during
the ensuing fifty years.

Mazarin rightly laid great stress upon this practical side of the King's education.   He was encouraged to hunt and to dance.   The woods at
Vincennes offered plenty of opportunities for the
chase ; the annual winter festivities of the Court
resulted in Louis becoming a very graceful and
skilful dancer.

By the time of Mazarin's death Louis had shown
himself worthy of all the care bestowed upon him
by the minister.   He had borne willingly the fatigues
and privations of many campaigns ; he had always
shown energy and vigour.

But Mazarin was not content with merely watching over the physical development of the young King. He was equally careful to instruct him in diplomacy and in knowledge of foreign countries. To the Spanish war and the opportunities it offered for discussing foreign relations Louis owed much of his very considerable acquaintance with the practice and policy of the leading European powers. During his stay at Metz in 1657 he received, as we have seen, invaluable lessons from Mazarin on this subject, which were supplemented by the general advice given him by the minister when on his death-bed.

In 1661 Mazarin could truly say that he had not only given France peace and glory, but had also bequeathed to her a King capable of continuing and increasing her national prosperity.

Louis' natural qualities, his seriousness, his dignity, his power of application, his firmness, had all been watched over and developed by the Cardinal who had also wisely accustomed him to the life of a soldier and had impressed upon him lessons in diplomacy and worldly wisdom.

There was no sudden transformation on Mazarin's death. Louis simply stepped into his minister's place. Hitherto Mazarin had ruled. Now the King ruled. Hitherto the country had been governed by a Prime Minister. After Mazarin's death Louis became his own Prime Minister. The saying, *L'État, c'est moi* marks accurately the character of his government from 1661.

6

CHAPTER III.

LOUIS XIV. RULES.

1661–1715.

ON the death of Mazarin in 1661 Louis had already reigned eighteen years. He was now in his twenty-third year, and up to this time had been content to let the Cardinal rule. Under the *régime* of Mazarin and Anne of Austria the King had been little more than a cipher to his subjects. Men were now to realise that a new epoch had been reached in the history of France, and that in the development in store for this country the personality of their sovereign would be an important factor.

In appearance Louis, though admirably proportioned, was slightly below the middle height. His eyes were blue, his nose long and well formed. His hair, which was remarkable for its abundance, was allowed to fall over his shoulders. With his handsome features and his serious—perhaps phlegmatic —expression he seemed admirably fitted to play the part of a monarch. He had all the kingly gifts necessary for the rôle. He was dignified, reserved, calm, and courteous. Majestic in person, his manners and carriage were above criticism. He was a graceful dancer and an excellent horseman. His tact even in the smallest matters was unerring, and his sense of propriety and order unusual in so young a man. He had cultivated with considerable success the habit of self-control; he rarely laughed, and seldom gave way to anger. His gravity of manner and habitual discretion impressed favourably those with whom he came in contact. "He would have been every inch a king," Saint-Simon tells us, "even if he had been born under the roof of a beggar," and Bolingbroke, writing from personal observation, declared that, "if he was not the greatest king he was the best actor of majesty, at least, that ever filled a throne."

He was, however, lacking in originality; there was in him no spark of genius. He loved details for their own sake. Flattery of the most exaggerated kind was ever acceptable to him. Though the Jesuits had superintended his religious training he was in reality ignorant of the rudiments of Christianity, and his general education had been scandalously neglected owing to the incapacity of Villeroi and Péréfixe. He remained ignorant all his life. Bolingbroke says he jested sometimes at his own ignorance; on the other hand, Saint-Simon tells us that on other occasions he spoke bitterly of his deficiencies. He certainly was inquisitive, and wrote to his agent Comminges, who was in England in 1663, for a report on English men of letters. "My intention is," he said, "to be informed of all that is best and exquisite in all countries and in all branches of knowledge, and to make the best of such information for my honour, and service, and glory." It followed naturally from his lack of knowledge and limited intelligence, that he was often, though unconsciously, guided by those who had stronger wills and more capable minds. His confessors, who were, as a rule, able and well cultivated men, shared, in turn with Colbert, Louvois, and Madame de Maintenon, a powerful influence over his actions.

As long as Colbert lived, the influences brought to bear on Louis were on the whole beneficent, but towards the end of his reign Louis allowed himself to be guided at times by the judgment of Madame de Maintenon, who herself was influenced by certain priests, whose opinions often lacked wisdom and discernment. Freed from Colbert's advice, Louis tended to promote to the highest offices of state men often incapable or untrustworthy. He always disliked brilliance of intellect, and distrusted men of distinguished abilities. Like Walpole, he preferred to see around him mediocrity of talent, and hated the assertion of individuality in any shape or form. When Chamillard was allowed to rule at Versailles, and Villeroi, Tallard, and Marsin were preferred to Catinat, Vendôme, and Villars, it was evident that Louis's successes in the early portion of his reign

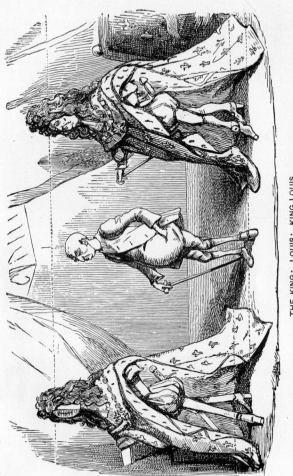

THE KING; LOUIS; KING LOUIS.

(From a sketch by Thackeray in his *Paris Sketch Book*.)

were due in great measure to his good fortune in finding round him a number of able men, trained under Mazarin's *régime*. It must, however, be remembered, in extenuation of Louis' later appointments, that he was always led to believe that the genius of Colbert, Louvois, and Lionne was but a reflection of his own, and that he was the moving spirit in all departments of government. Accordingly, when a minister died, Louis, convinced that all his subordinates were equal in talent and looked to him for the initiative, simply handed on the vacant office to a relative of its last occupant. What aggravated the faults engendered by Louis' bad education was his pride. This feature in his character rapidly became very prominent, and early developed into the worst form of arrogance. It led him to consider himself omnipotent and to delight in self-glorification. Through it he neglected the public good, and adopted a policy of mere personal passion and ambition. He imagined he had educated all his ministers, and that France owed her European position, her victories by sea and land, and her diplomatic triumphs entirely to his own skill, foresight, and resolution. As he grew older, the flaws in his character, pardonable as they might be in his earlier years, degenerated into very serious faults. His ignorance grew into something like stupidity, his firmness developed into obstinacy, his pride became mere arrogance and selfishness. Hence he considered himself above sworn contracts, hence he showed no regard for human life. He believed himself to be under the special care of

Providence, to be above all other men ; to be a privileged King among kings. Caprice at times seems to have dictated many of his actions. He becomes more and more impatient of opposition, and after the peace of Nimeguen he certainly for a time laboured under the delusion that he was permitted by God to undertake any scheme no matter how daring. The only justification for Louis is to be found (1) in his early education and surroundings,—even at an early age it was instilled in him that kings might do as they pleased ; (2) in the attitude of the clergy, who from Bossuet downwards vied with each other in the most abject flattery of the King; (3) in the atmosphere of the corrupt Court where adulation of Louis grew into one might almost say idolatry. He was assured that all his wars were justifiable ; the real condition of his kingdom was never brought to his notice ; he was always ignorant of the state of public opinion ; he had no friend in whom he could confide and from whom he could learn the truth. Like all despotic monarchs, he was liable to be influenced by Court intrigues. Two of his ablest generals were the victims of Court disfavour, and it was only the stress of events that forced them into prominence in the Dutch and Spanish Succession wars respectively.

His strength lay in his firm belief in himself, in his conviction of the divine origin of royalty, in his determination to be in reality a King, in his energy and honest desire to do his duty. Only a few of those about him had any idea of his true character, of his sense of responsibility, of his resolve to carry out conscientiously the duties of kingship. He was known to be fond of pleasure, to be timid, self-willed, and ignorant. The courtiers naturally looked forward to the reign of an easy-going, perhaps of a lazy monarch, to an age of fêtes; while the country hoped for a period of peace and prosperity after the late internal commotions and foreign wars.

But keen observers had already formed a different opinion of the King's aims and capacities. Le Tellier had noticed "the basis of severity and seriousness with which Louis knew how to strengthen the natural kindliness of his nature," and Mazarin had declared that "he will set off later but will go further than all the others," and that he had in him "the making of four kings and of one good man." Before his death, Mazarin had moreover taught him the duties of kingship and those rules of kingcraft to which he attached great importance. He had laid great stress upon the necessity of defending his crown and country against internal factions and foreign interference; he had induced him to be present at meetings of the royal Council; in a word he did all in his power to render Louis capable of taking the government into his own hands. And Louis fulfilled all the expectations of the Cardinal. He worked five hours a day till his death. "I gave myself as a law," he himself says, "to work regularly twice a day for two or three hours each time with various persons, without speaking of the hours I spent working by myself. There was no moment when it was not allowed to speak to me about business, if there was any urgency." "Those who believed," wrote Lionne, "that our master would soon tire of business were greatly mistaken; the further we go, the greater pleasure he takes in devoting himself entirely to it." The lessons of Mazarin had soon borne fruit and only confirmed the previous determination of the young King to rule absolutely and without a Prime Minister. He himself tells us that he always hated the idea of any limitation to his power, and that from his infancy the names of king *fainéant* and mayors of the palace were very distasteful to him. The events of the Fronde struggle had strengthened his resolution to make himself the real head of France. He never forgot the troubles of his minority, and especially that January night in 1649, spent at Saint-Germain, when the members of the Court had neither beds nor fires. Deeply impressed on his mind, too, was the connection between the Jansenists and the Fronde movement. Hence his consistent opposition to the Jansenist party. Under Louis XIV. then the absolute monarchy which had been revived by Henry IV. and organised by Richelieu was definitely established. Not only was the monarch absolute in fact, but a definite theory of absolutism was laid down.

The theory of the divine origin of kingship was firmly held by Louis and generally accepted in France. In his memoirs Louis lays it down that kings are God's lieutenants, answerable to him alone. The King represents the nation, and all authority lies in the hands of the King. " L'état, c'est moi " represents accurately Louis' conviction that in him were centered all the threads of internal government as well as of foreign policy, and that all Frenchmen were merely instruments for carrying out his wishes.

He was the embodiment of the power and greatness of France. He was convinced that a divine instinct would lead him to make right decisions. An absolute unlimited monarchy was especially agreeable to God. Thus Louis' policy both at home and abroad can be shown to have a distinctly religious basis. His wars of aggrandisement were excused on the ground that the victories of the French arms would lead to the advance of religion. In his attacks on the Protestants, Jansenists, and Quietists, he was merely carrying to its logical conclusion his theory of absolutism. But he only arrived at a decision in religious matters after very careful consideration. Painfully and laboriously he came to his conclusions, and unfortunately in each case—in the revocation of the Edict of Nantes, in the exile of Fénélon from the Court, in the demolition of Port Royal, and in the introduction of the Bull Unigenitus into the kingdom—Louis made a wrong decision, and inflicted in rapid succession a series of severe blows on the unity and prosperity of France. In his view of the divine origin of the royal power Louis was supported by the Church. Bossuet's celebrated declaration of the theory of divine right is well known. He asserted that kings were gods, that they carried on their brows the stamp of divine authority, and that they had to render an account of their actions to no man. The adoption of this theory of divine right, when joined to a consciousness of unlimited power, brought Louis to believe in his own infallibility.

On these principles then France was governed for nearly a century and a half. There was, however, a

striking difference between the reigns of Louis XIV.
and his successors which was well expressed by the
Maréchale de Richelieu when he said that "under
Louis XIV. one dared not speak, under Louis XV.
one spoke low, under Louis XVI. one spoke loud."

Louis XIV. was not content merely to accept the
theory of absolute power; he was resolved to be King
in fact, and carried out his determination during
the whole of his long reign. The first half of the
eighteenth century saw the government of France
directed by two prelates, Dubois and Fleury, while
in the seventeenth century till 1661 Richelieu and
Mazarin had controlled the destinies and administered the affairs of the country. Between these two
periods, that is from the death of Mazarin to the rise
of Dubois, Louis governed by himself. Under him
the absolute monarchy became definitely a distinct
form of government with its own institutions, organs,
and agents responsible to the King alone. All rival
authorities and jurisdictions were suppressed. The
States-General were never summoned. A government of divine origin had no need to consult the
people, and Louis himself tells us in his memoirs that
it is certain that the necessity of accepting the law
from the people is the worst calamity that can fall
on a man of kingly rank. In his memoirs too,
he notes the results of his meditations upon Parliamentary government in England. "This subjection,
which places the sovereign under a necessity to
receive the law from his people, is the worst evil
which can happen to a man in our position." And
in another place he speaks of "the misery of those

who are abandoned to the indiscreet will of *une populace assemblée.*" Louis could never understand the English government by King and Parliament, and was ever urging the later Stuarts to establish a despotism after the French model. He was himself convinced that an absolute monarchy was now established for ever in France, and he certainly did his best to prevent his successor from finding in existence any authority which did not owe its origin or character to the King, or any constituted body which wandered " from the bounds of respect." The *Parlement* of Paris, which in spite of Richelieu's severe edict of 1641 had during the Fronde period made an attempt to set limits to the royal power, was not likely to escape. The pages of its registers containing an account of its action during the late troubles were torn out, its political powers were taken away, and in 1673 an edict appeared forbidding the *Parlement* to make any remonstrance until the royal edicts were registered. Though destined in the eighteenth century to again play an important part in opposition to the royal power, the *Parlement* of Paris was compelled during the latter half of the seventeenth century to submit quietly to the despotic *régime* of Louis XIV.

Nor did the provincial Estates or the towns escape. Richelieu had taken advantage of the want of union between the provinces, and had struck heavy blows at their independence. The Estates of Languedoc, Burgundy, and Brittany alone preserved any semblance of their former influence, and these were compelled, partly by corruption, partly by intimidation, to submit to the dictation of the central power. From 1672 to the Revolution the provincial Estates have practically no history. In that year Colbert crushed some signs of independence in Provence and imprisoned ten deputies. In 1673 similar scenes were enacted in Brittany. A royal edict was sufficient to suppress what remained in France of the ancient municipal liberties. The task of securing the complete obedience of the nobles was equally easy. Louis had only to continue and develop the policy begun by Richelieu. Their powers in the provinces were jealously watched and limited, the Princes were not placed at the head of the French armies, the privileges of the great officers were closely curtailed. In 1662 the title of Colonel-General of the infantry was suppressed ; and the powers hitherto entrusted to the Colonel-General of the cavalry were curtailed. The importance of the marshals was lessened ; the right of nominating naval officers was no longer to be in the hands of the Admiral of France. What was more important was the exclusion of the nobles from all government offices. While preserving their obnoxious privileges, the nobles ceased to be a political power ; nay more, the King, sympathizing with the financial embarrassments of the aristocracy, was not unwilling to increase their privileges. They became mere courtiers and in many instances the King's pensioners. The great fault of the seventeenth century was that as a result of this policy all classes were dislocated and could not work together. The principal reason why the Revolution came about was not because the privileged classes had too much power but because they had none at all. The cleavage between classes in France grew wider and wider until the emigrations in 1789, and the succeeding years forcibly illustrated the real drift of the policy definitely begun by Richelieu and continued by all future rulers of France.

The power of the Church was not likely to interfere with Louis' plans for the establishment of a centralised government. On the contrary, Louis derived his despotic principles in great measure from the Church. To him the clergy looked for repressive measures against the Huguenots; on him the Jesuits relied for the suppression of the Jansenists, whose sympathies with the *Parlement* of Paris during the Fronde Louis never forgot; from him, too, the advocates of an independent Gallican Church hoped to obtain the realisation of their dreams. The establishment of a powerful Christian monarchy bent upon securing unity of doctrine was Bossuet's ideal government, and commended itself to the mass of the French clergy. Louis' reign afforded another proof of the truth of the *dictum* that "in France the Church could not divorce itself from the Crown."

Thus on the ruins of national, provincial, and municipal liberties was raised and organised a new administrative despotism which was to last till the Revolution. At the head of this royal administration was the King, and under him the ministers and secretaries of state, whose powers were greatly enhanced on the abolition of the post of Prime Minister. Over all the province were placed *intendants*, each of whom had under him assistants or *sub-*

délégués in each of his districts. These *intendants* were indefatigable workers taken for the most part from the middle class. Their influence was felt in all directions, and their supervision extended to every part of the province which was under their control. Though popular with the nation the despotism of Louis XIV. was hard upon individuals. A system of espionage was always in use and *lettres de cachet* were freely used. Liberty of the subject was unknown. The well known incident of the " Man with the Iron Mask " is an illustration of the tyrannical treatment which Frenchmen had to put up with under the Bourbon absolutism. In 1673 a man was arrested by Louvois near Peronne, and incarcerated in the Bastille. He was taken thence to Pignerol and placed under the care of Saint-Mars. In 1674 he was removed to Exilles, and after thirteen years' imprisonment there, was taken to the Isle of St. Marguerite. In 1698 Saint-Mars brought him to the Bastille, where he died in 1703. The name of this mysterious prisoner has never yet been ascertained. Among numerous suggestions as to his identity it has been urged that he was Fouquet, the Armenian Patriarch ; Avèdie, a twin brother of Louis XIV., Colbert's son, Cromwell's son ; Matthioli, a minister of the Duke of Mantua ; De Marchied, a Lorrainer, who was concerned in a plot to murder Louis XIV. His arrest took place simultaneously with the suppression of the liberties of the *Parlements* and the provincial Estates, and marks the time when Louis' system of government was in full working order.

It has sometimes been urged that in the States-General, in the *Parlement*, in the provincial Estates, in the corporations, and in the members of the noblesse and Church there could be found the germs of modern constitutional life. " The various institutions existed side by side, complicated and clumsy in their form, thwarting or supporting one another, according to the positions which the accident of their origin had given them." Some writers lament that no attempt was made to develop and vivify these germs of constitutional life, and so gradually to lead to the formation of a limited monarchy in which the representative principle had full recognition. The task of bringing the different institutions of France into harmony and friendly action, of establishing an equilibrium between the prerogatives of the Crown and the privileges of the nobles, could only have been effected by the King. The representative system had been well tried during the religious wars in the latter half of the previous century, and had been found wanting. It had then been recognised, even by advocates of constitutional government, that the States-General and the *Parlements* were incapable of giving France a good government. Henry IV.'s accession to the throne marked the desire of the vast majority of France for a personal monarchy. The feeling which led to the restoration of the power of the Crown under Henry IV. was, if possible, stronger at the close of the Fronde troubles. Even supposing that the establishment of constitutional government in France was possible before the Revolution, the hour and the man had not arrived in 1661. To begin with, the task of trusting the upper classes with a share of the government, and teaching them to prefer well-regulated activity to selfishness, and the task of raising the nation generally to a sense of its political responsibilities, required a man of different calibre from Louis XIV. The policy of Richelieu and Mazarin, too, had rendered any attempt to remove the deep divisions which separated the different classes in France peculiarly difficult. The Fronde had clearly demonstrated the worthlessness of the nobles, their want of any statesmanlike qualities, their sordid selfishness. It would have been impossible to secure their co-operation in any work of reform.

Besides, Louis' whole train of thought took him in an opposite direction. As King by divine right his suppression of national and provincial liberties was merely the logical outcome of his opinions. While vindicating his claims to absolute authority he was fired by the ambition to govern his country beneficently and gloriously. He intended to give France the blessings of a paternal despotism and to make her the leading power in Europe. There were many circumstances that tended to confirm him in this resolution. The French nation supported him with enthusiasm. They had no wish for any more constitutional experiments ; they had done with political theories and anti-monarchical sentiments. They were wearied of the struggles of the nobles for place and power ; they were sick of the petty ambitions of such men as Retz and Condé.

A hundred years later the struggles and divisions

among the Whigs caused the English people to show
a similar enthusiasm at the accession of George III.
Like George III., Louis XIV. had a firm determination not only to rule but also to rule well. Both
kings came to relieve their respective kingdoms
from the turmoil of factions and to make the royal
power felt through the length and breadth of the
land. The factious conduct of the Whigs brought
about the restoration of authority in England at the
hands of George III. The confused struggles of the
Fronde strengthened and firmly established the absolute monarchy in France. From Philippe Augustus to Louis XIV. the French nation had looked to
their kings to defend them from invasion, to check
internal anarchy, and to win glory. From the battle
of Bouvines to the treaty of the Pyrenees royalty
had been popular in France. The nation now expected at the hands of the King fresh achievements
and more military glory, and Louis found on Mazarin's death that he had the means in his hand of
satisfying the national aspirations.

France was the only country in Europe which was
capable of taking the initiative in Europe. The work
of Richelieu and Mazarin had been thoroughly done,
and there was practically no check to the royal power.
Louis had simply to follow the lines of their policy,
which in itself was no difficult task, for France possessed in Colbert the best administrator, in Lionne,
Servien, Grémonville the best diplomatists, and in
Condé and Turenne the best generals in Europe.
Corneille, Molière, and Descartes too were supreme
in the departments of heroic poetry, of comedy, and

of philosophy. Louis himself was as firmly bent on preserving the dignity of his Crown and on securing glory as any of his subjects could wish. " I will be found ready," he wrote to D'Estrades, his Ambassador in England, with regard to a *point d'honneur* in 1662, " to put my own state in jeopardy rather than tarnish by any faintheartedness the glory which I am seeking in all things as the principal aim of my actions." Already in 1661 D'Estrades, when establishing himself in England, had been carefully instructed " jealously to preserve the dignity of his Crown in any Court whither he is going." He was further " to preserve the pre-eminence to which the King is entitled, allowing no ambassador to go before him except the Emperor's in case he were to send one to England." The famous struggle between the French and Spanish ambassadors in the streets of London took place in October, 1661, and though temporarily defeated Louis' energetic action resulted in his triumph. No Spanish ambassador would henceforth compete for precedence with the most Christian King, and a medal was struck to commemorate the event. In August, 1662, the attack of the Papal guard upon Créqui, the French ambassador at Rome, took place, and again Louis successfully vindicated his honour and the respect due to etiquette. It was pretty evident to France, and indeed to Europe, that the honour of his country was safe in the hands of the elegant and vigorous young King.

Let us then sum up the aims of Louis XIV. on Mazarin's death. In the first place he desired to give

France a good government, and in spite of the many drawbacks of the old *régime* he may be said to have succeeded. In place of the old feudal disorganisation and independence France became well organised and well administered. The royal orders to the provinces were transmitted with rapidity and precision. Each branch of the administration obeyed the central authority. Justice was reorganised and greatly improved. Louis' code of civil and criminal law was in many ways admirable. The army was well disciplined and ready for the reforms of Turenne and Louvois; the finances were placed under a regular system, a strong naval power was created, trading companies were established, the French colonies in North America were strengthened, ports were opened, canals dug, and arsenals built. Industry and commerce were vigorously supported, manufacturing companies were patronised, public instruction was authorised, and literature and arts were favoured. The royal administration undoubtedly did great things for France. The royal power had found France divided; it gave her union. It found France a mere duchy; it made her a kingdom. From being composed of nobles and serfs, France became consolidated into a great nation.

In the second place Louis was bent on placing France in the forefront of European nations, and on giving to his House the position held in Europe by the Hapsburg dynasty for one hundred and thirty years. He aspired to found a strong Empire which should resemble that of Charles the Great.

Thus on the death of Mazarin the French nation looked forward to a period brilliant in military successes, in diplomacy, and marked by commercial and industrial development, to compensate them for the confusion which had characterised the government of the late Cardinal. In the young King the nation saw an epitome of itself, and it recognised in him a man who sympathised with all those aspirations which were peculiarly dear to the genius of the French people. Louis' youth, his handsome and attractive appearance, his dignified and royal air, appealed to his countrymen. He knew that their admiration was due to their expectation of success abroad, and of unity and prosperity at home. During the period ending with the death of Colbert in 1683, in spite of his boundless egotism and his exaggerated notion of absolute power, he satisfied these national expectations. For as long as he had good advisers, Louis was on the whole free from the commission of serious blunders such as marked the latter period of his life. Colbert, Turenne, and Vauban all belong to this period, and all contributed to making France the leading state in Europe. From 1683 to 1715 Louis becomes prematurely old, suffers at times from bad health, allows his egotism to increase, while freed from the wise counsels of his great Minister he yields more than ever to the advice of Louvois, of Madame de Maintenon, and of Le Tellier. He advances such men as Chamillard and Villeroi. By his mistakes he endangers the political edifice reared in the earlier portion of his reign. On the other hand the errors in taste which appear again and again between his mother's death and the death of his Queen are not repeated. The La Vallière and Montespan episodes are closed, and though the Court may become dull it is at any rate decorous. Apart, too, from his many mistakes, his diplomatic interests are as keen as ever, and he shows over and over again remarkable insight into the position of European politics. His courage during the Spanish Succession war was worthy of all praise, and it received its reward in the firm establishment of Philip on the Spanish throne.

In spite, then, of much that goes to show that Louis was a second-rate man ; in spite of the saying that he was like his own Versailles, splendid, showy, but essentially heavy, commonplace, and vulgar, in Louis' character can be found many elements of greatness. His firm belief in himself, his sense of duty which led him to bear " the trade of kingship " on his shoulders for some fifty-four years, the patience with which he carried out his aim of making France the leading power in Europe, all go to prove that Louis was far from being a mere commonplace man whose ideas were shallow and whose acts were showy and pretentious. He worked regularly and conscientiously all his life. He had a very elevated conception of the responsibilities of the kingly office. No amusement, and not even illness, prevented him from performing his regular duties. " We are not private persons," he once said ; " we owe ourselves to the public." In his private life he was during most of his reign considerate, thoughtful of others, courteous to women. He had all those qualities which go to make a gentleman. A great King he was, and western civilisation owes much to his reign.

Under him France was to Europe what he himself was to France. She gave the tone to European society, she laid down the canons of taste in literature and the arts, she spoke the decisive word in politics.

NOTE.—"The Man with the Iron Mask" (see p. 94) is now said to have been a certain Lieutenant-General de Bulonde who was struck with panic at Coni in 1691 and raised the siege. Louis XIV. was so infuriated at his conduct that he incarcerated him in Pignerol. The literature on this subject is considerable. It may be well to remember Louis XIV.'s own words : " If you knew who it was, you would find it not in the least interesting."

CHAPTER IV.

THE FALL OF FOUQUET AND THE RISE OF COLBERT.

1661.

MAZARIN died at Vincennes between two and three o'clock on the morning of the 9th of March, 1661. On being informed of the fact Louis, about two hours later, held his first Council, which sat for some three hours. Only three ministers in addition to Louis were present: Le Tellier, the Secretary for War, Lionne, who was practically the Secretary for Foreign Affairs, and Fouquet, the *Procureur-général* and the Superintendent of Finance. The latter was at that time living at his house at Saint-Mandé, and it was necessary to send the younger Brienne to summon him. Brienne met Fouquet crossing the Park in great haste, and very angry at not having been told of the Cardinal's serious condition.

Later in the day the King returned to Paris, and the next morning, March 10th, he held at the Louvre a second Council, there being present, in addition to Le Tellier, Lionne, and Fouquet, the Chancellor Seguier, the two Briennes, and the other Secretaries of State, Duplessis-Guénégaud, and La Vrillière. At this Council Louis made his memorable declaration. "Sir," he said, addressing the Chancellor, "I have summoned you with my Ministers and Secretaries of State to tell you that hitherto I have been right willing to let my affairs be managed by the late Cardinal ; in the future I shall be my own Prime Minister *(Je serai à l'avenir mon premier ministre)*." He then forbade the Chancellor, the Secretaries of State, and the Superintendent of Finance to seal any agreement, to sign any despatch, or to pay any money without his knowledge and order. "I have already explained to you my wishes," he said to Fouquet ; "I request you to make use of Colbert, whom the late Cardinal had recommended to me." At this meeting of the Council Louis arranged the order of each day's work. From nine to eleven each morning his inner Council, composed of Fouquet, Le Tellier, and Lionne, should meet. The finances should be dealt with in the afternoons. Every other day the Chancellor was to consult with him on judicial matters. Henceforward Louis worked about five hours a day at public business, never allowing himself to be diverted by any amusement whatever. Henceforward he had no Prime Minister, no independent statesman near him. The government was carried on by agents—*gens d'affaires*—who were merely heads of departments answerable directly to himself. George III. had a somewhat similar ideal in part realised during the administration of Lord North.

The same day on which Louis held his celebrated Council, the Archbishop of Rouen had an audience. "Sire," he said, "I have the honour of presiding over the Assembly of the clergy of your kingdom; your Majesty ordered me to consult the Cardinal on all matters; he is now dead; to whom does your Majesty wish that I should address myself in the future?" "To me," was the reply of the King.

The reign of Louis had in reality begun; he united in his own person the power and prestige of the monarchy, as well as of the prime ministership. From his ministers he could expect little help. Chancellor Seguier, then seventy-two years of age, had no statesmanlike qualities, and was avaricious and wanting in firmness. Of the four Secretaries of State, La Vrillière and Duplessis-Guénégaud were trusted by Louis, but had no great capacity. The Count of Brienne, the Secretary for Foreign Affairs, was sixty-six years old and incapable. His son—a mere boy—had the right of succession to his father's post. For some time past, owing to the importance of the foreign policy of France, and to the incapacity of Brienne, Lionne had acted as Secretary of State for Foreign Affairs. And he was now confirmed by Louis in his position. Le Tellier, the Secretary for War, was a hardworking, reserved man, more attached to his own interests than to those of the state. He had a thorough knowledge of the working of the governmental machine, but he was essentially a second-rate man, and his son-in-law, Louvois, was before long associated with him in his office. Fouquet remained Superintendent of Finance. He knew that Mazarin had mistrusted him; he had some idea that the Cardinal had warned Louis against him. He therefore acted cautiously. He made a sort of confession to Louis, pointing out that the necessities of the time were in great measure answerable for the abuses that had crept into the management of the finances. Besides, nothing had been done without the authority of the Cardinal. Fouquet's vindication of himself was accepted, and Louis, apparently satisfied with his promises for the future, evinced no desire to disinter the past. The King's attitude was, according to Fouquet himself, benevolent and reassuring, while his words were clear, precise, noble, and worthy of a great King.

Louis himself says that Fouquet was indispensable to him at that moment. He was aware of the grave and ruinous defects in the financial system of France, but Fouquet's credit was good, and the death of Mazarin had been followed by what amounted to a great financial crisis. Till the new government was firmly established, men were indisposed to lend.

Besides Fouquet's acquaintance with the internal economy of France, he had also a very considerable knowledge of foreign affairs. Louis therefore was willing to use the ablest man of the day in spite of his predisposition against him, at any rate till the governmental machine was in full working order.

To guard himself, however, from any deception, Louis had followed the dying advice of Mazarin, and, while employing Fouquet, confided in Colbert. By making him Intendant of Finance, Louis gave him the supervision of Fouquet's accounts. The day of his Council at the Louvre, the King had a secret interview with Colbert, who, according to the Abbé Choisy, informed him that the Cardinal had concealed at Sedan, at Brissac, at La Fère, at Vincennes, and in the Louvre nearly fifteen millions of ready money ; that apparently his intention was not to leave it to his heirs, and that therefore he intended it for the King.

Money to the extent of about eighteen millions was, it is said, found in all the places indicated, with the exception of the Louvre. This discovery was of great importance in two ways : in the first place it aided the advancement of Colbert in the royal favour, but, what was more important at that moment, it rendered Louis independent of Fouquet.

The events following the death of Mazarin had taken France by surprise. Louis' declaration that henceforward he would rule without a Prime Minister was scoffed at. The people generally applauded his attitude, but those about the Court never believed he would carry out his intention. After the first outburst of joy at the death of Mazarin, there was a widespread feeling that France had been deprived of a statesman who, by giving her peace with Spain, had begun to grapple with the difficulties from which France was suffering.

Though at peace at home and abroad, France was exhausted, and in financial matters had been scandalously mismanaged. Abuses of all sorts were rampant ; manufactures and commerce languished ; the lower orders were heavily taxed, justice was corrupt at its source ; the clergy neglected their duties ; bands of discharged soldiers ravaged the country ; the finances were in inextricable confusion. Gambling was popular, and licentious manners were everywhere prevalent. In this deplorable state of things men doubted the young King's will or ability to restore prosperity to the country. He was apparently given up to amusements of all sorts. It was also to be feared that under the influence of Condé or Turenne he might plunge France into war.

The King being an unknown quantity to his subjects, it was natural they should doubt if he would carry out his resolution, and, breaking with the tradition of the last fifty years, dispense with a Prime Minister.

They did not know that for some time Mazarin had been in the habit of giving Louis valuable advice. They had no idea of Louis' resolution not to be a mere *roi fainéant*. They were also unaware that Louis' attachment to Mazarin was the sole reason for his not having taken the government of France into his own hands sooner. The power which the courtiers believed would be wielded by Louis for three months remained in his hands fifty-four years.

Not, however, till the fall of Fouquet in September, 1661, was it realised the King was in earnest. Till then the ministerial system was hanging in the balance. With the arrest and overthrow of Fouquet, ministerialism received its death-blow, and the re-establishment of the royal power in all its ful-ness was effected. Between March 9th and September 5th, the revolution was organised and carried out. These months between the death of Mazarin and the fall of Fouquet constitute a most momentous episode in the history of France. The circumstances leading to his fall, the greatness of the man, his magnificent ideas, the splendour of his possessions, the blindness of his confidence, the suddenness of his overthrow, and his weary imprisonment, all give a dramatic and melancholy interest to the attempt of Fouquet to become Prime Minister.

Till Fouquet's fall the French world in general showed no indication that it realised the import of the King's firm determination. Convinced that he would soon tire of his devotion to work, the courtiers devoted their energies to discovering the successor to Richelieu and Mazarin. Opinions were widely divided on this question. The nobles had hoped to see Villeroi or Condé take the first place in the royal Council. When neither of these men was summoned to advise Louis, it was thought that the Cardinal de Retz would be chosen. His talents fitted him for the post, he was the one man in France whose power Mazarin dreaded to the last. But Louis was as opposed as Mazarin to De Retz and his friends the Jansenists. Some thought that the solid qualities of Le Tellier marked him out as the successful candidate. But of the three ministers to whom Louis had openly given his confidence, Lionne, Le Tellier, and Fouquet, the last named was the only one who possessed the qualities necessary for a Prime Minister.

" It was generally believed," says Madame de La Fayette, " that the Superintendent would be called upon to take the Government into his hands." There is no doubt whatever that Fouquet himself expected eventually to succeed Mazarin. He did not believe in Louis' perseverance ; he was convinced that in a few months the King would gladly delegate his power to a minister. What rival had Fouquet to fear? He was well aware of his intellectual superiority to Le Tellier and Lionne ; he had already been entrusted with important matters touching not only the internal condition but also the foreign relations of France ; he had frequent confidential interviews with the King. His relations, too, with the Court gave him every confidence. The number of his friends and clients and pensioners was enormous ; he was favoured by the Queen-Mother ; in the Council itself, though Le Tellier might be hostile, Lionne was practically in his pay.

His way seemed so clear, the confidence of the King so assured, that Fouquet neglected to take any precautions, and believed that within a very short time he would be at the head of affairs.

As first minister of a great king he saw opening out before him a wide field for his talents. He was resolved to begin his life over again, to make a fresh start, to enter as it were upon a new career. If he could only become Chancellor he would have a splendid opportunity of carrying out his ambitious projects. The Chancellor had great power ; nothing could be be done without his knowledge, for he signed and sealed all documents. He was present, too, at the meetings of the *Parlement*. Fouquet therefore aimed at ousting Seguier from the Chancellorship as soon as possible.

The restoration of the finances begun by him shortly after the peace of the Pyrenees was, however, his immediate care. He aimed at nothing less than a complete reorganisation of the whole financial system. He drew up a series of tables showing the expenditure of each department for a number of years. He formed plans which were afterwards adopted and carried out by Colbert for the abolition of many glaring abuses in the system of taxation.

But he took no precautions against the machinations of his enemies : he was unaware that Colbert, implicitly trusted by Louis, was occupied in pointing out the shortcomings in his career, and undoubtedly making the worst of the case against him. Colbert also watched Fouquet's accounts very closely in every respect. It was shown at a Council held at Fontainebleau for the reorganisation of colonial commerce that Fouquet had been negligent over details, while on a suggestion made by him that Belle-isle could provide a good harbour for the fleet, Colbert sent spies to Belle-isle to report on the works then in progress.

The history of that eventful summer of 1661 is then full of interest. The continuous series of gaieties at Fontainebleau proceeded as though ministers and King were not simultaneously engaged in laborious and anxious work. And all through these summer months the overthrow of Fouquet was being quietly planned, while the minister himself, unconscious of the seriousness of the crisis, was counting the days to the time when he should govern France as the Prime Minister of Louis XIV.

On April 20th the Court moved to Fontainebleau, where it was joined a few days later by Fouquet. The memoirs of the times fully describe its doings. Round the young King was a galaxy of rank and beauty. Anne of Austria, the King's mother, and Marie Thérèse, his wife, were there. There, too, was Henrietta of England, the bride of the King's brother, the Duke of Orleans. The Duke of Lorraine was there to render homage for his duchy, and among the princes and nobles were to be seen Beaufort and Condé, both so celebrated during the King's minority. It was a time of fêtes and of dances, of expeditions on land by day, and of entertainments on the lake and promenades in the woods by night, these latter often lasting till two or three in the morning. The future was bright with many a hope ; the present was dazzling and fascinating. Men gambled recklessly with borrowed money ; the King himself was not averse to high play. A theatre was erected in the park at Fontainebleau, and a new comedy was played. Lulli was installed superintendent of the royal music. In the *Ballet des Saisons* the King himself represented Spring, and danced with his usual grace and skill.

This mode of life at Fontainebleau—"a delirium of ambition, pleasure, and love"—lasted through the summer months. The King's open admiration for his sister-in-law, followed by his attachment to Louise de la Vallière, are well known incidents of this visit of the Court to Fontainebleau.

LOUISE DE LA VALLIÈRE.

The other side of the picture is of more interest to the historian. The King never allowed his love of pleasure to interfere with his self-imposed duties. His persistent will, his power of work, his delight in grappling with details, his untiring energy, and withal his capacity for dissimulation was never so clearly evidenced as during the summer of 1661. Working with his ministers five or six hours a day, he read all letters from ambassadors and answered them himself.

Negotiations were in progress with Sweden, Poland, Holland, and England. Fouquet's acquaintance with foreign affairs, only equalled by that of Lionne, was fully appreciated by Louis, who employed him specially in the attempt to bring about a marriage alliance between England and Portugal.

Both Turenne and Fouquet were of opinion that greater advantages should have been secured to France by the treaty of the Pyrenees. That treaty rendered France unable to aid Portugal directly, and it was of great importance to France that England should aid the Portuguese to secure their independence. On June 22, 1661, the marriage contract was signed between Charles II. and the Infanta of Portugal. The promise of large subsidies by Louis had won over the English King, and the weight of England was thrown on to the side of Portugal.

In Poland Fouquet aided, with men and money, the party headed by the Queen, who had been a French princess, in their endeavours to get the Duke of Enghien named as successor to the reigning monarch. With Sweden and Holland intimate relations were renewed, though with the latter country a treaty was not made till the following year.

The internal affairs of France also occupied much of the King's attention. He gave large sums to the German Princes; he enlarged and adorned Fontainebleau, Vincennes, the Tuileries, and Versailles. Fouquet had to provide for this expenditure, and all this time his work was closely supervised by Colbert, who criticised and undoubtedly made the most of, any shortcomings in the Superintendent's accounts. The Abbé Choisy declares on the authority of Pellisson, the ablest of Fouquet's clerks, that Fouquet persisted in making the state of things worse than they were, that Colbert pointed out daily to the King Fouquet's errors, and that when Fouquet, ignorant and unaware of Colbert's advice to Louis, adhered to his original statements, the King, not unnaturally enraged at this trickery, resolved on his overthrow as early as the 4th of May. In writing to his mother on the evening of September 5th, the date of the arrest of Fouquet, he says that the Minister's overthrow had been decided upon for four months. Fouquet seems to have had no notion either of the King's feelings towards him, or of the schemes of his enemies. He was apparently trusted by the King; he saw him daily in the course of business. Public opinion seemed in favour of his appointment as First Minister. The leading merchants were avowedly convinced that he was the only man capable of restoring order in the finances.

But Fouquet had no adequate justification for trusting blindly to mere appearances. It is said that on the occasion of his so-called confession to Louis, his intimate friends, Pellisson, who acted as his head clerk, De Lorne, and Bruant, urged him to give the King a full and accurate account of the financial state of the kingdom.

Though Fouquet ridiculed the idea of any danger, he received, about the time of the arrival of the Court at Fontainebleau, two very distinct warnings. The appointment of Colbert to the post of *Contrôleur-général*, and the presentation of the government of Touraine to the Duc de Saint-Aignan in preference to Fouquet's brother, Gilles, should have been sufficient to show him that it was advisable to walk warily. Many indirect warnings had already reached him. One of Colbert's clerks had asserted that his master would be the next Superintendent; another had in a wine-shop declared that Fouquet's fall was imminent, and that the Superintendent himself neglected his duties and allowed his underlings to rob the State. On another occasion several members of the household of the Prince of Condé boldly said that France had never been governed more disastrously, and that they were a hundred times worse off than in the days of Mazarin. These vague accusations and still vaguer threats were in the air. They came no one exactly knew whence, but they were taken up and repeated even in the ante-chambers of the Queen, and of Anne of Austria.

In those days, owing to the absence of a free press, it was difficult to obtain accurate information. Hence it was absolutely necessary for a minister to provide himself with spies, taken, not only from the lower orders, but also from the royal attendants. Ladies-in-waiting were much sought after for *espion-*

age purposes, as they possessed unrivalled opportunities for observation. Fouquet, though over-confident to an extraordinary extent, had not entirely neglected this valuable source of information. He had already in his employ Mademoiselle de Menneville, whom he interviewed secretly in Paris at his hotel in the Rue Croix-des-Petits-Champs, and at Fontainebleau, at the house of a woman called La Coz, who lived on the canal. In addition, he employed Mademoiselle du Fouilloux, who also belonged to the Court.

But with his hands full of business, and his mind undisturbed by any presages of coming evil, Fouquet was hopelessly beaten in the game of intrigue, and by his mistakes played into the hands of his enemies. He was engaged, though he was unaware of its significance, in a struggle for supremacy with Le Tellier and Colbert. Of these the former, a prudent, hard-working, avaricious man, had little in common with the audacious Fouquet. Nothing could be more repugnant to him than the possibility of working under the Superintendent. " He thought moreover," says Madame de Motteville, " that Colbert, who had been his agent, would always refer to him." He therefore warmly supported Louis' intention of having no Prime Minister, and joined with Colbert in a great effort to overthrow their common rival. The latter had, on Fouquet's appointment in 1653 to the post of Superintendent of Finance, become his enemy and rival. During the last year of Mazarin's life, the struggle between the two had become fiercer than ever ; Colbert had gone so far as even to demand a Chamber of Justice to overhaul the finances. In his celebrated memoir of September, 1659, he openly accused Fouquet of malversation, and of advancing his relatives and friends by means of the public money. It required all the arts of Mazarin to patch up this quarrel. Whatever were the faults of Fouquet, whatever the merits of the memoir, Colbert's hostility stood revealed. After the death of Mazarin, Colbert, as Intendant of Finance, had excellent opportunities for undermining his rival. In fact, between Louis, Colbert, and Le Tellier, there was practically a conspiracy, (though Louis asserts in his letter to his mother on September 5th, that she and Le Tellier alone know of his project, and the latter only two days before its execution), and probably as early as the beginning of May the fall of Fouquet was determined upon. Unfortunately for Fouquet, a powerful cabal had been formed against him by the famous intriguer of the seventeenth century, the Duchess of Chevreuse. Nothing is known definitely of the motives which prompted this lady, now sixty years of age, to take the lead in the plot. The only clue is to be found in the fact that in 1657 she had married for the third time a certain De Laigne who had a grudge against Fouquet. On June 27th, Anne of Austria paid the Duchess a visit at Dampierre, where it is said she met Le Tellier and Colbert. At any rate, the Queen-Mother was won over to the ranks of Fouquet's enemies. Warned by Pellison, Gourville, and other friends, of the intrigues of the Duchess, the infatuated Fouquet made two great blunders. In the first place, he taxed

Anne with caballing with his enemies. So cutting was his language that Anne refused to hold any further intercourse with him. And secondly, though warned by Madame de Fouilloux of the relations existing between the King and Louise de la Vallière, he endeavoured to gain over the latter to his interest. So clumsily did he make the attempt, so entirely did he misjudge the character of the young maid of honour, that, regarding herself insulted by his remarks, Louise de la Vallière complained bitterly to the King. Louis was hurt in his tenderest point, and from that moment Fouquet's overthrow was certain. Colbert, Le Tellier, and Seguier were opposed to him ; he had broken with Anne of Austria ; he had mortally insulted Louis. Had he been simply Superintendent of Finance, he could have been attacked and overthrown at once ; but being *Procureur-général*, he was under the protection of the *Parlement*, and could only be attacked through the *Parlement*. As long as he remained *Procureur-général* he was safe. In order to induce him to resign his office of *Procureur-général*, the King and Colbert resorted to a stratagem. It was pointed out to Fouquet that it was desirable to reduce the power of the *Parlement*, that in this work the King relied on Fouquet's assistance, and that obviously it was inconvenient for him to continue to hold the office of *Procureur-général* during an attack on the *Parlement's* privileges. It was hinted, moreover, that he could not be Chancellor and *Procureur-général* at the same time, and it was openly spread abroad that he was to be appointed Chancellor. In spite of the warnings of his friends, Fouquet, on August 12th, sold his office to M. de Harlay, and presented the King with a million livres. " Tout va bien," said Louis to Colbert, " il s'enterre de lui-même."

On August 17th Louis was present at the celebrated fête given in his honour by Fouquet at his splendid residence of Vaux. Even if the story of the discovery by Louis of a picture of La Vallière in one of the rooms be not true, the magnificence displayed on all sides only increased further the determination of the King to ruin his powerful subject.

After three weeks of intermittent anxiety on the part of Fouquet, who, till the last, was uncertain whether he was going to be Prime Minister, or whether his fall was imminent, whether he should fly to Venice, or whether he should remain, the blow fell on September 5th at Nantes, whither Louis had gone to meet the Estates of Brittany.

The arrest itself was organised by Louis. In order to lull the suspicions of Fouquet, he gave his orders verbally to a subaltern, D'Artagnan, on the morning of Sunday, the 4th of September. The next day, under pretence of hunting, the King held his Council earlier than usual. After a short meeting, Colbert, Lionne, and Tellier retired, but the King kept Fouquet back for a short time under various pretexts, pretending to look for papers, until he saw from the window that D'Artagnan was at his post. But whether he had been warned or not, certain it is that Fouquet escaped the notice of D'Artagnan, who thereupon sent a messenger to Louis informing him of the Superintendent's escape.

Louis fell into a violent rage; but was relieved shortly afterwards by hearing that D'Artagnan had succeeded in arresting Fouquet in the "Place de la Cathédrale." Thus fell Fouquet on the third anniversary of his acquisition of Belle-isle. The formation of a special court to try him, the length of his trial, which lasted three years, the obvious falseness of most of the charges, the influence exercised by Louis over the judges, the courage and ability shown by the prisoner, his intimate relations with all the ablest men of the day, his numerous and varied interests, all combined to focus the interest and the sympathy of France upon Nicolas Fouquet. This sympathy was considerably augmented when Louis refused to abide by the verdict of the judges, and changed the sentence of exile to one of perpetual imprisonment.

The charges fell roughly into two heads, malversation and treason. He was accused of corruption and dishonesty in the management of the finances, of appropriating to himself public money, of preparing to revive civil war in France, and for that purpose of fortifying Belle-isle. The charges for treason were absurd, those of malversation were to some extent true. But dishonesty was rife among all the official and ministerial class. Judged by modern standards, Mazarin was as guilty as Fouquet. The whole financial system was rotten, and remained so, with intervals of improvement, until the Revolution and after.

The trial of Fouquet was a seventeenth-century Warren Hastings trial. It was necessary to make an example in the case of the French Finance Minister as it was in the case of the Indian Governor-General. Had Fouquet been proved innocent it would have been difficult, if not impossible, to punish smaller men, or to annul the ruinous engagements into which he had entered. Louis, moreover, simply dared not allow Fouquet to be at large. He feared that the powerful and captivating minister might somehow interfere with his scheme of governing France after his own method. Of Fouquet's many friends La Fontaine remained especially faithful to him in his misfortunes, and dared to address Louis in favour of the fallen minister now about to undergo imprisonment for the rest of his life.

> "Lorsque sur cette mer on vogue à pleines voiles,
>   Qu'on croit avoir pour soi les vents et les étoiles,
>   Il est bien malaise de regler ses désirs :
>   Le plus sage s'endort sur la foi des Zephyrs.
>
>   .   .   .   .
>
>   Il est assez puni par son sort rigoureux,
>   Et c'est être innocent que d'être malheureux."

The fall of Fouquet marks an epoch in the history of France. The reign of Louis XIV. really began from the date of the Superintendent's arrest. The fall of Fouquet was not the fall of an ordinary minister, it was the fall of a system of government which had lasted half a century. It was the end of the period of Richelieu and of Mazarin, of the Hôtel de Rambouillet and of the Fronde, with all the intrigues and activities of that time. Resistance to

Louis' scheme of government was now over. Henceforward he could exercise his power without control or interference. Louis' determination to have no Prime Minister was revealed to the world. The manner in which Fouquet's overthrow was brought about throws much light on the King's character. During the period from April to September, Louis' capacity for combining work and amusement receives abundant illustrations. The whole episode too proves that Louis had not only thoroughly imbibed Mazarin's lessons on statecraft, but had also a natural gift for dissimulation which the Cardinal himself might have envied. His dislike of anybody who had been connected with the Fronde movement was strong, and this no doubt affected his attitude towards Fouquet as it did his relations with De Retz and the Jansenists. And Louis had ample justification for his watchful and suspicious attitude. Even as late as 1659 the spirit of insubordination had reappeared during the negotiations with Spain. Normandy was averse to the treaty of the Pyrenees, and gave Mazarin no little anxiety. Turenne, in direct contravention to Mazarin's orders, had sent money and men to the Duke of York to aid the restoration of Charles II. In order to check any reawakening of the old Fronde spirit, it was necessary to strike hard. The whole tenour of Louis' policy towards the great nobles forbade the existence in France of a man as powerful and independent as Fouquet. Dependence on the King was to be the sole avenue to advancement open to the noble class.

The precautions adopted by Louis to avoid failure, and the measures taken after the arrest to secure Fouquet's papers, would seem to show that Louis either tended to overrate the influence of Fouquet in the West, or was only dimly conscious of the extent of his own power. The influence of women, and the constant use of intrigue in this, as in most periods of French history, is amply exemplified during the months preceding Fouquet's fall, while the practical impossibility of arresting the Minister as long as he was *Procureur-général* shows that the privileges of that legal corporation, the *Parlement* of Paris, could not lightly be infringed, even by the most despotic of kings.

Fouquet's fall may unquestionably have been hastened by the machinations of his enemies who kept in the background. For while these three months can be characterised as a struggle between the King and the ministerial system as it existed under Richelieu and Mazarin, they can also be described as a struggle for supremacy between rival ministers. The Dutch envoy had noted that Fouquet was the most formidable man in France: the merchants were agreed that he alone could restore order in the finances.

So formidable a subject could not exist in the new monarchical system which Louis intended to inaugurate. And the justification of Fouquet's fall is to be found in Colbert's administration, which conclusively proved that the opinion of the leading merchants in France was erroneous.

Fouquet was, with all his faults, a magnificent

figure. But while he essentially belonged to the Fronde period, Colbert was a man after Louis' own heart. He represented what was dear to Louis— precision, order, regularity, and certainty. He was, moreover, honest and exact. Whatever were his motives in attacking Fouquet in 1659, he had at any rate justified that attack by showing in his memoir to Mazarin that not half of the taxes reached the King.

The existing financial system, for which no one was especially responsible, was an utterly rotten one. The country was going through a period of financial chaos. Those who had the fiscal administration in their hands, from the Superintendent to the meanest of the tax-farmers, robbed and misappropriated just as they pleased. The government loans were arranged so as to aggrandise most the individuals who were interested in them, while not only the nobles, but many others who had no legal exemption from taxation, paid no taxes.

It is true that Colbert, in his anxiety to succeed Fouquet as Finance Minister, made the worst of the case against his rival. There is no doubt, however, that France benefited enormously from the change of ministers, and the years from 1661 to 1672 were among the most prosperous that France had ever seen. In 1665 Colbert was made *Contrôleur-général* and in 1669 Minister of the Marine, and also Minister of Commerce, of the Colonies, and of the Royal Buildings. Over every department except that of War, Colbert was practically supreme. And Louis was justified in placing this confidence in his minister.

To Colbert Louis owed much of his military and other successes, to Colbert was due the immense impetus now given to the manufactures and the commerce of France. Colbert first set to work to establish order in the finances, to "unravel the terrible confusion in which Fouquet had entangled his affairs," and to reorganise the system of taxation. But though he could not diminish the number of privileged individuals, he resisted fraudulent claims to exemption from taxation, he lightened direct by an increase of indirect taxation, from which the privileged classes could not escape, he improved the methods of collection, and by these means he introduced order and economy where chaos had before reigned. Not content to merely reorganise the finances, he turned his attention to augmenting the sources of national wealth, and determined to enrich France by improving her trade and commerce. In 1665 the Council of Commerce was reorganised, and Colbert began his great work. Manufactures were fostered and new industries were introduced, inventions were protected, foreign workmen were invited into the country, and French workmen were forbidden to emigrate. Good roads and canals were projected, Dunkirk and Marseilles were declared free ports, and the duties levied on the passage of goods between the several French provinces were equalised. Unfortunately, he did little for agriculture, in which lay the true wealth of France. Moreover, he maintained the old corporation system by which each industry remained in the hands of a certain number of privileged *bourgeois*, and thus the

lower orders had no opportunities for advancement.
But apart from his steady encouragement of manufactures, Colbert certainly did much for French commerce.   He was ever an advocate of hostile tariffs
and protection, but he encouraged trade and supported the colonies.   Several new companies were
founded.   A privileged East India Company was
formed in 1664, followed in the same year by a
West India Company, and later by the Company of
the West, and commercial companies to trade in the
North and in the Levant.

The colonies were equally cared for and extended.
In the West Indies France held St. Domingo, Mar-
tinique, Guadaloupe, Tobago, Grenada, and the Bar-
badoes ; in Africa, Senegal, as well as interests in
Madagascar ; in America, Canada, Nova Scotia, Newfoundland, Louisiana.

Colbert's schemes of placing the West India
Islands under a company failed.   The company was
dissolved in 1674, the islands were put under a Government department, and the administration was
given to the Minister of Marine.   The French plan-
tations, however, grew steadily and flourished more
than did the English ones.   In their struggling infancy Colbert relieved them of taxation, gave lands
to poor and industrious emigrants, and advanced
money to the planters.   He defended their trade
and built fortifications.   In the East Indies he was,
if possible, more active, and success seemed likely to
attend his efforts.   The East India Company received special encouragement from Louis XIV. and
his minister.   It was declared that trade with India

COLBERT.
(From an old portrait reproduced in Philippson's
Das Zeitalter Ludwigs XIV.)

was not derogatory to a man of noble birth, and nobles were persuaded to participate in the enterprise. In 1668 a French factory was established at Surat, the richest mart in India; in 1669 another factory was established at Masulipatam, and in 1674 Pondicherry was founded. But other European nations had interests in the East and the monarchy of Aurungzebe was at the height of its power. It was not till the break-up of the Mogul Empire that there was room for the schemes of a Dupleix. As it was, the French were obliged to confine themselves to trade and to safeguarding their interests in the face of European competition. Throughout the century the interests of the French and Dutch clashed in India and Siam, and though the latter at one time took Pondicherry, the French regained it at the peace of Ryswick.

An attempt was made in 1665 to colonise Madagascar, but the climate and the hostility of the natives, which showed itself in a massacre of many of the colonists in 1672, practically ruined all Colbert's hopes of carrying out his scheme successfully. Colbert's greatest colonial success was in North America. In 1664 the famous Company of the West was formed, and a serious effort was made to expand the French colonies in New France. But though the structure of power was imposing, it was always a creation lacking in real vitality. The emigration was nearly always forced, the administration of New France was venal and bad, the home government was continually meddling, feudalism was introduced and proved ruinous to the young colony, and the Crown and the Church kept the people in leading-strings and prevented self-dependence. For a time indeed New France seemed to flourish, and towards the end of the century the French claimed all the country from the Mississippi to the St. Lawrence, and formed the famous plan of uniting Louisiana and Canada.

For the protection of French commerce and colonies a strong navy was required, and Colbert proceeded at once to form a strong fleet. The King only cared for the army, and to Colbert the French navy owes everything. With the aid of Vauban he made and fortified the ports of Calais, Dunkirk, Brest, Havre and others ; he reconstituted the arsenal of Toulon, founded a port and arsenal at Rochefort, and established naval schools at Rochefort, Dieppe, and St. Malo.

In 1661 France possessed but few ships ; in 1667 she had 50 men-of-war ; in 1672, 196 ; in 1683, 276 ; in 1690, 760, and she could hold her own against the English fleet.

Colbert was equally active in other departments. He interfered in ecclesiastical matters, and though he well appreciated the industry and value to France of the Huguenots, he supported Louis in his attempts to secure their conversion. He improved the system of justice, codifying the laws, diminishing the number of the judges, lessening the expense and length of trials, and establishing an organised system of police. He improved the buildings of Paris, erecting the Colonnade of the Louvre, and some boulevards and quays. But here he was checked by Louis, who preferred that Marly and Versailles should receive more attention than Paris. He also encouraged art and literature, founding the Academy of Sciences, now known as the Institute of France, the Academy of Inscriptions and Medals, the Academy of Architecture and Music, and French academies at Rome, Arles, Soissons, Nîmes, and other places. Painting and sculpture were patronised, and pensions were given to literary men such as Molière, Racine, and Boileau. It is easy to criticise his administration. It was characterised throughout by the spirit of protection, it was a system of order and supervision. France was treated as if she was a large school.

But in spite of his many errors, Colbert raised France to the first rank among commercial nations. He increased her wealth, he successfully established manufactures, he raised the credit of the nation. In 1678 Sir William Temple was much impressed by the wealth and prosperity of France, and this was due entirely to Colbert. He may have seized every opportunity for personal advancement, but France profited immensely from his administration. He was distinctly a statesman, for he conceived a magnificent and at the same time a practicable scheme for making France the leading power among European nations. And he was above all admirably suited to Louis XIV. Like his master, he had a matchless faculty for work, not scorning the smallest details, nor shrinking from the vastest undertakings. To his ability, energy, and laboriousness he owed a position for which he was admirably adapted. To Colbert Louis was indebted for much, if not all, of

9

the success of his enterprises during the twenty-five years succeeding Mazarin's death. In 1661 the receipts were eighty millions of livres, of which thirty-one millions reached the Treasury. The expenditure was fifty-four millions, and the deficit was therefore twenty-two millions. In 1667 the receipts amounted to sixty-one millions, and the expenditure to thirty-two and a half, leaving a surplus of thirty-one millions. With such a minister Louis XIV. felt justified in carrying out an ambitious and a not wholly impracticable foreign policy.

CHAPTER V.

LOUIS' FOREIGN POLICY TO THE END OF THE
DEVOLUTION WAR.

1662–1668.

T is difficult to describe accurate-
ly the drift of Louis' foreign
policy. Religious interests
were so continually mixed up
with the question of European supremacy that it is
dangerous to make definite
generalisations. That France
was the first state in the world
from 1661 to 1700 is undisput-
ed; that she owed her position in great measure to
Louis' consummate diplomatic skill is equally true.
He undoubtedly intended that France should be
supreme on land and on sea; he looked forward to
the time when he should succeed to Leopold as
Emperor. With a royal disregard of all the teach-
ings of history he regarded himself as the true

descendant of Charles the Great. He wished to be the leader and protector of Catholic Europe.

That France should be mistress of the world, that a great French Empire should rise on the continent which should dictate the law to Europe was undoubtedly the central idea of Louis' policy. But the means requisite for the consummation of this ideal varied as his reign proceeded. From 1661 to 1700 is a period distinct from that extending from 1700 to 1715. In the latter period his efforts were directed to preserving the Spanish Empire intact for his grandson, and by uniting in close alliance Spain and France, to secure for the Bourbons the supremacy of Southern Europe.

During the earlier period his aims and hopes lay in a different direction. He seems to have wished:

(1) To extend the French frontier to the Rhine, by completely absorbing Lorraine and by the conquest of Franche Comté. Though he failed during his reign in securing Lorraine he succeeded in acquiring Franche Comté, and Alsace with Strasburg.

(2) To extend the French frontier to the Scheldt. The French frontier was weak on the north-east. To make Paris safe against a sudden attack, and to give her a complete barrier had been one of the aims of Mazarin's foreign policy. He had failed to carry out his design, and thus entailed on Europe long wars, for until Paris had secured a strong barrier on the north-east frontier there could be no lasting peace between Spain and France.

(3) To extend the colonial Empire of France by fresh acquisitions in the West Indies, in Madagascar

and in North America, and to increase her trade and possessions in the East Indies.

(4) To secure the Imperial title and to pose as the head of the Catholic Church.

In attempting to extend the French boundary in the direction of the Rhine Louis was simply continuing the policy of Richelieu and Mazarin. Certain risks would have to be faced and definite preparations would have to be made. In carrying out this policy he would again find himself in conflict with the Empire and with Spain; he ran the risk of incurring the hostility of the Swiss. To neutralise the opposition of the Emperor it would be necessary to preserve the French connection with Turkey, Poland, and Sweden, and by stirring up those powers in the rear of Austria to paralyse her efforts on the Rhine. It might be advisable to develop the policy of Richelieu and Mazarin towards the North German Princes and to pay large subsidies as a price of neutrality. It was advisable and also possible to gain Bavaria.

But a move in the direction of the Scheldt was a far more hazardous undertaking. It implied the conquest and inclusion into the French monarchy of that county known then as the Spanish Netherlands, now as Belgium. Mazarin had made a definite attempt to effect this conquest, and by reviving the theory that the Scheldt and the Rhine were the natural boundaries of France he bequeathed to Louis XIV. a *damnosa hereditas* which has affected French foreign policy to the present day. Mazarin's attempt not only failed but resulted in the loss of the friendship

of Holland.   That country, alarmed at the prospect
of a strong power like France on her borders, made
the treaty of Münster with Spain in January 1648.
Checkmated for the moment, France under Louis
XIV. again returned to the policy of Mazarin.   The
Powers firmly opposed to any fresh advance of the
French towards the Scheldt were the Empire, Spain,
and Holland ; and French statesmen had always to
reckon with the fact that England might in pursu-
ance of her true policy, as she did in 1667, and again
after the Revolution of 1688, enter the lists against
France.   But Mazarin by the marriage of Louis XIV.
to Maria Thérèsa of Spain had bequeathed to the
King that policy of uniting France and Spain which
coloured to a more or less extent the whole of Louis'
reign.   Had Louis indeed foregone his policy of
aggrandisement in Europe for a time and devoted
himself to the acquisition of a colonial empire he
would have been consulting the true interests of
France.   Colbert had already done much for her
colonial development, and France had entered into
competition for the New World with England.   To
gain any real success in this struggle France would
have to concentrate all her energies and husband
all her resources.

Louis XIV. had like his successor in 1740 and again
in 1756 to decide between two lines of policy.   The
choice lay between the policy advocated by Colbert
and that of which Louvois was the chief representative. Colbert's policy meant careful abstention from
all European entanglements, a commercial war with
England and Holland by means of hostile tariffs, the

extension and development of the French colonies, the increase of the French navy, and if necessary war by sea. On the other hand the policy represented by Louvois was one of aggrandisement in Europe, and of the extension of the French frontiers at the expense of the Empire and Spain. It was only to be expected that a young and enterprising monarch, who in his desire for glory accurately expressed the national passion of the French nation for feats of arms and foreign wars, should prefer to follow the policy which had already brought France glory, increase of territory, and a great European position, to the slower, more inglorious, though safer methods of Colbert. Till 1685 Louis followed successfully the former policy, which gratified his love of conquest and popular worship and more than satisfied the national thirst for military successes. The frequent assertions of French supremacy, the purchase of Dunkirk, the Devolution War, the attack on Holland, the *Réunions*, the seizure of Strasburg, the war in the Spanish Netherlands in 1682–4, the apathy of Louis at the time of the siege of Vienna, his intrigues or alliances with Sweden, Poland, Hungary, Turkey, and the German Princes, are but a few illustrations to show how thoroughly the King pursued a policy of aggrandisement at the expense of Spain and the Empire. Till 1685 though at times he neglected the methods of Richelieu and Mazarin and seemed to desert the lines which they laid down, as when he invaded Holland in 1672, he carried on their policy. He endeavoured to force from Spain a complete rampart for Paris on the north-east frontier, and he ostensibly continued to carry out the old axiom in French politics of being Catholic at home and Protestant abroad. " The principal object of the foreign policy of Louis XIV. during this period of his personal government was the development of the two treaties of Westphalia and Pyrenees." He always however looked forward to the time when he could throw over his Protestant allies in Germany and appear to the world as the zealous leader of the Catholic party in Europe. It was not till the death of Colbert in 1683 that he cast aside that policy of religious toleration at home and abroad which had been so successfully followed by Henry IV. All through these twenty-five years from 1660 to 1685 there are numerous examples to be found bearing evidence of Louis' anxiety to aid the extension of Catholicism. His desire to secure the conversion of England and his bitter hatred of the Dutch both show how little he sympathised with the tolerant policy of his predecessors Richelieu and Mazarin. Till 1685, too, the interests of the navy and of the colonies were not neglected, though with the opening of the Dutch war of 1672 there is a distinct tendency to starve the navy and relegate colonial expansion to the background. But with the ministry of Seignelay the navy again took an important position till La Hogue dealt a serious blow at its attempt to rival the English fleet. During these years Louis' startling and almost uniform series of successes, won often in spite of the baneful effects of his personal influence, were in great measure due to the admirable instruments which he possessed in the generation of men formed during the years of his minority and inheriting the traditions of the days of Richelieu. But with the death of Colbert, and with the Revocation of the Edict of Nantes, a marked change passes over his fortunes. He had reached the high-water mark of prosperity. From 1685 to 1697, he found that the results of his championship of the Catholic Church at home and abroad, were distinctly disastrous for France, and that his audacious aggressions in the direction of the Rhine had aroused universal suspicion. The revocation of the Edict of Nantes dealt a serious blow at French prosperity ; the devastation of the Palatinate completed the alienation of his German allies, already alarmed by the seizure of Strasburg and his other high-handed acts. At the conclusion of the war against the European coalition brought together by the League of Augsburg he found himself while supported by the Pope compelled to give up territory and postpone indefinitely his scheme for extending the boundary of France to the Scheldt. As opposition to Spain was the necessary result of attempts to seize the Spanish Netherlands, Mignet's statement, that the " Spanish Succession question was the pivot which turned the whole foreign policy of Louis XIV.," is apt to prove misleading.

There is no doubt that, owing to the weak health of Charles II., the Spanish Succession question might be opened any day ; it is quite true that for some forty years Louis looked forward to the opening of that question, and that in his dealings with the Elector of Bavaria, with the Hapsburgs, and even with Rome he always kept the question before his eyes.

But till 1700 he never allowed the seeming imminence of the question to interfere with his schemes in other directions. His attitude towards the whole matter was very different to that adopted after the acceptance of the famous Will of Charles II. of Spain. Till the death of that monarch he was resolved to take advantage of the weakness of his kingdom, and while on the one hand appropriating portions of the great Spanish Empire, on the other hand by treaty arrangements to provide for the partition of the bulk of the Spanish possessions. The war of Devolution, the French gains at Nimeguen, the war of 1682, all illustrate his determination to seize as much as possible of the Spanish Netherlands, while his secret treaty of Partition in 1668 with Leopold, his treaty of 1670, his negotiations in 1687 with Bavaria, followed later by the two famous Partition treaties, show plainly that though the question of the Spanish succession was before his eyes, though it entered into his negotiations with European powers, it had not assumed the great importance which it did after the peace of Ryswick.

Louis' refusal to recognise his wife's renunciations and his long negotiations on the subject tended undoubtedly to familiarise Europe with the French claims to the Spanish inheritance, while the formation at Madrid of a French party ready to support the interests of France in Spain and the pretensions of the French Crown, testifies to the fact that Louis was fully alive to the importance of the Spanish Succession question. In 1667 he openly asserted his wife's claim, not only to the greater part of Flanders and to Franche Comté by the *Jus Devolutionis*, but also in the event of Charles II.'s death to the Spanish Empire. But the failure of his attempts to get his wife's renunciation formally annulled, the marriage of the Infanta Margaret to Leopold, the possibility that Charles II. might live long, all confirmed Louis in his intention of strengthening the position of France on the north-east by seizing a part, if not all, of the Spanish Netherlands, and of devoting himself to his general schemes of religious and political aggrandisement. Upon the formation of the League of Augsburg in 1686 it was far more important for Louis to assure himself of the neutrality of Spain than to make preparations for the close union of the two countries in the event of Charles II.'s death.

In carrying out his policy, Louis was greatly aided by the position in which he found France on Mazarin's death, by the weakness of some of the European powers, by the isolation and neutrality of others. The Emperor was hampered at home by the League of the Rhine, and was already occupied on his eastern frontiers by an attempt of the Turks to seize the whole of Hungary. England, under Charles II., was about to retire from the commanding position in Europe which she owed to the firmness of Cromwell. Spain was so weak that she could not reduce the revolted Portuguese, while Italy, Denmark, and Sweden were from different reasons unable to interfere, much less thwart any scheme of foreign policy which Louis might entertain. Louis' first object was to illustrate in a very

practical way his own views as to the position which
he proposed that the monarchy of France should
take in Europe. He claimed and secured the right
of his ambassador to take precedence of the Spanish
ambassador in London; he forced Alexander VII.
to make ample reparation for an insult offered to his
envoy, Créqui, at Rome; he successfully obtained
from England a declaration that her claims to the
supremacy over the sea should not extend beyond
Cape Finisterre. Before the end of 1662 Europe
recognised that the French preponderance was an
accomplished fact, while the aid given by Louis to
the Emperor in 1664 at the battle of St. Gothard,
and the successful expeditions against the Barbary
Corsairs in 1665, demonstrated clearly the military
power, as well as the active Christian character of
the new *régime* in France.

In 1665 the death of Philip IV. of Spain gave a
definiteness to Louis' foreign policy, and brought
out clearly and distinctly his views with regard not
only to the Spanish succession, but also with regard
to the future development and extension of France.
He at once determined to occupy the whole of the
Spanish Netherlands on behalf of his wife, whose
claims were formulated in a most elaborate manner
for the benefit of the astounded European nations.

Louis claimed the Spanish Netherlands on the
ground that by the *Jus Devolutionis*, a local custom,
his wife, who was the only daughter of Philip IV.
by his first marriage, was the heiress of the Low
Countries, to the exclusion of the Infanta and
Charles II., the children of Philip's second marriage.

LOUIS XIV. AT THE AGE OF 41.
(From an illustration, based on an old print, in Philippson's
Das Zeitalter Ludwigs XIV.)

Now this custom, in accordance with which, if a man married twice, the succession went to the children of the first wife to the exclusion of those of the second, referred only to private property, was a purely local custom, and was in force in Brabant, Malines, Namur, Hainault, and perhaps one other province. In Luxemburg, according to the custom then in vogue, two parts would go to Charles II., and one part to each daughter. In Franche Comté the custom was gavelkind. So even allowing that Louis was right in appealing to a local and private custom as holding good with regard to the succession, he could only enforce it in the case of a very few of the provinces, and not throughout the Low Countries.

Thus, then, the objections to Louis' claim were absolutely unanswerable. His claim, such as it was, was abrogated by the Act of Renunciation, which annulled all the rights of succession. It only rested on a custom applicable to private rights and did not refer to political rights, and moreover the Law of Devolution had nothing whatever to do with the succession to Brabant. But even in modern times flimsier claims have often been successfully upheld if made with sufficient audacity and supported by clever diplomacy. And at this epoch Louis was fortunate in his ministers and diplomatic agents, while the political condition of Europe favoured the success of schemes of a filibustering and blackmailing character. French diplomacy was directed by the capable Lionne, whose ability renders him almost worthy of being ranked with Mazarin. And it was

Lionne who, by his ever watchful diplomatic skill and extraordinary energy and activity, removed many of the difficulties during the ten years from 1661–1671, and contributed very largely to Louis' successes during that period.

The object of this diplomacy was, while advancing French interests in the Netherlands and elsewhere, to keep England and Holland neutral, to aid Portugal in its revolt against Spain, to conciliate the Emperor, and to overawe or gain Sweden, Denmark, and the German Princes.

After Mazarin's death French diplomacy certainly did not sleep. During the years 1661 and 1662 Louis at first endeavoured to induce Spain to annul Maria Thérèsa's renunciations, and, beaten on this point, he used every effort to make himself safe on the side of England. He employed Fouquet to assure Charles II. that he would not combine with Philip IV., and that he regarded a marriage between Charles and the Infanta Catherine of Portugal and an Anglo-Portuguese alliance with favour. Both England and France were enemies of Spain, and both were friendly to Portugal. So, in spite of a feeling of displeasure at Louis' amicable attitude towards the Dutch, there was little reason for fearing that Charles II. would oppose any scheme against the Spanish Netherlands, especially as Louis had already intimated that he would be prepared to make Charles independent of the grants of Parliament. In November, 1662, England had sold Dunkirk to the French, and though the Protestant world were alarmed, Charles II. was delighted at the price paid, and Louis acquired fresh popularity in France. During the years 1663 to 1664 the main effort of Louis' diplomacy lay in the direction of Holland. He hoped, as Richelieu and Mazarin had hoped before him, to persuade the Dutch to agree to a partition or to some arrangement favourable to the French plans with regard to the Spanish Netherlands. The neutrality of Holland was of even greater importance than that of England. DeWitt was ready to ally with Louis if certain obstacles could be cleared away. In 1661 the Republic had made a treaty with Portugal, and in 1662 one with England. But up to 1662 the attitude of France had been hostile. Lionne opposed the Republic on political, Colbert on commercial grounds. Between a despotic and a free government, a Catholic and a Protestant people, there was little in common. There were outstanding difficulties about fishing rights, tonnage duties, and the Dutch claims on Rhynberg and Ravenstein. Louis' anxiety, however, to gain the Dutch, caused these difficulties to be smoothed over, and in April, 1662, the treaty of Paris was made. It was a mere nominal alliance, it is true, but it now became of great importance to the Dutch to know precisely the nature of Louis' schemes on that debateable land—the Spanish Netherlands. Richelieu had desired in 1635 either the establishment of an independent Belgium or a partition of the Low Countries between Holland and France; Mazarin had thought of annexing the country to France as a rampart of Paris, and had attempted to exchange Catalonia—then in the hands of the French—for the

Spanish Low Countries and Luxemburg. The
Treaty of Münster, in January, 1648, between Holland and Spain, had ruined this plan, and he had
then fallen back on Richelieu's idea.

DeWitt was in favour of a modern Belgium. Realising that the security of the United Provinces
demanded the establishment of a free and independent country between them and France, he wished
to take the debateable Provinces away from Spain,
but did not propose to hand them over to France.
Towards that country his policy may be summed up
in the words *Gallum amicum sed non vicinum.* His
constant fear was lest Spain should exchange the
Provinces, or should be powerless to prevent their
annexation by France. Louis' policy, on the other
hand, was either to annex all the country, or at any
rate to arrange a partition with Holland which would
destroy the buffer between the Republic and the
French monarchy. DeWitt's fears were thus amply
justified, and, moreover, when he had cleverly obtained a declaration of the Devolution plan from
Louis, he found that his fears were fully confirmed.
Though he boldly objected to the scheme he could
do nothing more, and in 1664 the negotiations came
to an end. He hoped, however, by remaining loyal to
the French alliance to impose on Louis the necessity
of making concessions, to prevent him from precipi-
tating the execution of his plans, and generally to
arrest or restrain his ambition. These negotiations,
like those with Spain, had one effect anticipated by
Louis. Europe became accustomed to the evidence
of the French claims, and " the most intelligent fore-

saw that Louis XIV. would take the first opportunity of conquering the Spanish Netherlands." His diplomacy, too, had another important effect. By his nominal alliance with the Dutch he had prevented them from making any preparations against his aggressions, while by placing obstacles in the way of the conclusion of peace between Spain and Portugal the former was hindered from offering any resistance to his schemes.

From 1664 to 1667 Louis endeavoured to gain the Emperor. Leopold had in 1663 arranged to marry the Infanta Margaret, and naturally was expected to support Spain in opposing the policy of the French Court. But Louis' diplomacy hampered the Emperor at every turn. In 1664 Louis had concluded treaties with Sweden, Brandenburg, Saxony, and Mainz. In 1667 he stirred up Leopold's Hungarian subjects to rebellion, and after the outbreak of the Devolution War he made fresh alliances with Mainz, Cologne, Neuburg, and the Bishop of Münster, so as to check the passage of the Austrian troops into the Spanish Low Countries.

Not only was Spain helpless by her defeat at Villa Viciosa, the death of Philip IV., and the continued struggle with the Portuguese, not only was the Emperor neutralised, but the outbreak of the war between England and Holland tended still further to aid Louis. It was distinctly for the interests of France that this war should last as long as possible. Its prolongation would weaken both countries, and during its continuance the Spanish provinces would be left defenceless and open to Louis' attacks. Though

bound by treaty to Holland, he pursued a hesitating policy till he was forced, by fear of reconciliation between the belligerent powers, to declare war
on England in January, 1666, and to send a force
against the Bishop of Münster. The French assistance was in itself of little value to the Dutch. But
indirectly it led to some not unimportant developments.

The Swedes decided to join the English, the Danes
allied with the Dutch. The Great Elector became
alarmed at the prospect of Dutch dependence on the
French, made a treaty with Holland in February,
1666, and in October a quadruple alliance was formed,
consisting of Holland, Brandenburg, Lüneburg, and
Denmark, the object of which was to relieve Holland
of the necessity of having to place so much reliance
on the French power. But both England and Holland were ready for peace at the beginning of 1667,
and in May a conference at Breda was opened.
Louis realised that it was time for him to begin his
invasion of the Spanish Low Countries. Death had
lately freed him from the restraining influence which
Anne of Austria might have exercised upon his
schemes, France was prosperous, the Spanish Netherlands were practically defenceless, while Spain was
exhausted, at war with Portugal, and governed by
Père Nithard, the confessor of the Regent. There
was no immediate danger to be anticipated from
England, but it was important, even though Charles
II. had as early as February, 1666, secretly engaged not to interfere with Louis' designs, to strike
the expected blow before peace had actually been

concluded between England and Holland. Louis was himself extremely desirous to win some military successes. He never considered that the glory of the battles won and the towns taken during Mazarin's *régime* belonged to himself. Already in 1666 he had begun to hold inspections of his troops, and at Saint-Germain, at Fontainebleau, and at Vincennes military spectacles were included in the programme of amusements. With these serious preoccupations he combined, as he always did during most of his reign, a participation in the carnivals and fêtes which took place almost every winter. The following list is a good example of the sort of life led by Louis during these years: 1667, Jan. 5, A Pastoral Ballet; Jan. 6, Expedition to Versailles; Jan. 6–10, Ballet of the Muses; Jan. 12, Ballet at Paris; Jan. 22, A Review at Houilles; Jan. 24, Ball at Versailles; Jan. 25, Ballet of the Muses; Jan. 30, Grand Ball at Saint-Germain in the *Château Neuf*; Jan. 31, Ballet of the Muses; Feb. 4, Review; Feb. 5, 14, 16, 19, Ballet of the Muses; Feb. 20, 28, Carnival at Versailles. This Ballet of the Muses was first produced in Paris on January 2, and the King had intended to dance in it himself. But at the last moment, when he was already in costume, he was compelled to hurry off to see his mother, who had been taken suddenly ill.

On the 18th of May Louis left Saint-Germain to join the army under Turenne at Amiens. Turenne had formed his force into three divisions: the central body of 35,000 men was to operate between the Lys and the Meuse, and to move in the direction of Brussels; 8000 men under Marshal D'Aumont were to operate between the Lys and the sea ; while, to another corps of about the same strength under Créqui devolved the duty of covering the right flank, and of observing the movements of Germany in the direction of Luxemburg.

In this war there were two distinct campaigns ; the first in the Low Countries during the summer of 1667, the second in Franche Comté in the early part of 1668. The war is remarkable on account of the ease with which the French reduced, not only a large number of towns in the Spanish Netherlands, but also a populous and wealthy province. It is interesting as being the first war in which Louis himself took a leading part, and during its continuance Louis' aptitude for combining work and pleasure are as clearly illustrated as are the military skill of Turenne, the diplomacy of Lionne, the administrative ability of Louvois, and the engineering talent of Vauban.

To allay the apprehensions of Europe, Louis spoke of the invasion of the Spanish Low Countries as a journey he was taking in order to obtain possession of his wife's inheritance, and no declaration of war was made. Everything seemed to augur success. Spain, taken by surprise, could send no succours ; there was little to fear from any resistance in the Low Countries. Castel Rodrigo indeed some time previously had attempted to raise troops in Germany in order to be in a position to offer some opposition to the invasion which he had long foreseen. But Louis' representations at Madrid, coupled with the blindness and lethargy of the Spanish Court itself, had rendered ineffectual these and other attempts of Rodrigo to prepare for the inevitable struggle.

He had, moreover, neglected to seek allies, and had not taken any steps to utilise the services of the Count de Marsin, then in command of the Spanish forces in the Spanish Netherlands. With only 20,000 men at his command, and those scattered throughout the country, it was impossible for Rodrigo to attempt to defend every strong place. He therefore determined to concentrate the larger part of his available forces for the defence of Brussels, and to dismantle the fortifications of many of the towns, such as Condé, Armentières, Charleroi, and others which for lack of troops could not be defended.

On the 24th of May, two days after the election of Alexander VII., a French candidate, to the Papacy, the central portion of the forces, under the nominal command of the King, crossed the frontier and occupied Armentières. Then Turenne, in order to mislead the enemy, left untouched the strong places of the Scheldt, Cambrai, Bouchain, Valenciennes, and Condé, and meeting with no resistance, led the army to the Sambre, taking Binche on May 31st and Charleroi on June 2nd, six days after its evacuation by the Spaniards.

The outer works were still intact, and Turenne was so impressed by the strength of the place, lying as it does between Namur and Mons, that he advised Louis to remain there while the defences were restored under the direction of Vauban. Fifteen days later, on June 16th, a powerful garrison being left

under the Count de Montal in Charleroi, the French
army fell back on the Scheldt and in a fortnight captured a number of strong places. D'Aumont had
taken Bergues and Furnes, and Turenne now took
Ath and Tournai before the end of June. Douai
yielded on July 6th, and with its fall the active operations of Turenne's force came to an end for a short
time. While D'Aumont was employed in investing
Courtrai, the capture of which was effected on July
18th, Turenne's army was taking a well-earned rest,
and Louis returned to Compiègne in order to escort
the Queen and Court back with him to Flanders.
Douai, D'Orchies, and Tournai were enabled to appreciate in some measure the glories of Saint-Germain
and of Versailles, when they witnessed the arrival in
their midst of the pageant of the French Court.

As soon as the Court had departed to Arras, operations of war recommenced. Oudenarde, after two
days' siege, fell on July 31st, and a detachment of
troops was sent to take Dendermonde, the key of
Brussels, Ghent, Malines, and Bruges. But here the
Spaniards showed timely energy: fifteen hundred
men were thrown into the town and the sluices were
opened. Turenne, on his arrival on August 3rd, found
that the approaches were cut off by the water, and
after two days was forced to retire. Dendermonde,
like Amsterdam a few years later, was saved by an
inundation. This check to the French arms was
magnified in Vienna, and Louis' pride was wounded
by his failure. But Europe had little time to con-
gratulate itself on the Dendermonde episode. On
August 10th, Turenne, who had rapidly redescended

FRENCH
BARRIER TOWNS

S. OMER	VALENCIENNES
AIRE	LANDRECIES
BETHUNE	AVESNES
LILLE	MAUBEUGE
DOUAI & Ft. SCARPE	MARIENBOURG
BOUCHAIN	CHARLEMONT

AUSTR

FRONTIE

the Scheldt and effected a junction with D'Aumont, invested Lille, a place of great importance and hitherto deemed impregnable. The siege lasted seventeen days. It was defended by 2500 foot and about 650 horse. The Governor, the Count de Brouay, a man of energy and resource, was aided by able officers and supported by the burgher guard, which numbered 1500 men. It was known that Castel Rodrigo would do all in his power to succour the besieged town, and as a matter of fact 12,000 men had been collected by Marsin at Ypres for that purpose. But Turenne was also aware of the possibility of relief being sent to Lille. Créqui was ordered to bring his men from the Moselle to reinforce the royal army, and the siege, under the superintendence of Vauban, was opened with vigour. The latter's mode of investing a town showed a great advance on previous methods, and such was the rapidity with which the works were carried on that in a fortnight further resistance was seen to be impossible. Early on the 27th, the burghers realising that there was no hope of the arrival of reinforcements from Castel Rodrigo and dreading the pillage which always in those days followed a successful assault on a town, begged the Governor to surrender.

On his refusal they manned the ramparts and stopped the firing. The Governor then yielded to their demand, opened the gates, and Louis made a triumphal entry. Marsin, with some Spanish cavalry, arrived too late to prevent the capitulation of the city and retired northwards. Turenne, however, had arranged for the annihilation of Marsin's horsemen at the hands of Créqui and Bellefonds. These officers succeeded in surrounding Marsin, cut a portion of his force to pieces, and captured fifteen hundred prisoners. The unexpected success of Turenne at Lille so alarmed Leopold that he consented to send troops to oppose the French, and ordered levies to be prepared. The French envoy at Vienna, Gremonville, at once took a high tone and made him rescind the order. Delighted with his brilliant success at Lille, Louis retired to Saint-Germain, and Turenne completed his share of the campaign by the capture of Alost on September 12th, after a sharp struggle, in which five or six hundred French soldiers were killed or wounded. The defeat of the garrison of Mons at the end of October by Bellefonds, then in command of a detachment on the frontier of Hainault, definitely brought the campaign to a conclusion.

France had gained a line of strong places which, fortified by Vauban, would give her an " iron frontier " on the north-east. Early in September Louis joined the Queen at Arras, and then returned in triumph to Saint-Germain. Though, according to eye-witnesses, he bore his success with great modesty, a marked change was observed in his manner. Previous to this, his first, real experience of war he had shown shyness, especially when in the company of the Court ladies. This shyness and awkwardness now disappeared; he began like other men to take the lead in conversation. His youthful period had come to an end; Louis was now a man. This change may be partly attributed to his cam-

paigning in the Low Countries; it was in some
measure due to the influence of Madame de Montespan, who was rapidly supplanting Louise de la
Vallière in his favour.

Throughout the latter half of 1667 the diplomatic
activities of Louis never slackened. It was of
supreme importance that the Rhine and its various
passages should be closed against the possible arrival
of the Austrian troops. It was requisite to allay by
bribes or threats the uneasiness shown by Brandenburg and Sweden at the successes of the French.

In August the Duke of Neuburg signed a treaty
with Louis, in October the Elector of Cologne did
the same, while at the same time the Diet at Ratisbon
refused to oppose him. Brandenburg, won over by
gold, and Sweden, influenced by threats, declared
their neutrality, and in January and February, 1668,
Louis made treaties with Münster and the Elector
of Mainz. These alliances were secured at a very
heavy cost. French gold was not only poured
into the pockets of German politicians, but Louis
agreed to withdraw the candidature of Condé for
the Polish throne on the abdication of Casimir, and
to support that of the Duke of Neuburg, a relation
of Brandenburg.

Lastly he brought to a conclusion his negotiations with the Emperor Leopold, and on January
19, 1668, a secret treaty of Partition was signed.
By it it was agreed that, on the death of Charles II.
of Spain, Leopold was to have Spain, the West
Indies, Milan, and the Tuscan Ports; Louis was to
receive Naples and Sicily, the Low Countries and

Franche Comté, Navarre and Rosas, the Eastern
Philippines and the Spanish possessions in Africa.

Thus secure against the intervention of Leopold,
Louis was in a position to enter upon the second
campaign of the Devolution war, and to carry out
his projects on Franche Comté. It was well known
in Paris that negotiations between London and
Amsterdam were in progress ; Castel Rodrigo, too,
had adopted a confident tone, and had haughtily
refused the offer of a truce. A sudden attack on
Franche Comté would, it was thought, astonish the
world, punish the Spaniards, and prevent a coalition
between England and Holland. During the winter
of 1667–68 preparations were made rapidly, and
with the utmost secrecy. Condé, the Governor of
Burgundy, was received into the royal favour, and
entrusted with the execution of the design. Early
in December he returned from the Court to Burgundy and, with Louvois, made most elaborate
preparations. He informed himself of the condition
of the principal towns in Franche Comté, and of the
number and character of the troops available for the
defence of the Province. From the Swiss alone was
there any chance of real opposition to Louis' attack
on Franche Comté, and very explicit warnings had
reached the Swiss Cantons from Paris. The Swiss
were very sensitive on the subject of Franche
Comté, for they regarded it as a valuable barrier
against French aggression. But the Swiss were, like
the rest of Europe, completely taken by surprise.
Winter campaigns were practically unknown in
European warfare. The measures of Louvois had

been skilfully prepared, and the victor of Rocroi was again to electrify Europe. He had collected in Burgundy a force of fifteen thousand picked men, and on February 3rd he crossed the frontier. Within a fortnight Franche Comté was in his hands. On January 18th the serious, indefatigable, and hard-working Louis danced as *Pleasure* in a royal masquerade, and as in the winter of 1666–67 concealed under the appearance of devotion to amusement his design of taking an active part in the ensuing campaign. On the 2nd of February he left Paris, and arrived at Dijon on the 7th, having performed on horseback the journey of eighty miles in five days by roads more than usually detestable, owing to the winter season. Rochefort, Besançon, and Salins had already capitulated, and Louis received at Dijon their submission. On February 13th he was himself present at the capitulation of Dôle, the capital. The fall of Gray, on the 18th, was the final blow to the Spanish rule. On the 19th, the conquest of Franche Comté being completed, he returned to Saint-Germain, leaving to Condé as Governor of the two Burgundies and to Louvois the task of organising the administration of the new Province, which, as if by magic, in less than three weeks had been won by France. A populous country had been freed from its artificial connection with Spain, a continual danger to the French capital had been removed, and a fresh proof had been given of the power and resources of the French monarchy.

Louis' schemes did not end with the conquest of

Franche Comté. He meditated a further advance
into the Low Countries, and a large army was rapidly
concentrated on the frontier ready to operate in
April.

But these aggressive designs were suddenly
checked. Louis' rapid successes had alarmed Europe, and resistance to his schemes was openly prepared. He now found opposed to him not merely
Castel Rodrigo's men of straw, but a great European
coalition. On his return to Paris from Franche
Comté he received the formal announcement of a
Triple Alliance concluded on January 13th between
England, Holland, and Sweden.

De Witt had long been convinced that the possession of Spanish Flanders by the French would
mean destruction to the prosperity of the United
Provinces. The hostile tariff imposed by Colbert in
1667 had roused the strongest opposition in Holland, and the Dutch agreed with De Witt that it
was absolutely necessary to arrest at once the
progress of the French arms. A coalition alone
could resist Louis successfully. And De Witt
turned to Sweden and England.

In the former country a strenuous opposition had
arisen to the policy of friendship with France, and
De Witt succeeded in securing the promise of adhesion to any alliance formed by England and Holland
in favour of Spain. With England his task was
equally easy. Alarmed by the attack on the Low
Countries, England and Holland had hastened to
conclude the Peace of Breda in the summer of 1667,
and a sense of common danger tended to draw the

THE GREAT CONDÉ.

(From an engraving reproduced in Philippson's
Das Zeitalter Ludwigs XIV.)

two countries still closer together. The fall of Clarendon lost to Louis his most powerful English supporter just when the national feeling in England, irritated by the sale of Dunkirk, was showing itself fiercely opposed to the conquest of the Netherlands by the French. The Triple Alliance arranged by Sir William Temple, John De Witt, and Count Dohna expressed a firm determination on the part of England, Holland, and Sweden to resist any further encroachments of Louis XIV. The three powers bound themselves to obtain a cessation of arms till the end of May, on the basis of the proposals already made by Louis for the restoration of peace between Spain and France, to prevent any further extension of the French conquests, and agreed, if Louis refused to adopt their proposals, to attack him by sea and land.

The three powers had, however, a difficult task before them. To induce Spain to allow the greater part of the Low Countries to be saved from conquest was as difficult a task as to check a powerful king like Louis in his victorious career. Fully conscious of the seriousness of a crisis which had become of European importance, the allies compelled Spain to agree to peace and to accept one of the " alternatives " already proposed by Louis six months previously, viz., that he should *either* keep his conquests in the Netherlands, *or* receive Franche Comté with Aire, St. Omer, and Cambrai. After many delays Castel Rodrigo, who was averse to peace and hoped to continue the war with the assistance of England and Holland, decided to leave to Louis the towns which he had already conquered. While the country which was being saved against its will was accepting the terms of peace with a very bad grace, the negotiations at Paris were beset with difficulties. Louis' advisers were divided on the question of peace or war. Turenne, Condé, and Louvois were anxious to take the allies by surprise, to overrun the Netherlands, and to refuse the proposals of the Triple Alliance; Colbert and Lionne advised moderation on the ground that for a general European war France was not prepared in the matter of funds, military stores, or alliances. Finally, after much doubt and deliberation, Louis consented to treat on the basis which he had already indicated, but only agreed to a cessation of arms till the end of March. A large and imposing army in several divisions was assembled on the frontier ready to march as soon as the negotiations broke down. The feeling in Paris was decidedly warlike. Louis was furious on discovering the existence of the article in the secret treaty in which the allies had agreed, if Louis refused their proposals, to attack him by land and sea, and he was especially irritated at the attitude taken up by a small republic like Holland. Hence he readily listened to the counsel of those who pointed out that Spain was exhausted and could not send any reinforcements, that the allies would be powerless to prevent the entire conquest of the Netherlands, and that he could trust to his diplomacy to sow discord and dissension among his foes.

On the other hand there was much in the condition of Europe to make Louis hesitate before uniting the great powers against him in a strong coalition. Spain had on February 13, 1668, hastened to make peace with and to recognize the independence of Portugal. The influence of France in the latter country had been replaced by that of England. Sweden had definitely confirmed the engagement already provisionally made to join England and Holland, and the Triple Alliance had become an accomplished fact. Moreover military operations in Spain, England, and Holland were being steadily pushed on, and this fact undoubtedly contributed to decide Louis to postpone the continuance of the war and the attempted realisation of his plans to a season when there should be less unanimity among the great European states.

Holland, England, and Spain were indeed fully aroused, and Louis' decision was probably a wise one. In Holland naval and military preparations went hand in hand, in England the Parliament was prepared to vote large additional sums for the equipment of the fleet, even in Spain it was arranged that Don John of Austria as Governor of the Netherlands should at once take ten thousand men with him to the Low Countries and offer a strenuous resistance to the French armies.

But what probably weighed more than anything with Louis in favour of a peaceful solution was his secret treaty of January 19, 1668, with Leopold. Charles II. of Spain seemed likely to die any day; he had no children, and in the event of his death the succession to the Spanish dominions would be thrown open. For this contingency Louis was ready. He and Leopold had agreed upon the terms of the division and by those terms Louis would become owner of Franche Comté and the Low Countries.

At length on the acceptance by Castel Rodrigo of the second alternative, the treaty of Aix-la-Chapelle was signed on May 29, 1668, and the war which had fallen so suddenly upon Europe came almost as unexpectedly to an end. Louis' wisdom in making peace admits of little doubt. Had he persisted in war he would most certainly have brought upon himself a powerful coalition of which England would have been a leading member. English and Dutch writers have till quite lately been almost unanimous in ascribing Louis' decision in favour of peace to the efforts of the Triple Alliance. French writers are equally certain that the existence of the secret treaty with Leopold was the main cause of Louis' moderation. The truth probably lies between the two assertions. The Triple Alliance gave force to the advice of Colbert and Lionne; the knowledge of his treaty with Leopold decided Louis to postpone for a short while the realisation of his schemes and to take what seemed to be a step backward; the peace between Spain and Portugal impressed upon him the advisability of waiting till he could by diplomacy break up the coalition which had been formed against him, while the fear of a rising of the Huguenots in France may have strengthened his decision in favour of peace. The peace of Aix-la-Chapelle was only an armistice, but an armistice which proved invaluable to France and disastrous to the United Provinces. The Triple Alliance had been the result of a combination of circumstances which were not likely to repeat themselves. Of the three allies Holland had by her action incurred the greatest risk, for Holland lay in a precarious position between the commercial hostility of England and the political, religious, and commercial antagonism of France. Louis had every intention of continuing his annexations at a very early date and indeed at the expense of the United Provinces. When the hour of her trial came Holland was to find that of the great European nations the only ally on whom she could depend was her former enemy Spain.

II

CHAPTER VI.

THE WAR OF 1672.

1672–1678.

HE treaty of Aix-la-Chapelle
was merely a truce. The alli-
ance between England, Holland, and Sweden was built
upon no sure foundation, and
was unlikely to hold good for
any length of time. The interests of England and Holland
were in the matter of trade di-
ametrically opposed; Charles
II. himself disliked the Dutch on account of their
republican tendencies; the necessity of offering a
determined resistance to French policy was by no
means fully realised in England, and the aims and
general tendency of Louis' schemes were in no
degree understood. Sweden had, as it were, been
accidentally drawn into the Triple Alliance, and it
was unlikely that Sweden, since Richelieu's days so

closely allied to France and always so keenly appreciative of the pecuniary advantages of the French connection, would long remain in a position from which she could gain little or nothing. Though it is easy at the present day to analyse the causes for the isolation of Holland in 1672, he would have been a very wise man who could at that time have foretold that within three years a League which had been celebrated with bonfires would be broken up, and two of its members in open hostility to the third. Clifford had indeed asserted that there must be another war, but he never for a moment expected that the Triple Alliance would crumble away so soon. The men of that day had not yet realised the extent of the resources of Louis XIV. Though throughout his long reign Louis showed an extraordinary aptitude for diplomacy and remarkable wisdom in his choice of agents, he never showed more consummate diplomatic skill than when he set to work to isolate the Dutch Republic. Everything connected with the war, the diplomacy that preceded it, the elaborate military preparations, the skilful manner in which the peace of Nimeguen was concluded, the constant ebb and flow of the struggles between rival cliques at the Court interfering often considerably with successes in the field—all admirably illustrate Louis' strength and weakness. We note the enormous trouble taken about the smallest details, the precision with which the carefully planned arrangements were carried out, and the bombastic manner with which small successes were translated into brilliant victories.

The motives which led Louis into making his famous attack on the Dutch well exemplify the curious mixture of greatness and pettiness which meet us at every turn in studying the life of the *Grand Monarque*.

Though the Dutch had frequently proved most useful allies of France, they had incurred the resentment of Louis for their action on two occasions. By making with Spain the treaty of Münster in January, 1648, they had checkmated Mazarin and saved the Spanish Netherlands from annexation or partition. Again, in 1668, by joining in the Triple Alliance they had checked France in the realisation of her schemes against the Low Countries. In addition, the close proximity to France of republicans whose publications were strongly antimonarchical, and whose commerce had brought their country to a high pitch of prosperity, jarred upon Louis' tenderest feelings. The republic was founded upon a revolt from the King of Spain and from the Church of Rome. Colbert had already attacked the United Provinces by hostile tariffs, which, he expected, would ruin their trade. To destroy this republican nest and to restore the Catholic religion seemed to Louis an object worthy of a Catholic king.

But behind the political and commercial jealousy and the intolerant hatred which made the attack on the United Provinces seem a mere act of revenge, there were deeper and more statesmanlike forces at work. The object of the Devolution war had been to acquire the Spanish Netherlands, and the four years succeeding the treaty of Aix-la-Chapelle had only increased the determination of Louis and his advisers to annex that country. The real object of the war against the Dutch was the annexation of the Spanish Low Countries, though the various circumstances already mentioned diverted attention from the real meaning of the attack.

Had the ultimate intention of Louis been even suspected, his carefully erected system of alliances would have fallen like a pack of cards. His plan of operations was, however, so arranged as to hoodwink Europe. The surest way to annex the Spanish Netherlands was first of all to conquer, if possible, the Dutch, and that being accomplished the helpless Spanish Provinces could offer but a feeble resistance to the French arms. Viewed in its relation to the ultimate annexation of the Spanish Netherlands by France the Dutch war was a mere continuation of the war of Devolution, and Louis was carrying on by new methods the policy of Richelieu and Mazarin. In 1672 Holland was the only obstacle in the way of the realisation of the policy of extending the French boundaries on the north-east. But after the campaign was begun passion and arrogance carried Louis and Louvois too far, and instead of being content with weakening Holland to the extent of rendering her unable to aid or to defend the Spanish Netherlands, they appeared to Europe to be bent on the annihilation of a Protestant country merely on grounds of political, commercial, and religious jealousy.

Neither Richelieu nor Mazarin would probably have attacked the United Provinces. Not being blinded by religious enthusiasm they were able to appreciate the effect of religious forces upon the stability of old alliances. It was Louis' inability to gauge the strength of religious conviction that resulted in his failure to secure the main object of the war, and in his ultimate desertion of many of the principles which had guided Richelieu and Mazarin.

In arriving at the determination to subdue Holland, Louis, though acting consistently with his own programme, was in part deserting the policy inaugurated by Francis I. and followed by Richelieu and Mazarin. Hitherto France had taken up a moderate position—Catholic at home and Protestant abroad. She had held the balance between Protestantism and Catholicism on the continent. She had been careful to ally with the Dutch and to keep up friendly relations with the North German princes, and by this means to hamper and weaken the House of Hapsburg.

In attacking Holland Louis was adopting a policy which was sure in the end to alienate his North German allies. It was just at this time, too, that Louis, deserting the tolerant policy of his predecessors, began that course of persecution of the Huguenots which, culminating with the revocation of the Edict of Nantes, entirely alienated Protestant Europe. The process of converting France into a Catholic as well as an absolute monarchy, went on simultaneously with his attempt to undermine if not to annihilate Protestantism on the continent.

Carried away by a sincere desire to win brilliant

triumphs for the Church and by a wish to pose as
the leading supporter and benefactor of the Church,
he entered upon a course which was destined to
bring immeasurable evils upon France, and to unite
Europe in a determination which grew in intensity
from 1672 to 1713 to repress the Bourbon power.
"In Holland," says Mignet, "the old political system of France made shipwreck."

But Louis, young, ardent, surrounded by flatterers, and well served by generals and able ministers,
recked of none of these things. No sooner was the
peace of Aix-la-Chapelle signed than he began to
undermine it. "The years between 1668 and 1672,"
says Camille Rousset, "were years of preparation,
when Lionne was labouring with all his might to find
allies, Colbert to find money, and Louvois soldiers
for Louis." England was first gained. But the
secret negotiations which were undertaken in this
important affair lasted two years. Charles II. was
convinced that he could never hope to be absolute
until Catholicism was tolerated and recognised in
England. He himself followed the example of
his brother James, and became a Catholic early in
1669, and that step taken Louis at once offered him,
on condition of aid against the Dutch, every possible assistance in establishing despotic government in
England.

The conduct of the English Parliament in voting
him an inadequate sum of money in the autumn of
1669, and the influence of Henrietta of Orleans
swept away Charles' last scruple, and on June 1,
1670, the treaty of Dover marked Louis' great diplo-

matic triumph and the break up of the Triple Alliance. Without England a successful attack on Holland would have been impossible. The English ships alone were capable of coping with the Dutch fleet, which could easily have destroyed the French commerce. The alliance with England was, indeed, of incalculable value to Louis, who would have had little chance of carrying out his schemes had Cromwell and not Charles II. ruled in London. Thus was accomplished the first and most important step in the realisation of a policy of shattering the Triple Alliance, gaining or neutralising the European states, and destroying a small republic.

Lionne was largely responsible for the success of the negotiations for securing England's withdrawal from the Triple Alliance, but the final scenes of the drama which ended with Charles' assent to the treaty were enacted by Henrietta of Orleans. To cover her mission to England, Louis made a triumphal progress through the newly conquered towns in the north, taking with him his Queen and Madame de Montespan.

Greater difficulty was experienced in detaching Sweden from the Triple Alliance, and Lionne died before his negotiations had been brought to a successful issue. But the ill-judged economy of the Dutch and the efforts of Lionne's successor, Arnauld de Pomponne, ably supported by Courtin and the English Coventry, at last won an important diplomatic victory over the ambassadors of Austria, Brandenburg, Spain, and Holland. Sweden, poor and intensely jealous of Denmark, was to receive a large

sum of money down and an annual subsidy of
£150,000, and Denmark was not to be included in
the alliance. For this she was to hold North Germany in check, and to send an army into Pomerania.
The treaty was only signed in May, 1672—a month
before the attack on Holland began.

The untimely death of the attractive Duchess of
Orleans hardly a month after the completion of the
treaty of Dover, had not checked Louis' preparations in the slightest degree. In August he occupied
Lorraine, asserting as a justification the Duke's intrigues with Holland. He had already succeeded—
where Mazarin had failed—in securing the neutrality
of Bavaria, and hoped to obtain the Elector's assistance in the execution of his schemes with regard
to the Imperial throne and the Spanish succession.
In October, 1671, Osnabrück promised aid, and in
November of the same year the Emperor Leopold
signed a treaty of neutrality. In the early months
of 1672, the alliance with England was drawn still
closer, and Cologne and Münster made offensive
treaties with Louis. The Elector Palatine was
secured, and at the end of the year Brunswick-
Lüneburg joined in the opposition to Holland.
Louis had nothing to fear from Germany ; Mainz and
Trèves were, like Denmark and Saxony, neutral,
though the neutrality of the two latter was of a hostile character. The Dutch could do little to avert
the storm, in spite of the fact that De Witt had been
from 1671 well aware of the attack about to be made
on his country. In March, 1672, a Dutch merchant
fleet was attacked by Admiral Homes without warn-

ing, and four days later England declared war. The Dutch could only rely on Brandenburg and Spain. The latter had made a defensive treaty with Holland in December, 1671, and the former promised, on May 2, 1672, to bring to their assistance 22,000 men.

Louis' military preparations were no less minute than his political arrangements had been. The occupation of Lorraine assured him the frontier on the side of Germany, and a quarrel between the inhabitants of Cologne and their Archbishop gave Louvois an excuse for making the strong positions of Neuss and Kaiserwerth depôts for the French army. There, after three skilfully contrived treaties with the Elector of Cologne, he had stored in 1671 large quantities of grain, powder, and arms of all kinds.

Just before the actual outbreak of the war a curious attempt was made to divert the elaborate preparations into another channel. The philosopher Leibnitz was sent by the Elector of Mainz to present to Louis a scheme for the conquest of Egypt—the Holland of the East—and of the Indies. Had Louis followed the advice of Leibnitz the control of the Mediterranean trade would have fallen into French hands. Bonaparte's famous attempt to ruin the British Empire by occupying Egypt came too late. We have no proof that Louis gave any attention to this proposal of Leibnitz. Pomponne, however, wrote to the Elector that " projects for holy wars had ceased to be fashionable since the days of Saint Louis." Having thus failed in his endeavour to preserve the peace of Europe the Elector took up the cause of the Dutch and prepared to aid them by diplomacy.

War was declared against the United Provinces on April 6th and a medal was struck commemorating the victory which Louis was about to win. The inscription bore the motto *Evexi sed discutiam* and the medal represented the sun dispersing by his beams the vapours from a morass. On April 28th Louis left Saint-Germain, and went by Nanteuil, Soissons, Laon, Marle, and Aubenton to Rocroi, arriving there on May 2d. From Rocroi were issued the first set of the elaborate orders which regulated the campaign of 1672.

The army, a portion of which Louis met at Rocroi, was worthy of a mightier foe than Holland. Under Louvois and Turenne it had been completely reorganised and was in a high state of discipline. After the conclusion of the peace of the Pyrenees very drastic changes had been brought about. Up to this time the armies were either bodies of free lances collected round a particular general, and looking to him for pay, or a kind of armed militia which regarded soldiering as a sort of interlude, not as a profession. The army was now improved at the expense of the militia and organised into a standing force. It was divided into brigades, regiments, battalions, and squadrons. Generals were given absolute powers and the officers were placed under careful supervision. The household troops had been subjected to drastic reforms and were now an effective branch of the service, and a body of engineers was being organised by Vauban. Louvois also insisted upon the forcible enrolment of the nobility and gentry, he introduced a new system of drill which was

perfected by Martinet, he began a system of payment, he formed a commissariat, and made hospital
arrangements suitable for large armies.

Carefully trained under the eye of Turenne the
French infantry had become the best in Europe. It
had nearly trebled in numbers, and was far superior
to the cavalry in importance. As a fighting machine
the French army had no equal and Europe was soon
to recognise and imitate the changes which had
so completely transformed the military system of
France. The campaign of 1667 had first shown the
enormous progress made by the French army since
the death of Mazarin, but it was not till the Dutch
war that the full import of the reforms of Louvois
and Turenne was realised. The excellence of the
arrangements, the discipline of the regiments, and
the preponderance of infantry were clearly manifested during the invasion of the Dutch Provinces.
" It was," said Napoleon, " a new era in war."

Turenne and Condé were placed in command of
the forces and Vauban accompanied the army to
direct the capture of towns. Turenne's plans were
admirable and the campaign was in its earlier phases
one triumphal march. The King marched down the
Sambre and Meuse. At Viset he crossed the river
while Turenne masked Maestricht by capturing
Maseick and Tongres.

On the 31st of May, the main French army was at
Neuss and moving down the Rhine rapidly crossed
that river at Tolhuys on June 12th, after a slight
skirmish with the Dutch. Though Napoleon spoke
of this fact as " an operation of the fourth class," it

THE PASSAGE OF THE RHINE.
(From a collection of prints of Louis XIV.'s campaigns.)

was regarded by the inhabitants of Paris as a brilliant feat of arms. Up to this point the advice of Turenne had been followed. Had the army or even a small portion of it advanced rapidly the war would have been over in a few days. The Yssel had been crossed and there was practically no serious obstacle to the capture of Amsterdam. But the influence of Louvois acting upon the predilections of the King for siege warfare saved Holland and averted a step which would have changed the whole course of European history.

Against the advice of Turenne who rightly wished to push on and take Utrecht and Amsterdam, Louis insisted on turning aside and wasting precious time in reducing the forts on the Yssel—an easy way of securing certain triumphs which enabled him to pose as a great warrior. He failed at a critical moment to grasp the position and laid himself open to the charge of being defective in understanding and courage. Louvois must also take his share of the blame for this extraordinary blunder. Carried away by the mere pride of power, he seems to have thought that the complete overthrow of Holland was assured. His advice to Louis at this juncture proved most disastrous, and his presumption may be said to have destroyed all chance of a successful campaign.

It is difficult to understand why Turenne was unable to protest successfully against what he must have known was a most fatal blunder. But he had been sent to watch the movements of the Great Elector, while Louis who took up his quarters at Utrecht, failed to see the importance of seizing

Muyden, which commanded the chief sluices of the district, and before his advisers themselves had realised the effects of delay the dykes had been cut, the sluices had been opened, and Amsterdam was saved.

Three things, it has been said, saved the Dutch— an inundation, a revolution, and a coalition. No one could possibly have foreseen any one of these at the beginning of the year. Up to the " passage of the Rhine " the Dutch Republic had ranked with the great monarchies of Christendom, the rule of John de Witt seemed well established, and Europe generally never dreamt of a sudden catastrophe coming upon so prosperous and stable a government as was that of the United Provinces.

But Louis' rapid and successful march upset all calculations. A month sufficed to place at his mercy the flourishing republic. History affords few examples of so sudden a downfall of a hitherto prosperous state. " The great and astonishing progress which my armies had made in so short a time," writes Louis XIV., " the idea and forebodings of certain ruin and the general overthrow of the republic, the small reliance there was to be placed in a new and depreciated army, commanded by an inexperienced young man, all these sad and hopeless reflections bewildered the Dutch, and put them beside themselves." This was no doubt true as far as the Dutch population was concerned, but John de Witt had at an early period seriously considered the possibility of having to defend Holland by means of inundations. After the " passage of the Rhine " the Council of Amsterdam themselves admitted the seriousness of the crisis, but it was not till June 15th that it was decided that the country surrounding Amsterdam was to be inundated. The inundation begun on June 15th was nearly completed by June 20th. Such an act of heroism had not been expected by Louvois. " His Majesty," he had written shortly before the cutting of the dykes, " will be able in eight days to send troops to pillage The Hague and the towns of Holland which cannot be inundated in the dry weather we have now." Grémonville, the French ambassador at Vienna, was furious at the audacity of the Dutch in preferring " to ruin and destroy their country and their subjects, and to expose themselves to the danger of being drowned, rather than submit to so glorious and triumphant a conqueror."

Louis himself recognised the courage and heroism of the Dutch. " The determination to flood the whole country," he writes, " was certainly rather violent, but what would not one do to save oneself from foreign domination."

The immediate ruin of the republic had indeed been averted. She could now await the continuance of the war or make proposals of peace. But public opinion in Holland demanded a change of government. On July 3d the Perpetual Edict was abrogated, and on the 4th the Prince of Orange was proclaimed Stadtholder and Captain, and Admiral-General of Holland. On June 26th the States-General had unanimously voted for making peace with the King of France, and though the change of government implied a rising feeling in favour of resistance, William felt bound to continue the negotiations. But the baneful influence of Louvois was once more seen to the great disadvantage of France. The Dutch plenipotentiaries on behalf of the States-General offered to Louis, who was then at Ameron-gen near Utrecht, Maestrecht and the Rhine towns, undertaking also to pay 600,000 francs towards the cost of the war.

When Louvois treated these offers with scorn they increased their concessions. Louis in exchange for the towns conquered in the provinces of Utrecht, Oberyssel, and Guelders should have not only Maes-tricht and the towns on the Rhine, but also all towns held by the Dutch outside the seven provinces, such as Breda, Bois-le-Duc, and Bergen-op-Zoom. The sum offered should also be increased to 10,000,000 francs.

Had Louis accepted these terms he would have secured the country separating the United Provinces from the Spanish Netherlands from the Meuse to the mouth of the Scheldt, the subjugation of the Spanish Netherlands would only have been a matter of time, and ample vengeance would have been wreaked upon the Dutch. Pomponne strongly urged the acceptance of these terms. But by Louvois' advice Louis made additional demands. The frontier of the United Provinces was to be withdrawn to the Wahal, and all fortified towns on the river were to be placed at his disposal, or dismantled. Delfzyl and its dependencies were also to be given up and transferred by him to England. All edicts unfavourable to French commerce were to be revoked, and a treaty of commerce was to be concluded regulating the interests of the East and West India

Companies of France and Holland. A war indemnity of 10,500,000 florins was to be paid, and
lastly an embassy was to be sent to France once
a year to present Louis with a gold medal, the
motto on which was to convey to him thanks for
having " left to the United Provinces the independence which the kings, his predecessors, had
enabled her to acquire." These demands would if
complied with have destroyed the colonial power of
the United Provinces, ruined their trade, and overthrown their constitution.

There was a general impression at the French
camp and also in Paris that the King would obtain
all these demands. " The King will return Count
of Holland," wrote Madame de Sévigné—" the only
impossibility to his Majesty is to find enemies to
resist him." Louvois too was confident that the
Dutch dared not refuse the French terms. But
Louvois entirely misunderstood the character of the
Dutch people. In breaking off the negotiations with
Louis the States-General fully endorsed the avowed
opinion of De Groot that he " would sooner die than
accept such terms from France." Louis had taken a
false step and the consequences were serious. From
a military point of view the operations against the
Dutch will always be interesting. Turenne's plans
for the invasion of the United Provinces, the mask-
ing of Maestricht and the capture of Nimeguen are
in themselves sufficient to make the campaign celebrated. But the real object of the war had not been
gained, and a series of political blunders of the first
magnitude had been perpetrated.

12

Louis had failed through yielding to the advice of Louvois. His original intention had been to rest satisfied with a reasonable triumph. " The daily progress of my army," he had written to Grémonville, " puts me in a position to impose any conditions I please on the States, but I wish to listen to the promptings of my own generosity so far as is consistent with authority and the just rights of victory."

Even when he had had ample proof of the desperate resistance which the country was prepared to make he seems to have been carried away and intoxicated by success. This is his own explanation of the mistake he made in not accepting the terms offered him by the Dutch plenipotentiaries. " The proposals made to me," he wrote in later days, " were very advantageous, but I never could make up my mind to accept them." And as a further explanation he again wrote in his account of the campaign of 1672:—" Posterity may believe if it choose in my reasons for so acting, and can at its pleasure ascribe my refusal to my ambition and the desire for vengeance for the injuries I had sustained from the Dutch. I shall not justify myself. Ambition and glory are always pardonable in a prince, and particularly in a prince so young and so well treated by fortune as I was."

By the end of July the inundations had brought military operations for the moment to a standstill, while the rejection by William of the proposals of peace and the gathering together of an alarmed Europe necessitated Louis' return to France. But before he departed he again yielded to Louvois' baneful advice and released some twenty thousand Dutch prisoners. This course was adopted contrary to the counsel of Condé and Turenne, but apparently thinking he had nothing to fear from so feeble a power as Holland had proved itself, Louis with a misplaced generosity which some writers have described as bravado followed the recommendation of Louvois, though he soon regretted his resolution.

"I took my departure for France," he wrote, "having nothing to reproach myself with excepting the extreme indulgence which I showed to nearly twenty thousand prisoners of war by sending them back to Holland, where they formed the principal force which that republic has since employed against me." With this last blunder to ponder over Louis returned early in August to Saint-Germain, leaving Turenne in command of the army, Luxemburg governor of Utrecht, Lorge governor of Guelders, and d'Estrades governor of the Rhine towns. He received an enthusiastic welcome, as a conqueror returning from his victorious campaign. A triumphal arch was erected in Paris, while a gate at Saint-Denis and paintings in Versailles perpetuated the remembrance of his victories. Medals, too, were struck in his honour, one of which represented him "mounted on the Chariot of the Sun passing rapidly through its twelve houses exemplified by twelve of the towns he had conquered."

But fêtes could not conceal the real failure of the French policy and the dangers which in consequence threatened France. Louis had indeed lost a magnificent chance of bringing the war to a glorious

conclusion, and he had now to face the results of
that mistake.

The safety of the republic which had been partly
provided for by the inundation and the revolution
was now to be amply secured by the formation
of a powerful European coalition. In face of the
alliances which were being made to aid the United
Provinces Louis' presence at Saint-Germain was imperatively demanded. " The entry of Louis XIV.
into the Spanish Low Countries (in 1667) had," says
Mignet, " alarmed the United Provinces ; the invasion of the United Provinces alarmed Europe."

Leopold had already on June 23d made an alliance with the Great Elector for the preservation of
the peace of Westphalia, and in October he made
another with the States-General. Henceforward the
object of the war is changed. It is no longer a mere
contest against Holland ; it becomes a war between
France and a European coalition. In this—a practically new war in which Europe showed that it
fully realised the danger from the French monarchy,
Louis worked to achieve military glory, and he had
the satisfaction in the summer of 1673 of being
present when Vauban besieged and took Maestricht.
It was unlikely after such an event, and especially
when Turenne had compelled the Elector of Brandenburg, who believed himself abandoned by the
Emperor and feared for his possessions in Westphalia, to make peace in July, that Louis would consent to any reasonable arrangement with the Dutch,
such as might have been come to through the
mediation of Sweden at the Conference of Cologne,

which sat from June, 1673, to March, 1674. And so
the war went on fiercely at three centres, in the Low
Countries, in Franche-Comté, and in Alsace and the
Palatinate.

A new coalition was formed in August, 1673, consisting of the Emperor, the Dutch, Lorraine, and
Spain. The capture of Bonn by the allies in November was an event, the importance of which cannot be overestimated. Cologne and Münster were
forced to withdraw from their association with
Louis, while Trèves and Mainz readily joined the
coalition. The whole of Germany began to show
signs of opposition and England's alliance wavered.
In spite, however, of these defections, in spite of
the adhesion of Denmark to the coalition in January,
1674, and in spite of the still more important fact
that Charles II. in February was compelled by
Parliament to make peace with the Dutch, Louis
entered lightly upon the celebrated campaign of
1674.

The great event of the early portion of the year
was the invasion of Franche-Comté, while in the
later portion the strategy of Turenne was in itself
sufficient to create and establish a reputation. The
King himself took part in the reconquest of Franche-
Comté and enjoyed to the full, his favourite amusement of town-taking. After the French troops had
retired in 1668, the province suffered at the hands
of the Spaniards, who attacked all French partisans
and increased the taxation. When the Dutch war
broke out it was felt that a French invasion was inevitable. The towns were only half fortified, the

troops few in number and mostly composed of recruits. In spite, however, of the general feeling of
the hopelessness of resisting the inevitable, and in
spite of the weakness of the military arrangements,
the second conquest of Franche-Comté was only
completed after a struggle of six months and after
the French had experienced severe losses.

The operations were conducted by Enghien, Luxemburg, Vauban, de la Feuillade, Duras, and Resnel,
and were seriously hampered by the stern resistance
of such towns as Arbois, Salins, Besançon, Ornans,
and Dôle, ably seconded by the guerilla warfare
of bands of peasants. At the siege of Arbois the
women and girls fought side by side with the men,
and the same spirit animated the defenders of most
of the towns in Lorraine.

The campaign which began in February, 1674,
was at its height when Louis left Versailles on April
19th and proceeded to Besançon. Gray, Vesoul,
and Lons-le-Saunier had fallen and Besançon was
now besieged by the Duc d'Enghien. The Prince of
Vaudemont, son of the Duke of Lorraine, conducted
the defence ably supported by the population and
notably by one Père Schmidt who commanded the
artillery with such success that two hundred French
soldiers were killed and Vauban's efforts were for
the moment foiled. For twenty-seven days Besançon defended itself and only yielded when Vauban
succeeded in placing forty cannon on the heights
overlooking the town and so rendered further resistance impossible. It was feared that an army of
Austrians and Lorrainers under the Duke of Lorraine

might now arrive and interfere with the subjugation of Franche-Comté, but the skill of Turenne prevented the Duke from carrying out his purpose, and the capitulation of Dôle on June 7th, and of Salins on the 22nd marked the close of the sharp struggle for Lorraine.

During this time the Duke of Luxemburg had taken Ornans on May 5th and Pontarlier on May 8th. The conquest of Franche-Comté was practically accomplished and Louis left the seat of war on June 19th and arrived at Fontainebleau on the 25th. He had intended to proceed to Flanders, but satisfied with the news received from Condé and with the submission of Franche-Comté he decided not to appear again that year at the head of his troops. The importance of the capture of Franche-Comté was very great, and at the peace of Nimeguen it remained part of France. Its Estates were no longer summoned but the *Parlement* was allowed to exist, though its duties were confined to civil matters. It sat henceforth at Besançon, which fortified by Vauban became the well administered capital of the province. Franche-Comté in spite of heavy taxation on the whole gained by its subjection to the central authority. It soon became completely merged into the French kingdom, and its conquest prepared the way for the future possession of all Alsace and Lorraine and for the extension of the French frontier to the Rhine. When Louis returned to Fontainebleau in June, he had carried out for France a very important operation. Henceforth the Jura was to be the eastern frontier to France.

The war had by the middle of 1674 assumed increased proportions. The Elector Palatine and the
Elector of Saxony, with the Dukes of Brunswick and
Lüneburg had joined the coalition. In May the
Empire declared war against France and in July
the Great Elector joined the League of The Hague.
Louis had indeed made strenuous endeavours to
hamper Austria by forming an alliance with Bavaria.
But he could only succeed in making a treaty
early in 1673, which was of a very unsatisfactory
and vague character, the Elector refusing to be
drawn into open hostility to the Hapsburgs, and
in spite of a promise in 1675 to aid the Swedes he
abstained from taking any active part in the war,
and none of Louis' agents were able to shake him
in this resolution.

Sweden was the one active ally left to Louis,
but it was not till 1675 that Sweden made a useful
diversion in the north, which resulted in a severe
defeat at Fehrbellin in June and the temporary loss
of the Swedish conquests in Germany. In spite,
however, of the want of allies the French held their
own during 1674. All the recent conquests in Holland
had been abandoned except Maestricht and Grave
and the war assumed a defensive character. Condé
who made head against the Dutch and Spaniards on
the northern frontier fought in August the bloody
but indecisive battle of Senef, and though William
of Orange succeeded in taking Grave he had to relinquish his intention of invading France. The real
interest, however, of the year 1674 centres round
Turenne's famous campaign.

The redeeming feature of the invasion of Holland in 1672 had been Turenne's skilful operations. But at Saint-Germain his detractors had raised their heads and disputes had broken out between him and Louvois. To excuse his own shortcomings and errors Louis acquiesced in the attacks on his ablest general. Though Montecuculi successfully out-manœuvred Turenne and though in the autumn of 1673 Bonn fell, the French general completely effaced his reverse by his brilliant campaign in 1674 and 1675. It was, indeed, due to his advice that Franche-Comté was reconquered ; but his great achievement was his defence of France in the autumn of the year 1674. His devastation of the Palatinate was justifiable according to the opinion of the time and was only carried out in order to check the invasion of France by the armies of the League. Despite of all his efforts, however, the allies crossed the Rhine in September and after effecting a junction with the Great Elector settled in Alsace for the winter and compelled Turenne to retreat. The alarm in Paris was great, the arrival of the foe at the capital was expected, and the ancient *arrière-ban* was called out. But Turenne was equal to the occasion, and by his winter campaign in the Vosges he saved France. Using the Vosges to screen him from his enemies he marched from Lixheim in Lorraine to Belfort in the depth of winter, arriving at the latter place on December 27th. He at once burst upon his astonished foes scattered through Alsace, defeated some of them at Mulhausen and the Great Elector at Turckheim on January 5th. A week

later not a German soldier remained on the left
bank of the Rhine.

The rest of the war was of a tamer character,
though as far as France was concerned it was carried
on at first with satisfactory results. Sweden attacked
the Great Elector in Pomerania and drew him from
the Rhine; John Sobieski, the King of Poland, had
French sympathies, and in 1675 made a treaty with
France. He agreed to aid Sweden against Brandenburg as soon as his hands were free from his Turkish
war. For this aid he was to have a large sum of
money and Ducal Prussia. But when the treaty of
Zurawna in 1676 ended his war with the Turks the
relations of France and Poland were no longer
friendly, and in 1684 Sobieski made a treaty with
Austria. In the west Turenne's movements against
Montecuculi were so successful that the King delighted with the bright prospects set out to join the
army of the north, intending to end the war with a
brilliant campaign.

Departing from Saint-Germain on May 11th he
proceeded to join the forces in the Netherlands.
After a campaign distinguished by no brilliant success, Louis left his army under the Prince of Condé
and arrived at Versailles on July 21st. But the death
of Turenne, on July 27th, destroyed all chance of a
successful campaign. The efforts of Condé in the
north and of Créqui on the Moselle were paralysed
and the latter was defeated on August 11th near
Trèves by the Dukes of Lorraine and of Zell-
Lüneburg.

In Paris the utmost consternation prevailed. The

TURENNE.
(From an illustration in Erdmannsdörfer's
Deutsche Geschichte von 1648–1740.)

opposition to the party of Louvois and Madame de Montespan had lost its leading member. Though Louis had latterly allowed Louvois to come between him and Turenne he fully appreciated the loss which France had sustained, and the necessity of increased exertions on his own part and on that of his generals. On July 30th he wrote to Condé giving him the command of Turenne's army and ordering him to hand over his force to the Duke of Luxemburg. On August 16th he wrote again to Condé relative to Créqui's defeat at Kond-Saarbruck, and on October 17th he wrote sympathising with Condé's weak health and allowing him to leave the army whenever he chose. Having driven Montecuculi from Alsace Condé retired and Montecuculi resigned his command.

. Thus the year 1675 saw the end of the military careers of not only Turenne but also of Condé and Montecuculi, the great masters of the art of war in Europe.

In 1676 Louis again took part in the campaign in the Spanish Netherlands with the army of the north. In was in this latter campaign that he "lost the very finest occasion he could ever have had for gaining a victory." He had left Versailles on April 16th and on the 21st joined the army which under Créqui and d'Humières was besieging Condé. Vauban directed the siege operations and Condé fell before the end of the month and Bouchain was in its turn besieged. William of Orange marched to relieve it and a battle seemed imminent. The Prince's troops lay between Valenciennes and Raîmes and

Louis began to draw his up between Saint-Léger
and Aubri. His troops numbered about 48,000
while those of the enemy only amounted to 35,000.
Never was there a better opportunity for winning
a battle with the minimum of risk. On a rising
ground was held a famous council of war. Louis
himself recognised that a victory lay within his
grasp. Some of his generals advised an immediate
attack; others feared to expose Louis to any danger.
The Marshal de la Feuillade threw himself at the
King's feet imploring him not to run any risk, while
Schomberg when appealed to by Louis refused to
accept the responsibility of advising a battle. Louis,
who always preferred besieging towns to fighting
pitched battles, allowed his better judgment to be
overruled with the words : " As you have more
experience than I have, I yield, but with regret."
It is said that he lamented all his life this momentary
weakness, which enabled his enemies to say that he
lacked courage, that he always avoided battles and
delighted only in sieges. Bouchain capitulated on
May 11th. After marching about the Netherlands
for some six weeks he left the command of the
army with Schomberg and departed for Versailles
on July 4th. In spite of her success in warding
off invasion, in spite of the brilliant achievements
of the French fleet in the Mediterranean where
Duquesne had defeated utterly the Dutch and
Spanish fleets off Palermo, France was discontented
and exhausted. Revolts had broken out in some
of the provinces, many districts near the frontier
had been wellnigh ruined, the continued war had

necessitated heavy loans, oppressive taxation, and the adoption of that most pernicious custom—the sale of offices.

There was, however, no immediate chance of the war coming to an end and though several of the combatants were ready for peace, hostilities were continued with vigour. Two events of a different sort irritated Louis beyond measure during the year 1677. In the first place his brother, the Duke of Orleans, won a pitched battle at Cassel against William of Orange—a feat far more brilliant than the continuous sieges of towns,—and in the second place William of Orange crossed over to England and persuaded Charles to agree to his marriage with Mary, the daughter of James, Duke of York. But though this latter circumstance showed that public opinion in England was forcing the hand of Charles II. no active interference in the Netherlands on the part of the English was apprehended, and during the year 1677 the French armies continued to win successes. Louis had left Saint-Germain on February 26th and had arrived before Valenciennes, then besieged by Luxemburg and Montal on March 4th. Vauban, who as usual directed the siege operations, was strongly of opinion that the final assault should be by day and not as was usual by night. Louis and Louvois strongly opposed this proposal but Vauban defended his view with such tenacity that Louis after much careful thought yielded. On March 17th at 9 A.M. the assault was made and the town capitulated. Cambrai fell on April 6th, and on April 22d Orleans who had been detached to take Saint Omer

defeated Orange at the battle of Cassel. There
seems little doubt that Louis was much piqued by
his brother's success. He carefully avoided visiting the battle-field, and Orleans was never allowed
another opportunity of winning any military successes. Jealousy of his brother alone explains such
conduct on the part of Louis. On May 31st he was
back at Versailles. Nothing more of great importance occurred after the King's departure. William
of Orange failed to take Charleroi, and in December
d'Humières captured Saint-Guilain without much
difficulty. It fell on the 11th, and on the 14th
Louis sent a letter of congratulation to the Marshal.

But affairs in England were becoming serious.
England's alliance, or, at any rate, her neutrality,
was of vital importance to Louis. Louis knew well
the real position of things in England. He knew
that as long as Danby and William acted together,
England's hostility was assured. To neutralise
their influence he intrigued with and received timely
aid from the opposition, who, bent on the overthrow
of Danby, were ready to join Louis, and sacrifice
their country. Louis, therefore, supported by the
English opposition, determined to act boldly, and
by forcing peace with one of the combatants to
bring the rest to terms in detail. He took Ghent
and Ypres in March, 1678, and these victories had
the effect he expected, viz., of hastening on peace
between himself and the Dutch. Ever since 1676 a
congress had been sitting at Nimeguen to discuss
terms of peace. The Dutch had been anxious to
end the war for some years. They hated the Spaniards, they were discomfited by the death of Ruyter

in 1676. But each side hoped for further successes, and time was on the side of Louis. There was little heartiness in the relations subsisting between England and Holland, and in both countries there was a strong opposition to the government.

By taking advantage of these circumstances, and by working upon the internal divisions in England and Holland, Louis undoubtedly gained better terms than he could have expected. In Holland William was continually abused, and his relations with England became the object of suspicion. In England party passion, fomented by Louis and his agents, was rising, and Charles II. was in great perplexity.

Alone of the combatants Louis, who was above criticism and unchecked by the presence of an opposition, had not only clear views, but the power to put them into execution. By concluding treaties with each of the allies separately, he emerged triumphantly from a war which seemed at one time likely to end disastrously for France. On August 10, 1678, Louis made peace with the Dutch, on September 17th with Spain, on February 2, 1679, with the Emperor and Empire, and shortly afterwards with the Duke of Brunswick and Lüneburg and with the Bishop of Münster. Sweden and Brandenburg made peace at Saint-Germain-en-Laye in 1679, Louis insisting that his ally, Sweden, should lose nothing, and Sweden and Denmark made peace a few months later.[1]

---

[1] Among the numerous works bearing upon the Dutch war the most useful are, *The Life of John de Witt*, by Lefèbre-Pontalis, and Rousset's *History of Louvois*.

By the peace of Nimeguen France was the gainer, and Spain the real loser. Though France restored Courtrai, Oudenarde, Ath, Charleroy, Ghent, Limburg, and Saint-Ghislain, Spain was forced to yield Franche-Comté and many strong places on the north-eastern frontier, such as Cambrai, Bouchain, Valenciennes, and Condé, besides Aire and Saint Omer in Artois, and Ypres, Cassel, Maubeuge, Charlemont, and Dinan in Flanders and Hainault. France thus obtained a line of strong places stretching from Dunkirk to the Meuse, and useful for purposes of defence or as a basis of attack. The questions at issue with the Emperor had been difficult to settle. Of these three only required considerable attention:—

(1) The imprisonment of the Prince William of Fürstenberg in 1674 by the Austrians.

(2) The future position of the Duke of Lorraine and of his duchy.

(3) The affairs of Alsace—the Emperor demanding arbitration with reference to Louis' claims in respect of the ten Imperial towns of Hagenau, Rosheim, Obernai, Landau, Wissembourg, Schlestadt, Colmar, Kayserberg, Turckheim, and Münster.

The Emperor, who refused to make peace till a campaign of Créqui compelled him to yield, gave up Freiburg and Old Breisach, and received in exchange Philipsburg. Fürstenberg was released, Lorraine remained temporarily in French hands, as the Duke refused to accept the terms offered him, and the position of the ten Imperial towns was left undecided.

Such is a brief account of the Dutch War, as it is

generally called. In the history of the development of Louis XIV. it holds an important place. During its progress many of those characteristics which marked him off from other monarchs of the time are presented to our notice. Though enamoured of Madame de Montespan, he never allowed her influence to interfere with public affairs. As he says in his *Mémoires*: "Our first object should always be the preservation of our glory and our authority, which can only be maintained by assiduous work." Louis as a lover and Louis as a sovereign were to be two distinct personalities. The amusements of the one were never to encroach in the slightest degree on the duties of the other. And certainly he never allowed his work to be interfered with during the war. He always held the theory that the army was the especial care of the King, and he took the army under his charge. Each month he satisfied himself that the regiments were complete, deserters were severely punished, the generals and officers were carefully supervised. All disputes were settled by the King, whose authority was never questioned. The smallest details, such as questions relating to the quarters of the troops, were referred to him, while the larger questions, dealing with the commissariat, were only decided after Louis had mastered all the points at issue. All appointments in the infantry, as well as in the cavalry, were made by him directly, and in this way the officers realised that the surest road to promotion lay in their devotion to the King. He was very fond of reviews, which he held frequently, and by means of them made himself acquainted with the life of each regiment, and was able to influence the officers by praises and rewards.

At the peace of Nimeguen his power stood at its greatest height. Though he had not trampled upon Holland, he had dictated terms of peace to all the other powers. He had united to France the important province of Franche-Comté and a large part of the Spanish Netherlands. The north-east frontier, increased and strongly fortified by Vauban, was an invaluable addition to the French monarchy; Lorraine was practically at his feet. Out of a great struggle against half Europe in arms Louis had emerged the only gainer. He had been well served by his commanders, his diplomatists, and his administrators, all of whom he had found to his hand on the death of Mazarin.

Since the time of Charles V. no European monarch had wielded so much power or been regarded with greater awe and admiration by Europe. The authorities of Paris conferred on him in 1680 the title of "the Great." Louis indeed stood before the world on a pinnacle of glory. He had baffled and tricked England, he had pensioned her king, and bribed the leaders of the English opposition. He had created a navy of two hundred and fifty ships, and his armies had in 1678 numbered three hundred thousand men. Since the days of Imperial Rome no such forces had been employed by any civilised nation.

The skill of Turenne ably seconded by Vauban and Louvois had increased the territory and strengthened the frontiers of France, while Colbert's vigilant genius had insured order and efficiency at home. With no fear of interruption from within, and with vast resources, financial, military, and naval, Louis was now in a position to pursue the work of external expansion.

CHAPTER VII.

THE TAKING OF STRASBURG.

1681.

TO make France "a central fortress of which he was commander and the approaches of which he vigilantly guarded and strengthened" was, says von Ranke, Louis' great aim. The peace of Nimeguen had not gone far enough. It was still necessary to complete the "ceinture de frontières." Vauban had already done a great work in fortifying the frontiers. Bayonne and Perpignan defended France against Spanish invasion; Pignerolo was an advanced post in Italy; while Freiburg and Huningen on the Upper Rhine, Saarlouis, to defend Lorraine, Maubeuge on the Sambre, Dunkirk, La Rochelle, and Toulon on the sea-coast, and Lille on the northern frontier, all testified to the thorough and practical manner in which Vauban had carried out his task. But German rights extended very considerably over the left bank of the Rhine, and Louis' object was as far as possible to extinguish these rights and to make the Rhine the boundary of France.

The possession of Luxemburg, Lorraine, and Alsace was therefore absolutely necessary for the fulfilment of Louis' ambitious schemes. Already during the negotiations at Nimeguen significant indications had not been wanting of coming aggressions. The French envoys had endeavoured without success to secure Lorraine, and, in anticipation of the settlement of 1735, to compensate the Duke with territory in Sicily or elsewhere. Attempts were also made to obtain Luxemburg, the possession of which would have doubled the value of Thionville and Longwy. The great aim, however, of French diplomacy was to gain full sovereignty over Alsace. With Alsace in French hands, Franche-Comté, Champagne, and part of the three Bishoprics would be safe from attack, and Lorraine could never be retaken. Consequently during the negotiations at Nimeguen the French absolutely refused to consent to any limitations of their rights over Alsace. No sooner was peace made and Europe had disarmed than Louis began to put into force his great scheme of *Réunions* by which he was enabled to annex to France in time of peace more territory than she had ever gained by war. According to the French theory he simply asserted rights which had since the treaty of Westphalia lain dormant.

The French pretensions were founded on their interpretation of clauses in the treaty of Westphalia. By that treaty certain places with their dependencies or districts were ceded to France. The sovereignty of Upper and Lower Alsace had been given to Louis saving the rights of the " immediate " nobles, while ten towns in Alsace which were termed immediate towns or Imperial cities also asserted their claim to independence. These indefinite rights and this qualified sovereignty Louis desired to abolish. He determined to sweep away by a *coup de main* these cobwebs of old claims and this shadowy independence, to bring within the boundaries of France the disputed territories, and above all to secure Strasburg, the key of the way across the Rhine into Alsace. Strasburg had, indeed, hoped to continue the neutrality which she had enjoyed during the late war. But weak, defenceless, surrounded by enemies and far from all help, it was obvious that this detached fragment of the Empire could not continue much longer to preserve her neutrality between France and Germany. She was bound to become either entirely French or German, and it seemed certain that she would fall a victim to the French schemes. In carrying out his designs Louis was aided by the fact that England was occupied with her own internal dissension. The quarrel between Charles II. and his Parliament had become very bitter, and while it lasted " external considerations fell into the background." Louis' army, too, alone of European armies, was kept on a war footing, and added weight to his pretensions. Moreover the Bishops of Metz,

Toul, and Verdun were his creatures and played into his hands. On being summoned to render homage to Louis, they asked for the institution of a tribunal to adjudicate upon usurpations which had taken place during the course of time. So many of their possessions, they declared, had been gradually taken from them, and so many of their rights had lapsed, that without a tribunal it was impossible for them to give a proper account of their lands and jurisdictions.

A committee of the *Parlement* of Metz were thereupon empowered to make the necessary enquiries, and this committee became the first " Chamber of Reunion." Before this committee the three Bishops laid a long list of those who had seized any part of their lands, and of those who owed and had not performed their feudal duties. The new chamber dealt with both these classes in a very summary fashion. The former were at once to justify their possession of any portion that had formerly belonged to the Bishoprics ; the latter were to recognise no other sovereign than Louis XIV. and no tribunal other than the *Parlement* of Metz.

The chamber, which was appointed in October, 1679, and began its work on December 11th, took it for granted that all the rights of the Empire within the limits of the three Bishoprics had passed to Louis, and that he was the suzerain of all the so-called vassals of the Bishops. In other words, " Louis, one of the parties, made himself judge in his own cause and by one-sided verdicts had everything which he desired granted him." Other

Chambers of Reunion were erected at Besançon,
Breisach, and Tournay. While the Metz chamber
examined into questions connected with the three
Bishoprics, that of Besançon acted for Franche-
Comté, Breisach for Alsace, and Tournay for Flanders. By their decisions a large number of towns
and a considerable extent of territory was handed
over to Louis who, if the owners refused to recognise
his sovereignty, promptly seized and occupied their
city or district. By this method France obtained,
among other acquisitions, Saarbruck, Saarwerden,
Falkenberg, and Gemersheim, belonging to the
Elector of Trèves; Wildentz, belonging to the
Elector Palatine; Deux-Ponts, belonging to the King
of Sweden; Lauterbourg, belonging to the Bishop
of Spires; Montbeliard, belonging to the Duke of
Würtemberg. The Breisach chamber especially distinguished itself by two decrees, one on March 22d,
the other on August 9, 1680, which declared the
absolute and exclusive sovereignty of Louis in Upper
and Lower Alsace; and in consequence all the immediate nobles (that is those who held directly from
the Emperor), and towns, princes, officers, and
estates of Alsace became vassals of the King of
France. The French arms were in 1681 put up all
over Alsace, and the nobles, unable to resist, sent to
Paris a deputation which gave in their submission to
Louis. The same high-handed policy was carried on
throughout the "reunited" districts. Oberstein,
which for five hundred years had belonged to the
Archbishops of Trèves, was occupied by French
troops; Homburg and Bitche suffered the same fate.

The Castle of Falkenburg, in the Palatinate, resisted, but was soon forced to surrender by the French artillery. There were however still three places the possession of which was deemed essential for the rounding off of French territory. These were Casale, Strasburg, and Luxemburg. By means of diplomacy, legal fiction, and the exercise of force, Louis managed to secure all three by the autumn of 1684, and Europe awoke to find that, during six years of nominal peace, the French power had made greater advance than during any previous war.

The two decrees of the Breisach court respecting Louis' sovereignty in Alsace extended of course by implication to Strasburg, which, if these decrees had any force, was now included in the French monarchy. Precedents were not wanting to encourage Louis in his design on the liberties of Strasburg. By the treaty of Westphalia Bremen had been ceded to Sweden in terms as vague as those which regulated the cessions to France. In 1666, in spite of a promise made by the Swedes in 1654 that her customs and government should be maintained, Bremen had been forced by Wrangel to bow her neck to the Swedish yoke. Again in 1671 Rudolf Augustus, Duke of Wolfenbüttel, had possessed himself forcibly of Brunswick, an Imperial town, and had introduced a garrison of three thousand men.

Strasburg was herself in an unenviable position. During the early part of 1679 Imperial troops had remained within her walls, and she had been the recipient of Imperial orders couched in very harsh terms. She certainly had no reason to desire that

her connection with and dependence on the Emperor should become closer.

On the other hand, the ever-increasing numbers
of French troops in Alsace filled her citizens with
disquiet and inclined them to retain the Imperial
troops. Their suspicions were far from being ground-
less. As early as January, 1679, Louvois himself
visited Alsace in order to make himself master of
the real position of affairs there. The three leading citizens of Strasburg—Zedlitz, Dietrich, and
Güntzer—paid him a formal visit at Schlestadt. It
has been asserted that at this time Louvois opened
secret negotiations with some of the leading Strasburg magistrates. Though no doubt bribery played
some part in the fall of Strasburg, no actual proof
exists to show that Louvois' visit to Alsace had any
other object than that of studying the best means
for effecting the capture of the principal city of the
province.

The first direct step towards this end was to insist
on the retirement of the Imperial troops. The firm
attitude of the French, who had occupied the Strasburg territory, resulted in a special treaty signed by
Leopold, regulating the execution of the articles of
the peace of Nimeguen, and placing Strasburg more
than ever at the mercy of the French. Strasburg
was to be evacuated by Imperial troops by August
10th, but no clause prevented the entry of French
armies into Alsace.

The departure of the Imperial troops so far from
rendering the relations between the French Court
and Strasburg more friendly was the signal for fresh

ARGENTINA.

Straßburg.

1. Der Rhein brück.
2. S. Claus v. Unda.
3. S. Wilhelm.
4. S. Stefan.
5. S. Catherin.
6. S. Clara.
7. Ecks Kawern.
8. S. Andreas.
9. Münster.
10. Brüning thurn.
11. Kauffhaus.
12. Prediger Closter.
13. Jung S. Peter.
14. Carthauß Closter.
15. Spital.
16. Aller Heiligen.
17. Frawen broder.
18. Alt Waan.
19. Alt S. Peter.
20. Jung S. Peter.
21. Holand.
22. Steinstraßer thor.
23. S. Nicola.
24. Ny S. Peter.
25. Hospthau Closter.
26. In Braich.
27. S. Margretha.
28. S. Elsbeth.
29. Deutsch Hauß.
30. Spital thor.
31. Cronenburger thor.
32. Rohen Hartmack.
33. Fischer thor.
34. S. Urban.
35. Spital Mühl.

STRASBURG.

(From an old print, and reproduced in Erdmannsdörfer's *Deutsche Geschichte von 1648–1740.*)

misunderstandings. The commercial regulations of
the Senate—the mere flickerings of a spirit of independence—irritated the French. Then the Stras-
burgers had burnt the Château of Schäffolsheim
belonging to the Baron of Wangen, one of the most
active of French partisans during the late war. It
was only by payment of a large indemnity that the
Senate could satisfy Louvois. The third difficulty
which arose was more serious. In 1672, the bridge
between Strasburg and Kehl which had been built
in 1388 and which was the last link between the city
and the Empire had been destroyed by Condé,
and in 1679 Louvois wrote forbidding as contrary to
the treaty of Münster the re-establishment of any
fortification between Bâle and Phillipsburg. This
question became so acute that the Senate determined to send a deputation to Versailles to explain
the true state of the case by word of mouth. From
Louvois the members of the deputation received
rude treatment; Louis, on the contrary, presented
them with gold chains. It was evident that any
serious attempt to rebuild the bridge or any portion
of the old fortifications would be at once crushed by
the troops which during 1679 were busy enforcing
the French domination throughout Alsace and at
the same time rapidly isolating Strasburg. Early
in July, Hagenau, and later in the month, Wissem-
burg and Landau, two important strategic ports,
were occupied by the French. Schlestadt, Turk-
heim, Kaisersburg, Münster, and Colmar all took an
oath of fidelity and obedience to Louis XIV. and
his representative Montelar. About the same time

(September, 1679,) the Marshal d'Humières was occupying the two Lorraine fortresses of Homburg
and Bitche.

In the beginning of 1680 a threat to fill all the
villages round Strasburg with French troops forced
from the Senate a distinct engagement to suppress
the works then in progress at the fort of Kehl.
Strasburg being now from a military point of view
practically isolated, the time was come for a definite
assertion of the sovereignty of Louis over the whole
of Alsace.

On March 22, 1680, the *Parlement* of Breisach
proclaimed the absolute sovereignty of Louis in
Lower as well as in Upper Alsace. In consequence
of this decree Strasburg was virtually united to the
French monarchy. On August 9th the Superior
Council of Breisach confirmed the doctrines enunciated on March 22d. Louis' pretensions to Alsace
thus received the support of legal authority, and it
was evident that the King would not be content with a
mere form of words, but would take the first opportunity of enforcing a claim which had been recognised as valid. In May the Senate, with the knowledge that their doom was upon them, sent a second
deputation to Paris to make useless complaints of
the exactions of French officers in their villages.

The action of the French in Alsace reassured
them. The March edict of the Breisach chamber
was put into execution with severity. Falkenburg
in the Palatinate was taken by assault; Strasburg
itself was warned that the reception of an Imperial
garrison would be considered as a *casus belli*. In the

autumn the villages round Strasburg were formally occupied and the arms of France were substituted for those of the Emperor on all public buildings. In each village were posted two dragoons and all arms were seized.

Thus the French with consummate skill had indeed not only secured the retirement of the Imperial forces from Strasburg, but had taken full possession of Alsace. Strasburg remained the last home of Alsatian independence, but isolated as she was and surrounded by foes, it seemed as if little less than a miracle could save her from sharing the fate of the rest of the province. The inhabitants of Strasburg were helpless to avert from themselves their impending doom. Warnings of the designs of the French government against their city reached them from Paris in the autumn of 1680, and the appearance of a comet increased and seemed to justify the fears of the superstitious. The vague answers of the French agent, General Montelar, to the pressing interrogations of the leading citizens as to the designs of Louis XIV., left no room for doubt in the minds of thoughtful men that before a year had run its course Strasburg would have fallen from its position as a free Imperial city.

The chances of help from without grew more and more remote as the months passed. The Court of Vienna, though appealed to by the government of Strasburg, confined its efforts in favour of the city to diplomacy. One diplomatist was sent to sound the Elector of Brandenburg; another, Count Mansfeld, was sent to Paris to combat the views of the French government with regard to the question of the *Réunions*. His interviews with Colbert de Croissy were of a most unsatisfactory nature, and the ambiguous answers he received convinced him that the only method of checking the progress of the French in Alsace was by proposing a conference and thus postponing if possible the outbreak of open hostilities, till the Imperial army was ready to take the field.

The fate of Strasburg depended on the immediate action of the Emperor Leopold. Frederick William of Brandenburg could not be relied on for assistance. His policy was one of opportunism tempered by occasional paroxysms in favour of Protestantism. He hated the Court of Vienna, for Leopold had not only refused to aid him during the late war in securing Pomerania, but had also turned a deaf ear to his demands for Jägerndorf, East Friesland, and the three Silesian Duchies of Liegnitz, Brieg, and Wohlau. Immediately after making the treaty of Saint-Germain-en-Laye he had become the ally and pensioner of France, and in consideration of an annual payment of 100,000 livres for ten years had agreed to support by his vote and interest the candidature of Louis XIV. or that of the Dauphin to the Imperial throne or to the position of King of the Romans whenever occasion required. That the Elector knew of the coming fate of Strasburg as early as the beginning of 1680 there is no room for doubt.[1]

---

[1] On this, and other matters connected with the fall of Strasburg M. Legrelle's work on *Louis XIV. et Strasbourg* can be consulted.

The jealousy between Brandenburg and Vienna, while peculiarly advantageous to the policy of France, was disastrous to the fortune of Strasburg. But Frederick William had no high ideas of his duty to Germany. The Archbishopric of Magdeburg, assigned to Brandenburg by the treaty of Westphalia on the death of the administrator, fell to Frederick William in 1680, and the Elector was far more occupied in entering into possession of his newly acquired territory than in raising any sentimental or other objections to Louis' acquisition of Strasburg. In May, 1681, Louis sent to Hamburg three vessels from Rouen laden with gifts for the Elector and Electress and their family : two carriages, suits of clothes, sweetmeats, and books. The carriages and clothes were to be used on the entry of the Elector and his wife into Magdeburg and Halle ; the sweetmeats were for distribution among the people. Like another well-known ruler, Frederick William, secure in his alliance with the Great King, busied himself with his own affairs, while the Empire was losing one of its fairest gems. Though Frederick William failed to appreciate the magnitude of the issues at stake, the feeling in Germany was rising in strong opposition to the annexation policy of the French government. The Electors of Saxony and Palatinate together with a crowd of smaller princes took up a national attitude and clamoured for a general arming as early as August, 1680. A coalition, to include the Empire, England, Holland, and Spain, was anxiously desired and at one time seemed likely to be formed. The Emperor pressed the Diet to arm for

the defence of the Empire, levies were raised, and
by May, 1681, 140,000 men had been collected by
the order of the Diet. William of Orange had an
interview with the leading princes of the House of
Brunswick, and on September 30, 1681, a convention
between Holland and Sweden to maintain the settle-
ments of Westphalia and Nimeguen proved the
germ of the League of Augsburg. War was on the
verge of breaking out, and had it done so Louis'
schemes would have been very considerably interfered with. That it did not break out was due
partly to his own wisdom in consenting to Mansfeld's suggested conference, partly to certain events
which for a time prevented the Courts of Vienna
and St. James from taking active steps in opposition
to his aggressive policy. England was the hereditary foe of France, and her rival on the sea; her
Protestant religion rendered her peculiarly antago-
nistic to Louis XIV. And his *Réunion* policy had
been viewed with dismay by English statesmen.
Charles II. strongly disapproved of his encroachments, and the words of Sunderland to Barillon the
French ambassador in England go far to show that
had King and Parliament been united, the European
league of 1686 might have been formed in 1680.
But the political and religious animosities of English parties checked these statesmanlike projects and
postponed their realisation some eight years.

The Exclusion question turned men's attention
from the crisis on the continent. Shaftesbury, the
defender of Protestantism in England, cared nothing for its fate in Europe, and the policy of his party

drove Charles II. into the arms of Louis XIV. As usual, the necessities of the later Stuarts proved the opportunities of the French monarch. The dissolution of the Parliament of Oxford on March 28, 1681, was immediately followed by an agreement between Charles and Louis in accordance with which the English king was to receive 500,000 livres during the ensuing three years, so as to carry on the government without having recourse to Parliament, and he on his part undertook to withdraw gradually from his alliance with Spain and not to allow Parliament to lead him into hostility with France. Louis had succeeded. No interference by the English nation in opposition to his policy was to be anticipated, for in spite of a visit to England, undertaken for the purpose, William of Orange had failed to reconcile Charles II. and the Parliament. Louis was now free to accomplish one of the great schemes of his life. He not only advanced claims to the county of Chiny, which embraced almost all Luxemburg, and marched his troops into the county, but he definitely prepared for the immediate seizure of Strasburg itself. Frederick William and Charles II. being his pensioners, the only other serious obstacle to the realisation of his designs was the Emperor. Leopold was in a difficult position. He had attempted to get Strasburg chosen as the seat of the conference, hoping that the fact of the city being the meeting-place of a European congress would give it a sort of inviolability. The French minister saw through this device and eventually Frankfort-on-the-Main was selected.

14

Leopold's only hope of any successful opposition to Louis lay in gaining time. His hands were fully occupied in Hungary. The *réunions* had forced from him concessions which he had hoped would conciliate the Hungarians, leave him free to deal with the French encroachments, and able to concentrate on the Rhine all his available forces. Unfortunately Tœkeli and his party refused to accept the concessions and drew still closer to the Turks. Louis was fully alive to the necessity of rapidity in his movements. In a despatch to Sebeville, his ambassador at Vienna, he says : " No sooner has the Emperor freed himself from his embarrassments which keep his principal forces on the Hungarian frontier than he will direct his steps to the Rhine." The French saw clearly through Leopold's design of gaining time, and when the Imperial envoys entered Frankfort on October 30th, Strasburg had been for a month in French hands.

The course of events had favoured Louis' schemes. England's desertion of the European cause, coupled with the inability of the Emperor, owing to the dangers on his eastern frontier, to take an active part in counteracting Louis' designs on Strasburg and Alsace, removed for the time all chance of any external aid being given to the citizens of Strasburg. The only chance of the preservation of the republican liberties of Strasburg lay in help from without, for within the city division and discord reigned, and rendered any successful defence against French armies impossible. Unlike Metz in the late Franco-Prussian war Strasburg was absolutely incapable of standing a siege. Isolated, for the Ten Towns were now definitely in French hands, she could not rely on her Town Council any more than on her Bishop and Chapter for effective measures of resistance. The circle of iron within which she now found herself was narrowing each day, and all the efforts of her patriotic citizens were of no avail. The Alsatian nobles had either been coerced or cajoled ; Francis Egon of Fürstenberg, the Bishop, was a mere creature of the French King. At the congress of Nimeguen by a declaration of the rights of his office he had brought down upon him all the fury of Leopold. On his flight from Germany Louis had diplomatically accorded to Fürstenberg a hospitable welcome at the Louvre, French officers in Alsace were forbidden to shoot any game on the episcopal lands, and all possible measures were taken to gain the full support of the powerful and cunning prelate. In May, 1680, Fürstenberg like Charles II. and Frederick William became one of Louis' pensioners, receiving a payment of 60,000 livres. In the following autumn with a suite of fifty horsemen he proceeded to Paris, where he took a leading part in the fêtes organised during the Carnival in the early spring of 1681. Louis' policy was successful ; the Bishop became an active partisan for the French cause ; the higher clergy in Strasburg declared themselves in favour of the sovereignty of France. This adherence of the Bishop and Chapter to the French side was recognised by the increase of the Bishop's pension on August 1, 1681, to 80,000 livres for four years.

But though the Bishop, the Chapter, and the Town

Council, influenced partly no doubt by bribes and promises, supported the French pretensions, the mass of the citizens, who were mainly strict Lutherans, were opposed to the abolition of the republican form of government. They desired the continuance of their local autonomy, they had no wish to snap the link which connected them with the Holy Roman Empire. They were proud of the unique position held by their city in Europe and had no reason to desire annexation to France. In their eyes their connection with the Empire was their only hope of security. Strasburg fell, but it did not fall through the corruption of its citizens. Its fall was brought about by superior force, by the sudden appearance of the powerful armies of France.

In May, 1681, the announcement of the arrival of the famous General Mercy at Strasburg startled Louvois. Already in March consultations had taken place in Paris as to the course to be adopted, should the Imperial forces march toward the Rhine. The arrival of Mercy at Strasburg seemed to imply that fresh projects against the French were in contemplation. Louvois was not the man to wait. Full instructions were sent to the generals and measures were at once taken to cut off all hope of relief being sent to the doomed city. Troops were posted at Altkirch, and on the borders of Flanders to check any hostile movement of the Swiss or the Spaniards. On the night of the 27th-28th September, d'Asfeld with three regiments of French dragoons seized the old dismantled bridge. The whole city was roused, alarm bells were rung, and fires made on the ramparts, which were manned by the affrighted citizens.

In the morning the French force was largely augmented, and though negotiations were opened by the citizens it was obvious that resistance was impossible. The defence of the city had been left since 1679—when from motives of economy they had dismissed their two Swiss companies—to a force of five hundred men, of whom at this moment one half were rendered useless by sickness. A large proportion too of the citizens capable of bearing arms were absent at the Frankfort Fair. The moat was also dry, and there was a deficiency of powder. To such a helpless condition was Strasburg reduced through the short-sighted economy, incapacity, and perhaps corruption of its leading men. The citizens, perceiving that they were unable to resist a power " so great and so terrible as that of His most Christian Majesty," sent a deputation to meet Louvois on Monday September 29th at Illkirch, and on the following day, September 30th, the French troops took possession of Strasburg, Louvois having agreed with some qualifications to the terms proposed by the city authorities.

Louis heard of the capitulation on October 2d at Vitry on his way to Strasburg to be present at its capture. He had left Fontainebleau on Saturday September 27th after making a public declaration of the object of his journey and his destination. Louvois' efforts to make the entry of the King as magnificent and imposing as possible were crowned with success. Amid the salvos of 265 cannons, the blow-ing of trumpets, and the ringing of bells, a carriage drawn by eight grey horses and containing Louis and his Queen, the Dauphin and his wife the Dauphiness, as well as the Duke and Duchess of Orleans, entered Strasburg in the afternoon of the 23d of October.

On arriving at their quarters, the King at once mounted a horse and attended by the Dauphin and other members of his suite rode off to inspect the bridge, about which so much had been heard at Saint-Germain. The day ended with a general illumination of the city. The next morning Louis attended a grand Mass in the cathedral when a magnificent Te Deum was sung. On entering the cathedral he was met by the Prince-Bishop Francis of Fürstenberg, supported by mitred abbots, the canons, and many of the clergy. Fürstenberg having delivered an address, in which he recalled the part taken by the early Frankish kings in the construction of the cathedral, the King and Queen proceeded to their seats in the choir. In Strasburg Louis remained four days, giving audiences to the leading men. As was his custom, he took the greatest interest in seeing everything, and in drawing up the minutest instructions with reference to the future government of his new acquisition. He crossed the Rhine and saw Kehl; he made a close examination of the defences of Strasburg and of the environs. On the 26th he held a review of his troops, and the next day the Court left Strasburg and went homewards by Saverne.

CHAPTER VIII.

THE TRUCE OF RATISBON.

1684.

HE news of the fall of Strasburg sent a shock through
Germany. Casale had fallen
the same day into the hands
of a French force under Boufflers and Catinat. Luxem-
burg was expected to follow
suit. The wildest rumours
found credence, and at Frankfort it was asserted that
Worms and Philipsburg had capitulated to the
French. There was nothing in the attitude of the
princes of Germany, lay or ecclesiastical, to cause
alarm to the French. Brandenburg was in Louis'
pay; the young Elector of Bavaria was occupied with
marriage projects; Hanover was bribed by the prospect of an electorate for himself; the Count Palatine

by the convention of Areillen (February, 1682) was
promised a pension of 200,000 livres a year in addition to a sum down of 600,000 livres; the three
ecclesiastical Electors were as usual devoted to
French interests. For a time indeed John George
III. of Saxony showed warlike tendencies. In April,
1681, he had made a treaty with Brandenburg and
the two Electors had agreed to unite forces in case of
necessity. The influence of Frederick William's
agent Meinders, who was sent to Dresden, succeeded
in calming John George. It was pointed out to him
that if he fought against Louis XIV. he must necessarily be beaten, and that the only result of a successful war on the part of the French would be to
transfer the Imperial crown to the House of Bourbon.

Though Louis could not rely on the support of
either Bavaria or Saxony he had by diplomacy secured a majority in the Electoral College. The
Bishop of Münster, too, had definitely made an alliance with Louis on December 28, 1680, and thus in
the north of Europe the French King could count
upon powerful supporters, though he had failed to
gain over Hesse Cassel and other north German
princes.

The Emperor Leopold seemed helpless. The
appearance of the Turks in Styria, and the continued discontent in Hungary rendered for the time
being any movement towards the Rhine out of the
question.

But each year the Emperor's position in Germany
was in reality becoming stronger. In many of the

small German Courts the aggressions of Louis had caused a deep feeling of uneasiness. For the moment, however, Germany seemed powerless to arrest any further invasion of her rights or territory. Men were rather dazed and stupefied than actually furious when they heard of the seizure of Strasburg. It was Louis' interest to allay this feeling, to calm all irritation, to pose as a monarch desirous of peace. He therefore not only attempted by strenuous diplomatic efforts to gain over individuals, but he definitely offered to the Empire an equivalent for the territory which it had lost since the treaty of Nimeguen. He proposed to yield Freiburg in Brisgau, a strong place and an ancient Imperial town, which had been in French hands since 1678. Had this offer been accepted, the arrangements made in 1713 would have been in part antedated by some thirty-four years.

But Louis' efforts for a general pacification were destined to fail. The *Réunions* had touched too many interests: the capture of Strasburg was too flagrant a piece of audacity to be allowed to pass unnoticed. Moreover, as though to see to what extent he could go, Louis in November, 1681, began the siege of Luxemburg.

The Chambers of *Réunion* had awarded to France, as belonging to the Bishopric of Verdun, Vireton and the county of Chiny which stretched up to the fortifications of Luxemburg. Louis also claimed Alost, with the intention of exchanging it for Luxemburg, the possession of which was, the French declared, indispensable for the safety of Thionville and Longwy.

Both England and Holland were by this new aggression attacked in a vital point. The capture of
Luxemburg would make the French from a military
point of view masters of both the Netherlands.
Charles II. of England proposed that the fortress of
Luxemburg should be razed, and in order to give
time for him to negotiate with the Spaniards Louis
agreed not to blockade it strictly for four months.
In Holland there was as usual a difference of opinion. The peace-at-any-price party advocated the
cession of the fortress to the French on condition
that it was dismantled or razed. William of Orange
and his followers, however, desired a close union with
Spain and England, and a firm opposition to Louis'
schemes. The States-General in accordance with his
views agreed to raise a force which should advance
to the relief of Luxemburg, whenever such a course
was necessary.

A European war appeared to be on the verge of
breaking out, and this would have interfered with
all Louis' arrangements. His constant aim was to
prevent any interference on the part of England in
opposition to his policy. It seemed likely that
Charles II. might be compelled to summon Parliament, which would insist on the weight of English
influence being thrown into the scale against Louis.
It was all-important therefore to keep Charles II.
true to his understanding with Louis. This could
only be done, in the opinion of the French King, if
James Duke of York was in England. In James
Louis had full confidence ; Charles II. he was convinced, could not be trusted. He therefore made it

a matter of great personal interest to secure the return of James. On the understanding that Louis should yield in the matter of Luxemburg, James was allowed to appear in England. By this means Louis had, as he hoped, removed all danger of the summoning of the English Parliament.

These were the true motives of his unexpected declaration early in 1682, that the siege of Luxemburg was raised. But these motives did not appear. "Louis XIV. possessed," to quote from von Ranke, "acuteness of observation, decision, and a grand manner." He loved to pose as a magnanimous monarch, he always studied effect. The Turks were threatening Germany. Louis therefore declared that, being anxious not to impede the efforts of the German princes in defence of their country, he was resolved, in order to bring to a conclusion the matters at issue in the Low Countries, to confide the decision of his claims to the arbitration of the King of England. This proposal, to allow the great European question of the day, viz. the fate of the Netherlands, to be settled by the decision of Charles II., was not likely to commend itself either to Spain or to the States-General. Orange's statesmanlike counter proposal in December, 1682, was to the effect that Charles II. should call a congress of ambassadors to London, and that before them should be laid not only the question of the Spanish Netherlands, but also the German matters. The opponents of Louis XIV. hoped to prevent the Empire from being compelled to cede Strasburg; they also wished to save Luxemburg.

But, as usual, circumstances aided Louis and afforded him an opportunity of carrying out his designs. On the very day on which Strasburg fell, Charles XI. of Sweden, furious at the loss of the Duchy of Deux-Ponts and determined to be no longer dependent on France, had signed a treaty with the States-General. In the spring of 1682 Leopold and Spain had joined this coalition, and in June Saxony, Bavaria, Hesse-Cassel, Lüneburg, and the leading members of the circles of the Upper Rhine and Franconia had given in their adhesion to it. We see here the beginnings of the famous league of Augsburg, which a few years later was to unite Europe against France. The reply of Louis to this coalition of his enemies was unhesitating. An envoy was sent to support Toekeli in his resistance to the Hapsburgs, attempts were made to stir up opposition in Sweden and Poland and Holland to the foreign policy of their rulers, (and in the case of the latter country with considerable success,) a treaty was signed with Denmark, which power with Brandenburg, Münster, and Cologne formed a powerful northern league devoted to French interests. It was even proposed to send an agent to rouse Russia. In the south the Swiss had been pacified, Venice had shown no objection to the occupation of Strasburg, and a treaty had been signed with the Duke of Savoy which in 1684 was to be ratified by his marriage with the second daughter of Monsieur. Louis consequently in the early portion of 1682 was far from being isolated; he was ready for a new war if his enemies desired it. But his aim was if possible to

secure his new possessions without further recourse
to arms.   He wished for a peaceful settlement of his
claims, he hoped that they might be definitely recognised and acquiesced in by Europe.   Since the
autumn of 1681 the conference of Frankfort had
been sitting.   But little progress was made toward
any conclusion.   The Hapsburg interests were served
best by delays.   Leopold looked for a speedy termination of the troubles in Hungary, when he could
at the head of a large armed force speak with authority on the Rhine.   Both Brandenburg and Denmark through their envoys attempted to induce the
Austrians to come to some arrangement at Frankfort such as Louis desired.   At length weary of
delays Louis ordered his envoys to leave Frankfort
on December 1, 1682, the conference having sat
for fifteen months and done literally nothing.

One more attempt Louis made at securing a peaceful recognition of his claims.   He authorised Verjus
his envoy at the Diet at Ratisbon to negotiate on the
same basis as had been laid down at Frankfort, up
to February, 1683, but in consequence of the Turkish
invasion of Austria the time was extended to August 31st.   Louis demanded a thirty years' truce
during which period he was to be left in undisturbed
possession of his recent acquisitions.   To the Emperor no less than to such men as William of Orange,
agreement with such terms was regarded as equivalent to a surrender of all the places and territories
in question.

At first the attitude of the Austrians was unac-
commodating.   A large number of troops had just

been assembled in Hungary, and Leopold hoped to achieve a decisive victory in the East which would affect the solution of the problems in the West. But in the summer his tone changed and the Diet, moved partly by the greater moderation of Louis' tone and partly by the Turkish designs, were more disposed to come to some arrangement. On August 31st, it was decided to accept the offered truce. The Turks were in full march on Vienna and all Europe waited anxiously for the result of this bold action on the part of the Porte. The questions at issue in the West were for the moment put on one side. The siege of Vienna absorbed the attention of all Christendom.

Louis has been frequently accused of alliance with the Turks, or at any rate of sympathising with their aggressive attitude in the East and especially with their attacks on the Hapsburg possessions. There is no doubt that the success of Louis' policy in the West was greatly facilitated by the difficult position in which the Hapsburgs found themselves owing to the disaffection in Hungary and the aggressions of the Turks. Since the times of Francis I. the French had deftly made use of their friendship with the Porte to harass the Hapsburgs on their eastern frontier. With Poland too a connection began in the same century, and a few years later France and Sweden fought in close alliance in the Thirty Years' War. Thus was built up that system of alliances with Sweden, Poland, and Turkey, which was supposed to unite these three powers in close union with France.

But this elaborate system with its centres at Stockholm, Warsaw, and Constantinople only existed in the minds of theorists. To bring three nations like Sweden, Poland, and Turkey different in so many respects into line at a given time against an astute power like that of the Hapsburgs was impossible. With Sweden France had during the first half of the century much in common, and Sweden had as late as the Dutch war of 1672 benefited largely from the French alliance. But the effect of the seizure of the Duchy of Deux-Ponts had converted Sweden into an open enemy, and one link in the chain stretching from Stockholm to Constantinople was broken.

Poland the centre of the chain proved to be the weakest part of the system and most difficult to manage. Opposed as a rule to Sweden either on territorial questions such as those relating to Livonia, Esthonia, and Courland, or on questions of succession, and equally opposed to Turkey on every possible ground, Poland was always an insoluble difficulty to French diplomatists. Between 1678 and 1683 Louis had tried hard to gain over John Sobieski. His efforts were in vain. The Polish King largely contributed to the salvation of the Austrian House at the siege of Vienna and in the following year made a definite alliance with Leopold.

Turkey was probably the most valuable of the three powers as a counterpoise against Austria. But with the beginning of the personal government of Louis XIV., a reaction had taken place against the policy, pursued by Francis I. and Henry II., of a

definite alliance with the Turks. Unlike these two
monarchs, Louis was permeated with strong religious
ideas. That he a great Christian King should form
a close connexion with an Infidel power was repugnant to his most cherished convictions. The very
notion of an alliance ran counter to the whole tendency of his policy : it could not be seriously entertained by the Head of Christendom. On the
other hand there was the influence of tradition.
The Ottoman alliance had powerfully contributed to
save France from the grasp of Charles V., it had certainly aided Protestantism in Germany, and from a
French point of view it had rescued the North German allies of Francis I. and Henry II. from subservience to Vienna. Friendship between the French
and the Turks might again be used to enable France
to strengthen her position at the expense of the
Empire.

Louis therefore was torn by two conflicting ideas.
The prospect of making an Ottoman alliance and of
using it for the furtherance of his own schemes appealed strongly to him as a politician. On the
other hand, to carry on a crusade against the
Turks, to advance the movement towards Christian solidarity, to attack the Ottomans by sea and
by land, was a course which commended itself to
Louis' religious and dramatic instincts. It was
under the influence of the crusading idea, that
the French took a leading part in the battle of
St. Gothard in 1664 and aided the Venetians in
Candia in 1668. It was this idea that led Louis
to entertain the project of taking Egypt, and

which caused him to attack the Barbary states, and to threaten even to burn Constantinople. But it could not be denied that France benefited greatly from the conflict between the Porte and the Hapsburgs. Though Louis did not support the Turks by a definite alliance, he derived great advantage indirectly from their invasions of the Austrian territory. While the march of French troops to aid the Hapsburgs in 1664 contributed to give lustre to the beginning of Louis' reign, the siege of Vienna in 1683 and the long war which followed, occupied the Austrians and enabled Louis to gain his ends at the treaty of Ratisbon. Louis did not actively support the Turks, and as a result they were overthrown at Vienna in 1683, at Mohacz in 1687, at Salankemen in 1691, at Zenta in 1697. They were furious at the conduct of France and refused to be included in the treaty of Ryswick. An alliance between the French and Turks was impossible in 1683. The French fleet was carrying on a struggle of considerable importance in the Mediterranean against the Barbary states, and this alone would have prevented any union between Louis and the Sultan. Colbert de Croissy declared that the French hoped that the siege of Vienna would last a long time, and finally would fail through want of discipline on the part of the Turks, and the ravages of disease. The French government, too, expected that the impression produced in the Empire by the siege would enable them to carry out their designs in Germany. In the event of the fall of Vienna, the Venetian ambassador asserts that Louis' intention was to march to the relief of that city, and having

joined forces with the Germans to drive back the
Turks.   He would thus have posed as the saviour
of Christendom, and on the death of Leopold
would have received the Imperial crown.

But events turned out otherwise. The Turks were
driven back, but the man who was hailed by Europe
as the deliverer of Christendom was not Louis XIV.,
but John Sobieski.   Louis had missed a great opportunity of taking part in one of the most important events of his day, the struggle between
the East and the West, between Christendom and
Mohammedanism.

During the period of the Turkish invasion the
siege of Luxemburg had been suspended. No
sooner was Vienna delivered than the Spaniards,
overjoyed at the event, regained confidence and
thought they could resist France. They relied on
receiving help from Germany and expected that the
armies which saved Vienna would also deliver Luxemburg. "With extraordinary and ill-timed temerity they nerved themselves so far as to make a
declaration of war against France." On October
26th, Charles II., then in his 23d year, drew his
sword and declared that he would never sheath it
till he had been avenged of all the injustices which
he had suffered from the King of France.

Louis replied with elaborate preparations and in
April, 1684, Créqui and Vauban besieged Luxemburg. It seemed likely that a general European
war would break out, and with the Turkish war still
on his hands, the Emperor would have found it very
difficult to resist the arms or the pretensions of

VAUBAN.
(From an illustration in Philippson's *Das Zeitalter Ludwigs XIV.*)

France. Louis had formed the plan of marching through the Cologne territory against Holland and Hanover. Fortunately for Europe this project was not carried out and the war narrowed down to a campaign against the Spanish power in the Netherlands and in Italy. Brandenburg, Louis' ally, was strongly opposed to a French attack on Hanover and was as strongly in favour of a general pacification. Holland, owing to the opposition of Amsterdam, was unable to aid the Spaniards, and Germany, still the prey to internal divisions, was not in a position to combat the French and Turks at the same time. The Spaniards, without money or even an army worthy of the name, could make no resistance when hostilities broke out on the frontiers and the French seized Courtrai and Dixmude. The Spanish Court fired with warlike enthusiasm at once arranged to send troops and money to the Low Countries. In order to show that reconciliation with or concessions to the Court of France was impossible, a solemn declaration of war against France was made in December. Courtrai and Dixmude had by that time fallen, Oudenarde was bombarded, while Luxemburg itself was captured on June 4, 1684, and Genoa almost destroyed by Duquesne was compelled to agree to humiliating conditions. The Marshal Schomberg advanced into Alsace with 20,000 cavalry, and Charles II. of England congratulated Louis on the fall of Luxemburg. That successful resistance to the French army was impossible was recognised by the Electors and Princes of the Empire no less than by the Dutch. The latter on

June 27th accepted a twenty years' truce and withdrew their troops from the Spanish Netherlands;
the former, conciliated by Louis' declaration that
he intended to adhere to the terms laid down the
previous summer, succeeded in impressing on Leopold the necessity of making an arrangement with
Louis.

The Spaniards, through the unreadiness of Europe
to oppose actively the French arms, were compelled
to agree to Louis' terms. On June 29th, by a pro-
visional arrangement, they yielded Bouvines, so celebrated in French history, Chesnay and Beaumont,
important possessions of Hainault, and Luxemburg
itself. Some thirty villages, half in Luxemburg and
half in Hainault, together with the Spanish protec-
torate over Genoa, completed the cessions resulting
from the unfortunate "War of Luxemburg." On
August 15th, the Empire and Emperor recognised
the existing state of things by the truce of Ratisbon,
which settled that for twenty years Louis should
retain his hold upon all the places—including Strasburg and the fort of Kehl—assigned to him by the
chambers of Metz and Breisach and by the *Parlement* of Besançon up to August 1, 1681.

For twenty years then Louis was to enjoy possession of his newly gained territories. Even with this
limit he had secured a great victory. His next aim
was to convert the truce of Ratisbon into a permanent definitive peace, so as to get legal and perpetual possession of his new acquisitions. He regarded
that truce as a step towards a general pacification

which should find France with her frontiers advanced and well-nigh impregnable, her reputation enormously increased, and Paris the centre of a powerful and united Christian monarchy of which he was the moving spirit.

CHAPTER IX.

THE truce of Ratisbon is an important landmark in the reign of Louis XIV. "This great diplomatic success," says M. Legrelle, "truly marks the apogee of Louis' long reign." It was "that glorious convention rather perhaps than the peace of Nimeguen" which "is the culminating point of this great reign." Von Ranke holds a similar opinion. "France," he says, "was obtaining at that time a position of incontestable preponderance in continental Europe," and again he speaks of the new power which Louis had called into life, uniform in its nationality and ecclesiastical system, with well defined frontiers, and admirably armed for offence and defence both by land and sea. And in another place he alludes to the truce as a magnificent diplo-

matic success which distinctly marks the apogee of
Louis' long reign.   Similar language is held by Saint-
Simon and by Lavallée.   "Here ends," says the former, speaking of the years between 1684 and 1688,
"the apogee of the reign and height of its glory and
prosperity. . . . We are now to see the second
age which will scarcely come up to the first."   And
the latter indicates the year 1684 as the culminating
point of Louis' life and reign.   "At this epoch," he
says, "Louis stood at the height of his prosperity
and at the apogee of his greatness.   The absolute
monarchy which had raised itself on the ruins of
the Fronde seemed unconquerable abroad and all-
powerful at home.   The Protestants were disarmed
and in subjection, the *Parlement* of Paris was discredited, and the nobles were reduced to complete submission.   While Colbert had restored the finances, had
formed a strong navy, and had stimulated not only
the industrial, but also the artistic and literary resources of France, Louvois and Turenne had reorganised and unified the army and Lionne had developed
and strengthened the diplomatic relations of France
with Europe.   With a well equipped army of 400,000
men, and with the frontiers defended by a hundred
fortresses restored or constructed by Vauban, France
might well feel able to defy the wrath of Europe.

After the peace of Nimeguen, the predominance
of France became each year more assured, and the
truce of Ratisbon found Louis occupying a brilliant
position both at home and abroad.[1]   He had still

---

[1] On the importance of the truce of Ratisbon, see Ranke, *Fran-
zösische Geschichte ;* and Legrelle, *La Diplomatic Française et la Succession d'Espagne.*   Vol. i.

further increased and strengthened the frontiers of France, he had conquered Strasburg, Casale, and Luxemburg, he had bombarded Genoa and Algiers. He was the terror of Europe and the admiration of his subjects. He was in full possession of all his faculties and thoroughly appreciated the glorious position to which he had attained.

Yet success seems to have blinded him to the tendencies of the time and to the actual condition of European politics. The death of Colbert removed a sagacious adviser, and henceforward Louis is usually served by men of mediocre abilities. " The secondary age," as Saint-Simon calls it, began with the truce of Ratisbon, an age which sees the commission of many fatal mistakes—mistakes which well-nigh ruin France and bequeath to her endless trouble and misery, and serious political complications.

The truce of Ratisbon itself was in reality a great blunder. Louis had hoped that it would prove the prelude to a general peace ; his enemies regarded it as affording them a valuable opportunity for gaining time and for gradually forming a powerful European league against him. Europe employed this breathing space for drawing together the threads of a general coalition which was to humble France and wrest from her some of her lately acquired possessions; Louis used the period of peace, partly to complete the extensive works at Versailles, partly to establish the French predominance in the Mediterranean, and generally to pose as a Grand Monarch, whose influence and prestige extended not only far

into the distant East, but over the American continent.

His authority was practically boundless. No
opposition to his will existed. In 1682 the residence
of the Court was definitely fixed at Versailles, which
henceforth became the recognised centre of the
monarchy. Louis had never liked Paris. That city
had been the centre of the troubles of his minority;
it had witnessed many of the episodes of his early
days, which he would have gladly consigned to
oblivion. Paris wearied him with its crowds, its independence, its many importunities. In the early
days of his rule, too, he loved hunting, open-air
fêtes, and out-of-door amusements. Hence, soon
after the death of his mother, he lived mainly at
Saint-Germain, the beauties and delights of which
are so clearly set forth by Saint-Simon. As years
rolled by Louis developed a passion for building
which, with his ever increasing love of splendour,
magnificence, and profusion, proved a ruinous matter
for his country. Colbert had in vain attempted to
check the lavish expenditure in Versailles; he urged
the completion of the Louvre, "the most superb
palace in the world," and did all in his power to keep
the King in Paris.

But Louis in addition to his dislike of Paris had
no sympathy with Colbert's view, which in later
days was forcibly enunciated by Danton, that Paris
was the head of France. He was jealous of the
capital and wished to be himself the centre of the
French nation.

Fontainebleau, Chambord, Saint-Germain had

been occupied by his predecessors, and reminded
him of their great deeds. Louis determined to build
. a palace which should be the glorification of himself.
It was through this strongly marked characteristic
combined with his passion for building that led Louis
to abandon Saint-Germain for Versailles,"la plus triste
et la plus ingrat de tous les lieux," and to create out of
a small hunting lodge a royal palace, his *chef-d'œuvre*,
" so ruinous and built in such bad taste." Versailles
was by nature treeless, without water, with a dry
sandy soil, but Louis, as Saint-Simon tells us, loved
to fight and conquer even nature. Everything at
Versailles was magnificent, uncomfortable, and in
questionable taste. The want of water " in spite of
sixty leagues of aqueducts " was a serious defect. To
remedy this drawback Louis determined to divert the
Eure between Chartres and Maintenon and to bring
its waters by means of a canal to Versailles. In 1681
22,000 soldiers and 6000 horses were employed on
the work, a great part of whom were soon rendered
by sickness unfit for service. No sooner was the
truce of Ratisbon signed than Louis sent a portion
of his army to the works. A third of them perished,
and this attempt to remedy the deficiencies of
nature was finally abandoned in 1688 on the outbreak of war, after the sacrifice of many lives and
an enormous expenditure of money,—nine millions
alone being spent on the aqueduct of Maintenon.
It was at Versailles that Louis resided during these
years when his power and influence were at their
height. It was there that he received embassies
from distant lands. There came in 1684 the Alge-

rian envoys to implore Louis' mercy and consideration. There was seen at the beginning of 1685 the
unusual spectacle of a Doge of Genoa and four Sena-
tors asking pardon of the King of France, while at
the end of 1684 and again in 1686 Versailles witnessed an event almost unique in the history of
western Europe,—the appearance of an embassy
from Siam. The arrival of this mission was the
result of Louis' far-reaching diplomacy and admirably illustrates the general aims of his policy.

During these years Louis was not content with
being supreme in Europe ; he aimed at the extension of his influence in the far East and discovered
an excellent opportunity of carrying out his purpose
in the success of Colbert's East Indian policy. In
India the position of the French was eminently
satisfactory. The French East India Company was
flourishing and the fame of Louis' victories and of
the peace of Nimeguen had penetrated as far as
Siam.

No better illustration of the general tenor of
Louis' policy could be found than in the history of
his relations with Siam. His motives in sending
embassies to Siam were partly religious, partly commercial, partly political. The rivalry between the
French and the Dutch raged in the East Indies and
Louis hoped to oust his rivals from Siam and to ruin
their trade with that country. At the same time he
undoubtedly hoped to effect the conversion of the
Siamese, and never realised how well-nigh insuperable were the obstacles to the success of such an
attempt.

Almost simultaneously with the revocation of the Edict of Nantes, the conversion of the Siamese was taken definitely in hand. A revolution in Siam coincident in point of time with the English Revolution of 1688 dealt with dramatic completeness a similar blow to French influence. The Roman Catholic religion in Siam received a shock from which it never recovered, the French prestige in that country was well-nigh ruined, and the Dutch influence triumphed in Siam at the very time that William III. was securing the English crown.

The history of the relations of France and Siam is short but piquant, and abounds with curious illustrations of Louis' methods, of his general attitude, of his belief in himself, and of the defects of his policy.

Official intercourse between the two countries began in Louis XIV.'s reign, but up to 1669 the French had only been represented by missionaries. The early missions seem to have been so successful that an additional number of priests were sent out and by 1677 five missions had been established and letters sent to Phra-Naraï the tolerant King of Siam from both the Pope and the French King. Phra-Naraï was greatly impressed with the power of Louis, and moreover was alarmed at the maritime tyranny of the Dutch and the menacing development of their eastern empire. He accordingly spoke of sending an embassy to France. The rapid growth of the Dutch power had for a long period been a source of great anxiety to French statesmen. This anxiety was in a special manner shared by Louis, whose antipathy to the Dutch on account of their political views and religious tenets only increased as years went on.

In Siam there was a splendid field for an attack on the Dutch East India Company, which, the mistress of Java and the Moluccas, not only had the right of carrying on trade, of building ports, of making alliances, and of founding colonies in the Indian and Chinese seas, but enjoyed a practical monopoly of the spice trade, and had in great measure driven the Portuguese out of India.

Colbert had in 1664 founded the French East India Company which was not at first received with any great favour. But in 1668 a French factory was established at Surat; a few years later Martin founded Pondicherry and the French Company entered upon fairly prosperous days. The commercial monopoly of the Dutch was at once threatened, and the French, overjoyed at the favourable reception accorded to their missionaries, determined to establish a factory in Siam. In 1680 the King of Siam having heard from the missionaries of the peace of Nimeguen with a highly coloured account of Louis' victories, and being moreover influenced by Constantine Phaulkon a Greek adventurer, who had gained his confidence and had practically become first minister, allowed the establishment of a French factory, and in 1682 made a treaty with the French East India Company on very favourable terms. He also resolved to send an embassy, and in 1681 the first expedition to France set out with numerous presents for the Pope, Louis, his Queen, the Dauphin, Orleans, and Colbert. Off Madagascar, however, their ship was

wrecked and all perished. In 1684 a second embassy
was sent, Phra-Naraï having in the meantime received a letter from Louis together with the King's
miniature. This embassy, composed of two manda-
rins and their suite, started in January, landed at
Calais towards the end of the year, and early in December had an audience of Louis at Versailles. On
being presented to the King the members of the
embassy remained so long on the ground that Louis
growing impatient asked if they were never going to
rise. They spoke fair words, hinted that Christianity was on the increase in Siam and that the King
was favourably disposed to it, spoke of commercial
privileges, and asked that a French embassy should
be sent. This request was strongly supported by
Père la Chaise, Louis' confessor, by the French
clergy generally, and by the most eloquent divines in
particular.

It was eventually decided that an embassy should
be sent and in March, 1685, it set out. The objects
aimed at by Louis and his advisers in fitting out a
costly expedition to a distant kingdom like Siam are
singularly in agreement with those for which French
policy was then struggling at home.

First, the embassy was to attempt the conversion
of the King of Siam. Just when religious unity
was being insisted upon in France, in the very year
which saw the revocation of the Edict of Nantes,
Louis thought the conversion of an Asiatic sovereign would clearly demonstrate to the world his
determination to advance the Christian religion, no
matter at what cost, in Asia no less than in Europe.

Then secondly the embassy was to leave no stone unturned to further the political and commercial interests of France. France was on the verge of a war in Europe. Foremost among her avowed enemies stood Holland. The greatness of Holland in large measure depended upon her eastern trade. A blow was therefore to be struck at once at that trade.

On September the 23d, after a voyage of six months and twenty days, the two ships conveying the members of the embassy—*L'Oiseau* and *Le Maligne*, arrived at Siam. But the expedition did not prove a conspicuous success. Its chief was the Chevalier de Chaumont, a hot-headed fanatic full of religious zeal, and he was accompanied by the notorious Abbé de Choisy, and twelve young Frenchmen of noble birth, four missionaries, six Jesuit Fathers, and an engineer. Like Louis XIV. and his advisers, the members of the embassy seem to have really expected the immediate conversion of the King of Siam. Nothing, however, was further from the thoughts of Phra-Naraï, and Chaumont, who only cared for the work of conversion and had no sympathy with commerce, soon found that, as far as he was concerned, he might have stayed in France.

The Siamese desired an offensive and defensive treaty with France; Chaumont made the conversion of the King a *sine quâ non*. Eventually Phra-Naraï declared that he had no intention of giving up a religion which had been held by the Siamese for 2229 years. Though the main object of the embassy was thus defeated, missionaries were still allowed to carry on the work of conversion, and a treaty favourable to French commerce was made. It was further arranged that the maritime places should be fortified *à la* Vauban and that new forts should be built at Bangkok and Mergui and garrisoned by French forces. In December, 1685, another Siamese embassy accompanied Chaumont back to France and arrived at Brest in June, 1686. In August a solemn entry was made into Paris and later the Siamese were taken to Maintenon and shown the troops still working at the aqueduct. On September 1st, a great reception was accorded to them at Versailles, and a picture of that very characteristic scene is still extant.

After once more seeing Louis the embassy started back early in 1687 accompanied by some 636 officers and men to garrison the forts of Bangkok and Mergui. This expedition had as usual the threefold character of a military expedition, of a commercial enterprise, and of a religious crusade. Only 492 arrived at Siam, the rest having succumbed on the way. Early the following year a reinforcement of 200 men were dispatched from France.

But the French fortunes in Europe and in the East seem to have been inextricably intertwined. The year 1688 was destined to be as disastrous to the French in Siam as it was to their fortunes in Europe. The priests and Siamese aristocracy had long been weary of the rule of Constantine, whose policy had uniformly been one of alliance with the French. In July, 1688, a revolution broke out. The King was deposed, French influence was overthrown, Constantine was ruined. The unpardonable indeci-

RECEPTION OF THE SIAMESE AMBASSADORS AT VERSAILLES.

(From a photograph of a painting.)

sion of the French commander, Desfargues, was in great measure answerable for the disasters to the French cause. Louis' relations with Siam remain, however, as a curious and interesting illustration of his zeal for conversion, of his hatred of the Dutch, and of his intense and overweening desire to seize every opportunity to pose as a Great King.[1]

But in 1685 there was no sign of coming disaster in Siam. The conversion of the King and his country was regarded as imminent, and Louis plumed himself with the thought of the profound impression which would be produced in Western Christendom when he, the strong supporter of the Christian religion in Europe, could boast of having converted a large and powerful kingdom in the far East. For while he was attempting to convert the Siamese, he was busy at home in proving to Europe his zeal for religion. He had resolved to proceed rapidly in carrying out his deepseated determination of securing at all costs religious and political unity at home. Political unity was practically assured, but as long as the Huguenots were allowed to enjoy the privileges accorded them by the Edict of Nantes, Louis could not regard France as united in a religious sense. Religious unity at home was the logical outcome and result of the political unity already won, and the necessary complement of the commanding position acquired by Louis in Western Christendom. His power dominated Europe. His navy swept the Mediterranean. All around him was

---

[1] On the subject of the French relations with Siam see L. Lanier's *Étude historique sur les relations de la France et du royaume de Siam : de* 1662 *a* 1703.

16

subservience and adulation. Religious unity at home
was to him absolutely necessary and seemed easy to
secure. In the East the Emperor was carrying on a
crusade against the Turks. It seemed to Louis a
happy idea to emulate him by leading a crusade
against the Protestants. He had moreover the sympathy of James II., who while pursuing his own
policy in England was acting in harmony with
the views of the French King. The flood of universal Catholicism seemed to be rising rapidly, and
in devotion to that Catholicism a great Christian
monarch like Louis could not allow himself to be
outdistanced by Austria or England.

But if Louis' motives are closely analysed, it will be
found that the existence of the Huguenot element in
France jarred upon his dogma of absolute authority
and did not imply any real sympathy with or devotion to the Papacy. His wish to realise an absolute
supremacy far outweighed any desire to uphold the
divine power of the Pope. He was convinced that
the royal authority was insulted by the presence in
France of the Protestant camp; he was equally
certain that the French people would be all the
better for the suppression of the heretical section.
And in his persecution of the Huguenots he was
completely at one with the nation. Never was
the King more in sympathy with the mass of his subjects than when he issued the order for the revocation of the Edict of Nantes.

The existence of a schismatic body within France
had always been a source of annoyance to Louis, and
it is possible that he hoped by expelling the whole

sect of Protestants to be in a position to claim " the
liberties of the national Church as a reward for his
crusade." A Gallican Church under the direct supervision of the King himself and free from all interference from Rome was undoubtedly Louis' ideal. It
was therefore an accurate appreciation of the King's
real motives that caused Innocent XI. to condemn the
revocation of the Edict of Nantes. By it the interests of Rome were as seriously imperilled as the interests of the national Church in France were
advanced. The revocation was from Louis' point
of view absolutely necessary, and was part of a general scheme. He had long been preparing for the
event. Mazarin had treated the Huguenots with
tolerance. With his natural prudence he saw the wisdom of pursuing a conciliatory policy. Besides, they
had not supported the Fronde and for that he was
grateful. The Edict of Nantes had in consequence
been confirmed in 1652 and the future seemed assured
to the Huguenots for the exercise, not only of their religious rites but also of their political functions. But
the hatred of the French clergy never slept. With pas-
sionate language they besought Louis even while he
was a mere child to check the progress of this heretical society. In 1655 the Archbishop of Rheîms
declaimed against the declaration of Saint-Germain in
1652 and alluded to the Huguenot temples as " Syna-
gogues of Satan " and to the Huguenots themselves
" as heretics, persecutors, and schismatics."

Soon after the death of Mazarin the policy which
culminated in 1685 began in real earnest. The young
King yielding to his clerical advisers abandoned once

and for all the liberal-minded policy of Henry IV. and inaugurated the era of persecution. In April, 1661, Louis agreed to the demand of the clergy that commissioners should be sent into the provinces to report on the Protestant churches built since the Edict of Nantes; for the clergy claimed that Article 9 of that Edict only allowed the Protestants to exercise their worship in certain places and therefore that all churches built since 1597 should be pulled down. The result of the commission was favourable to these views and numerous churches were demolished. Not only was public worship gradually proscribed but many vexatious restraints were imposed on the Protestants. The signal had been given and preparatory measures were taken which made quite apparent to farsighted men the nature and meaning of the King's policy. In 1666 the first series of emigrations took place and in 1668 it was reported that 800 French Protestant families had arrived at The Hague. The Elector of Brandenburg ventured to protest against the infractions of the Edict of Nantes, but Louis replied that no churches which had been in existence in 1597 had been destroyed. A system of semi-persecution was thus continued in accordance with the strict Jesuit interpretation of the treaty of Nantes. Already burials in the daytime were prohibited on the ground that no clause could be found permitting interments by day. In 1670 schoolmasters were forbidden to teach any subject save reading, writing, and arithmetic on the ground that the Edict contained no list of subjects which the Protestants might teach. On such frivolous in-

terpretations of the Edict many schools were closed
and only one master was allowed in each school.
These regulations were severely enforced through
the instrumentality of the clergy, and the Protestant
schools were practically ruined.

In 1669, the violent and persecuting spirit shown
by the Bishop of Amiens resulted in a large emigration of the Protestants of Picardy to England. In
1675 the clergy demanded that Protestant children
should be converted at the age of fourteen, and in
1681 a royal edict declared that such children could
be converted at the age of seven. The Protestants
had to choose between ignorance or conversion.
They were thus treated like Turks or infidels. They
were loyal French subjects ready and willing to fight
for their country, they were the backbone of the
commercial prosperity of France. But Louis had
always dreaded as well as disliked them. In 1668 he
feared a revolt of the French Huguenots, and in
1680 he ordered that the Protestant officers should
gradually be dismissed from the navy. The King
had evidently been entirely misinformed as to the
strength of the dissidents, for as a political party
the Huguenots do not seem to have been well organised or in any way dangerous. But after the
peace of Nimeguen a change had come over Louis'
life. He fell under the influence of Père la Chaise
and Madame de Maintenon. Colbert's influence was
waning ; that of Louvois was increasing. The lying
reports of the intendants notifying the conversion of
thousands rendered Colbert's advice fruitless, and
Louis' fresh persecuting measures—the result of his

religious and political ardour—were accompanied by
a rapid series of emigrations. In 1681 a large number of Protestants fled from the west and the north
and in 1683 after Colbert's death persecution and
destruction of churches continued with renewed
vigour till the culminating point was reached in the
Dragonnade of 1685 and the revocation itself.

In 1688 the largest emigration took place, and apart
from the thousands of good citizens who left the
country, we must notice the remark of Vauban that
France lost 600 officers and 12,000 soldiers better
seasoned than their Catholic brethren. And this
took place in 1688 the year of all others when Louis
required all his best soldiers to combat the rising
flood of European hostility.

The question as to Louis' own share in the responsibility of this fatal policy, which produced such incalculable harm and loss to France, has yet to be
finally determined. Louvois has been accused of
being the author of the fatal revocation; Madame
de Maintenon has been also charged with strongly
supporting the anti-Protestant policy and of being
the main cause of the attack of the Reformed religion. The Jesuits and clergy generally have in
their turn been regarded as mainly instrumental in
bringing about the greatest mistake of the reign.

There is no proof that Louvois played a leading
part in furthering a policy which had been in men's
minds all through Louis' reign. But there is no
doubt that he carried out with unnecessary violence
against the Protestants measures which were in
direct oppositon to Colbert's principles, and that he

THE REVOCATION OF THE EDICT OF NANTES, 1685.

(From an old print reproduced in Erdmannsdörfer's *Deutsche Geschichte von 1648–1740*.)

regarded the adoption of a policy of persecution as a means of supplanting that great minister and of recouping the exchequer at the expense of his victims.

Madame de Maintenon certainly did not play a leading part in the revocation. This is Voltaire's opinion, and there is no ground for disputing it. She, like almost all Catholic France, approved of the measures taken against the Huguenots, thinking with all the world that the revocation was a praiseworthy act and easy of execution. In a letter written on August 13, 1684, she says that the King has the intention of bringing about the entire conversion of the heretics, and that he had frequent interviews with Le Tellier the Chancellor and Châteauneuf, Secretary of State, with reference to *les affaires de la religion prétendue reformée.* She goes on to say that she was allowed to be present at these interviews and that she did not agree with the measures proposed by Châteauneuf. "One cannot," she writes, "precipitate matters; one must convert and not persecute. . . . The King is ready to do all that may be considered as tending to the benefit of religion. This enterprise will cover him with glory before God and before men." The atrocious persecution, due in great measure to Louvois, was repugnant to her nature. She would have trusted entirely to persuasion and not to cruelty. "The King," she writes, "is much touched by what has come to his ears—and he knows only a portion. . . . For fifteen years have I counselled moderation ; I have never injured any one, and the King

has often reproached me for my moderation."
When she told Louis that the persecution would,
so far from bringing about conversion, only inflame
the Protestants the more against the Catholic religion, Louis refused to listen. "I fear, Madame," he
said to her at one time, "that the mildness with
which you would wish the Calvinists to be treated,
arises from some remaining sympathy with your
former religion." Still she pressed her point of
view and succeeded in keeping her Protestant ser-
vants in spite of Louis' protests.

Louis was distinctly responsible for the revocation. The question of the conversion of all dissidents in France had occupied his thoughts for a very
long period. Throughout his reign, ministers, the
clerical assemblies, the *Parlements*, the great mass
of the kingdom, had pressed the matter upon his
attention. Public opinion had declared itself un-
mistakably for the revocation. As early as April
5, 1681, Madame de Maintenon writes: "If God
preserve the King there will not be one Huguenot
left twenty years hence." This is usually taken to
be a quotation from Louis' own lips, and would seem
to indicate that Louis was more than willing to regard himself, as in other cases, carrying out the
popular wish. Louis' responsibility was heavy, but
he was in great measure the tool of the clergy. Ever
since 1661 he was to a considerable extent unwit-
tingly influenced by some more powerful mind than
his own. Thinking he was acting best for his own
salvation, he allowed himself in this matter to be
guided by the Jesuits. The determining cause of

the revocation was the action of the clergy. "The conduct, the direction, the strategy of this great event was in the hands of the French clergy," says a modern French writer. "The real authors of this revocation carried out," says Saint-Simon, "with the least pretext and without any necessity, are assuredly those who inspired it."

Louis has in accordance with this view been described as a "glorious accomplice." On his deathbed, on August 26, 1715, addressing the three cardinals who stood round him, he declared, according to Saint-Simon, that he had always acted with regard to Church affairs by the direction of his clerical advisers, and that they were responsible for all that he had done.

Louis unquestionably hoped in 1685 to repair the past by one great act of religious intolerance, though he probably was in the hands of his agents throughout. There is no reason to doubt that he was deceived as to the amount of vigorous Protestantism in the country. The intendants sent lying reports of conversions to the King, and Louis, misled by the official information, imagined that the revocation would have no disastrous effect upon France. Louis lived on a pedestal and was to a great extent, if not entirely, ignorant of the horrors which attended the execution of his policy. This view receives some confirmation in the letter of Madame de Maintenon quoted above. And at the same time it must always be remembered that few even of the more sagacious minds ever realised the real import of the line of policy pursued by the government of France towards the Huguenots. Colbert never actively opposed the persecutions, and never showed any signs of an appreciation of the real drift and possible results of Louis' religious policy. But during his lifetime the persecution had not reached its extreme limits, and he was mainly occupied in the task of establishing an equilibrium between the expenditure and receipts—a task in which he was fairly successful even as late as 1683, the year of his death.

Louis succeeded in his object, but at what cost? The last remaining stumbling-block in the way of a centralised monarchy was removed. No jarring or discordant note disturbed the harmony which existed on the surface between king and people. The revocation was extremely popular. Louis like George III. represented the tastes and prejudices of the mass of his countrymen. The Huguenots were unpopular, they had always held their privileges " in the teeth of the majority of the nation," and their proscription by Louis was a popular act. The nation, like Nero, fiddled while France received a blow from which she has never recovered. Above 300,000 emigrants left the country, including the best men of France as regards " birth, substance, and reputation." The trade of the country went with them and the rest of Louis' reign is a period of economic decadence. Even in the year 1685, it is stated that a single parish in Rouen contained 5000 poor, while in Poitou, in Limousin and Languedoc, a large number of peasants subsisted on *chataignes, glands, herbes, boucliers.* And from this time the want and misery increased to an enormous extent. France could ill afford to see the entire Teutonic factor eliminated from her midst.

Centralisation was indeed secured, but the stream of national life was dried up. The educated middle class ceased to exist. The year 1684 saw Louis at the height of his power, the year 1685 saw the commission of this fatal error and the beginning of the decline of the greatness and influence of France.

The revocation of the Edict of Nantes gave the religious question a foremost place among all the affairs of Western Christendom and proved to be the prelude to the League of Augsburg. In 1684 Louis had given the law to Europe; in 1687 his domination in Europe was threatened on all sides. The explanation of this—one might almost say revolution in the general current of European opinion was due to the revocation of the Edict of Nantes. And Louis' whole conduct with reference to it was teeming with blunders. He had expected that the revocation proceeding simultaneously with the Imperial war against the Turks would disarm the hostility of the Emperor and bring about friendly relations. But the very reverse happened. The Empire and Emperor became united. The German Catholics remained faithful to their chief and the Protestants joined them. Louis moreover carried away by his ideas of exterminating heresy had forced Victor Amadeus of Savoy to assent to the expulsion of the Vaudois from their valleys early in 1686. He considered that the presence of Protestants living peacefully so near France would prove a bad example to his own Huguenot subjects. The Vaudois valleys too would afford a refuge for fugitives from France, and such a state of things could not be tolerated by the greatest monarch in Europe. The expulsion of the Vaudois was an act of blind and useless brutality and only aggravated the general feeling of Europe against the aggressive and all pervading domination of France.

The year 1685 then marks the time when Louis finally deserted the wise policy which aimed at preserving intact a circle of Protestant alliances in Germany. Though he and his successors endeavoured at times with success to return to the old and more statesmanlike system, it was left for the rising power of Brandenburg to enter upon the position which France had abandoned.

CHAPTER X.

THE LEAGUE AND THE WAR OF AUGSBURG.

1686-1697.

T was impossible for the peace of Europe to be much longer maintained in face of the "position of incontestable preponderance" acquired by France in continental Europe. "Everyone," says von Ranke, "knew what object the ambition of Louis XIV. was likely to pursue on the approaching extinction of the Spanish line of the House of Austria and on the expiration or breach of the armistice concluded with Germany. The old independence of the States of Europe could not be maintained any longer unless this prince found somewhere or other an energetic resistance."

The possibility of making such a resistance had

long occupied the minds of many of the European Princes. In the autumn of 1681 Charles XI. of Sweden, furious at the loss of the Duchy of Deux-Ponts, signed a treaty with the States-General, and to this early in 1682 Leopold gave his adhesion, his example being followed by Spain, Saxony, Bavaria, Hesse-Cassel, and the leading members of the Circles of the Upper Rhine and Franconia. This attempt to curb the *Grand Monarque* was, as we have seen, premature, and it was not till after the revocation of the Edict of Nantes that European opposition took a practical form. A deep feeling of sympathy was manifested in England for continental Protestantism ; in Holland the party of the Prince of Orange was strengthened ; the Elector of Brandenburg was thoroughly aroused. But as long as England's King was an ardent Roman Catholic, the issue of a struggle with Louis XIV. was regarded as doubtful.

It had been obvious for some years to all sagacious men that if Louis succeeded in transforming the truce of Ratisbon into a peace, and secured forever his *Réunion* acquisitions he would acquire complete military preponderance in Europe.

With England as his ally there is little doubt that Louis would have carried his point and established his predominance. On England's action then the fortunes of Europe depended. The alienation of James from his subjects was of the gravest European consequence. " The strife which awaited its decision in England was closely bound up with the great religious and political conflict which then di-

LOUIS XIV.
(From an old portrait reproduced in Philippson's
Das Zeitalter Ludwigs XIV.)

vided Europe." [1] James II. was bent on the restoration of Roman Catholicism in England. But even the Roman party in England was divided. The moderate Catholic party was in agreement with the views of Innocent XI., while the Jesuit faction which surrounded the King strongly advocated a close alliance with Louis XIV., whose policy they supported. The rival claims of Louis and Innocent placed James in an unpleasant dilemma, and at length he decided to mediate between the two. While James was busy endeavouring to wean Innocent from his antagonism to Louis, and to establish the Roman Catholic religion in England, the opposition to France had become European. On July 9, 1686, the League of Augsburg was formed—to preserve the treaties of Westphalia and Nimeguen and the truce of Ratisbon. It included the Emperor, the Kings of Spain and Sweden, the Dutch Republic, the Palatine and Saxon Electors, with the Circles of Bavaria, Franconia, and the Upper Rhine. In 1687 Innocent XI. secretly joined it, and the Dukes of Bavaria and Savoy openly. Calvinists, Lutherans, Catholics united so as to be ready for all possible contingencies. The League bore a European rather than a German character. It only required the adhesion of England.

Louis' answer to the League was a demand that the truce of Ratisbon should be at once transformed into a peace. James II. supported him, and it appeared likely that the European struggle would

---

[1] See Ranke. *History of England, principally in the Sixteenth and Seventeenth centuries.*

begin in the north of Europe by the allied English
and French forces attacking the Dutch Republic.

It seemed then possible that England and France
might early in 1688 unite against Holland, and that
the history of 1672 might be repeated. The relations between the government of James II. and that
of the Stadtholder were seriously strained. Colonial
disputes about Bantam in Java, and the recall by
James in January, 1688, from the Dutch service of
those English and Scottish regiments which had remained in Holland since 1678 boded no good to the
Protestant cause in Europe. At this very time too
Denmark and Sweden were on the verge of a struggle over the Schleswig-Holstein " affair," and as the
Dutch supported the Swedes, England and France
supported Denmark. It seemed more than likely
that this business might bring on a general war.

Louis had no time, however, to lose. The Turkish war still occupied the Emperor in the East but
it might be concluded at any moment ; Hungary
was firmly held by Austria ; on September 6th
Belgrade was carried by assault. Peace with the
Turks once made, the forces then employed on the
Danube would be an important factor on the Rhine.
Louis' policy ever since 1684 had been perfectly
clear. To unite permanently to France those districts, the possession of which was yielded to him
for twenty years by the truce of Ratisbon, was a
policy worthy of a great king. By so doing he
would acquire " complete military preponderance in
Europe both for defence and offence." His religious policy was equally clear. He intended to

force the Pope to confirm the ecclesiastical independence of France and thus the first position in the Catholic world would be assured to himself. To secure these objects it was necessary to strike at the newly formed League, while as yet the Turkish war occupied a great part of its forces. Opportunities for kindling a European war have been rarely difficult to find during the last three centuries, and Louis easily found more than one pretext which he thought would enable him to establish his preponderance in Europe on a permanent footing. The death of Maximilian Henry, Archbishop of Cologne, in June, 1688, was an opportunity seized upon by Louis to occupy Cologne, and to place his creature William of Fürstenberg in possession of the Electorate to which he had not been legally elected. The idea of the occupation of an Electorate, so important geographically as was Cologne to France, by Prince Joseph Clement of Bavaria, the candidate of the Emperor and Pope was not to be entertained for a moment, and while Fürstenberg took possession of his Electorate, French troops occupied Cologne. Then the question of the succession to the Palatinate opened a vast field for Louis' ambitious schemes. The extinction of the male line of Simmern in 1685 left Charlotte Elizabeth, the wife of Orleans, the only descendant of the Simmerns. Finding that the Pope and Emperor refused to recognise Fürstenberg and to transform the twenty years' truce into a peace, Louis determined to postpone the inevitable struggle no longer, and at once prepared to assert the rights of the Duchess of Orleans in the Palatinate.

17

Madame herself was furious at this claim set up
on her behalf, and, before the Dauphin started on
September 25th to invade the Palatinate without
any previous declaration of war, she told him that
he should be grieved and " not pleased at the
thought that her name should be used to ruin
her poor country." The decision to occupy the
Palatinate had not been come to without serious
deliberation. But after long consultations the
French ministers had decided that it was of the utmost importance to France that the Emperor and
Empire should cede definitely the territories placed
in Louis' hands by the truce of Ratisbon, and should
recognise the claims of Orleans to the Palatinate
succession. In order to obtain the cession of these
territories it was resolved to occupy the Palatinate
without further delay.

This decision has been severely criticised by many
able historians. By attacking Holland or even by
making a movement against Maestricht, the expedition of William would, it is usually said, have been
prevented. But it must be remembered that Maestricht was not in the heart of Holland, and though
its siege would have embarrassed the Dutch, there
is no reason for believing that it would have caused
the abandonment of the expedition to England.
The French arms had failed in 1672 in the attack
on Holland, though the Dutch were unable to offer
any organised resistance. In 1688 the Dutch were
fully prepared, they had powerful allies, and Maestricht itself was far better able to stand a long siege
than in 1672. French troops had already marched

into the Electorate of Cologne without causing any special disquietude to Holland or paralysing the efforts of William. There is no doubt that it would have been far better for the French cause had William's landing in England been prevented. But Louis' reasons for deciding to attack Philippsburg have not been fully appreciated by writers who speak of his great blunder in marching to the Middle Rhine. Louis' principal object at this time was to convert the truce of Ratisbon into a solid and definite peace. By seizing Philippsburg, the main doorway from Germany into France, he hoped to bring his enemies to treat, and he at once offered to restore it and Freiburg if they would agree to his terms.

Moreover his relations with the English Court had in the summer of 1688 become strained. To prevent the landing of William in England, Louis had proposed a junction of the English and French fleets and had this taken place William's plans would for a time have been frustrated. But the English ministers thought that William would be hampered by difficulties with the States-General, and they feared the effect of the junction of the fleets upon English public opinion. James and the Court too were indignant at Louis' attitude and the tone of the declaration made early in September. It was thought that he assumed the air of a protector and imagined that England could not defend itself without his aid. Such patronising manners on the part of Louis at once roused James' pride. He assured the Dutch envoy that no alliance existed between England and France, and that he intended to pursue a policy of neutrality ; shortly afterwards he offered the States General a treaty which had for its object the maintainance of the peace of Nimeguen and the truce of Ratisbon. The foreign policy of England was no longer in harmony with the aims of the French Court, and as James determined further to conciliate the Episcopalian party the English alliance seemed for the time lost to Louis.

Villars, describing the opinion held at Versailles, gives us some very valuable information : "The Court hesitated as to what should be its policy, whether it should give aid to King James about to be attacked, or should prevent the peace with the Turks, which was being made, and which would bring upon us the whole forces of the Emperor and Empire. M. de Louvois, upon his return from Forges, where he had been taking the waters for some days, decided to take the second course. In effect nothing was more important for us than to secure so powerful a diversion in our favour as that of the Turks. Besides, what prospect was there that so great a revolution could take place in England without much trouble and discord? This suited us better than a settled government under King James; the more so that we had already seen England at peace and under the authority of King Charles II., a devoted ally, compel that sovereign to declare war against us."* Though these views proved erroneous, still it was always quite possible that the English feeling might have forced James II. into

* Villars (Marechal de), *Memoires :* 1672–1734. Edited by the Marquis de Vogüé.

JAMES II. OF ENGLAND.
(From an illustration, based on an old engraving, in Philippson's
Das Zeitalter Ludwigs XIV.)

measures prejudicial to the French interests. It is easy to be wise after the event, and to say that Louis ought to have spared no efforts to prevent the Prince of Orange from landing in England, but when the circumstances of the time are clearly and fully examined, and when it is remembered that no one could anticipate that William III. would take possession of England, as Charles VIII. conquered Naples, with a piece of chalk, it will be found that there is more justification for the attack on Philipsburg than some historians imagine. On October 2nd Boufflers took Kaiserslautern; on October 29th the Dauphin received the submission of Philipsburg; in November Madame wrote " my troubles are increased by hearing all those around me discuss incessantly the preparations that are being made to burn and bombard the good town of Manheim, which my father, the late Elector, built with so much care. It makes my heart bleed, yet they are angry at my grief . . . now the King is sole master of the Palatinate."

On the very day of the fall of Philipsburg, William of Orange sailed for England, to save Protestantism and the balance of power in Europe. The decision to attack the Palatinate was, as it turned out, an enormous blunder. Had Louis elected to attack Holland or even to make a demonstration in the direction of Maestricht, William would have been paralysed and the Revolution in England averted or at any rate postponed.

The news of the siege of Philippsburg came as a great relief to the Protestant Princes of north Ger-

many. To them it had been long apparent that a
general struggle against the predominance of France
was inevitable. Frederick William, the great Elector of Brandenburg, had hoped that on the conclusion of the Turkish war, the forces of united
Germany would invade France and aided by disaffection among the French nobles would penetrate
to Paris. On his death his son Frederick III. continued to advocate his father's plans. With Charles,
Landgrave of Hesse, he formed a close alliance to
defend the whole course of the Rhine, which they
rightly thought was endangered by Louis' attitude.
It was evident to them as it was to the Duke of
Celle and others that the election of Fürstenburg
to the Electorate of Cologne must be prevented at
all cost, and that England must be won over to the
European opposition to Louis.

The invasion of the Palatinate decided many
hesitating Princes. The Elector of Saxony declared
he would carry the war on the Middle Rhine, the
Duke of Hanover was equally determined to come
to the aid to the Empire. It only remained for
William to succeed in his English enterprise. All
the events of the last three years had combined to
aid him. The revocation of the Edict of Nantes
had destroyed in great measure Louis' influence in
many of the small German courts; the continued
alliance of England and France had roused the fears
of every Protestant statesman in Europe; the affair
of the Cologne electorate would, it was believed,
end in the ruin of Germany; Louis' attack on the
Palatinate, while it convinced William of Orange

that the Anglo-French alliance must at all hazards
be broken, relieved his anxiety on the score of Holland and enabled him to set out for England, supported by the good wishes of not only the German
Protestants but of Pope Innocent XI. and the Emperor Leopold.

By the beginning of 1689, Louis' position was far
from being satisfactory. The Turks were unable to
create any serious diversion in his favour; Denmark
was surrounded by foes. Louis deemed it necessary to withdraw from the Palatinate. He had
seized on the four Rhine Electorates but realised
that he could not defend the whole breadth of the
annexed districts. His advisers therefore hit upon
a ghastly plan of wasting the Palatinate. Accordingly what is known as the Second Devastation of
the Palatinate took place—and this meant the total
destruction of its cities, and the ruin of its agriculture, trade, and prosperity, in order that the advancing Germans might find a desert between them and
France.

Madame was in despair at the fate of her beloved
country. "Should they kill me for it," she wrote
on March 20th, "I cannot help bitterly regretting
and deploring my share in my country's ruin. I am
seized with such a horror when I think of all that
has been destroyed that every night I think myself
at Heidelberg or Manheim in the middle of the
desolation. I wake up with a start and do not go
to sleep again for two hours. I think of it all as I
once knew it, and as it is now; also the change in
my own life, and then I cannot prevent myself

weeping." But Madame's despair could not save her beloved country. The French soldiers devastated the Palatinate, the town of Heidelberg was burnt, its magnificent castle was ruined. The whole country was ravaged ; cities and agriculture destroyed, the Rhine district left in great part a desert.

" The ravage of the Palatinate," says Mr. Lilly, " was one of those crimes which arouse inextinguishable hatred in the breasts of a people and leave to future generations a terrible legacy of vengeance." [1]

The memory of Turenne's devastation in 1674 was still fresh, and this second wanton infliction of misery on the inhabitants of the Palatinate roused Germany and infused new energy into the League. The Diet declared war at Ratisbon in February, 1689, and three armies were at once set on foot. This second devastation of the Palatinate well marks the end of Louis' culminating period of prosperity, which beginning with the peace of Nimeguen, closes with a deed unsurpassed in cruelty and lawlessness. A thrill of horror ran through Europe, and the patriotic feelings roused in Germany by this last manifestation of Louis' arrogance may be said to have never entirely subsided. Some fifty years or so later, when the French at the opening of the Austrian Succession War were proposing to intervene actively on the side of Prussia, it was found that there was " one point on which all Germans were agreed without distinction of the greater and lesser states, of Protestant or Catholic, one common feel-

[1] *Chapters in European History* by W. S. Lilly, vol. ii. pp. 84–5.

ing that could impose silence on their special dissensions; this was sullen and jealous irritation with France."[1] The soldiers of France "little knew to what an undying hatred on the part of Germany they devoted the very name of their country, when they inscribed it in letters of blood and fire on all the hills of the Palatinate."

Some of the most eminent of French soldiers like Villars condemned this devastation as opposed to the true science of war and contrary to humanity. Villars himself tries to excuse Louis on the ground that Louvois over-persuaded him. "The King," he says, "whose merciful nature was never really understood, had been over-persuaded that the safety of the State depended upon creating a desert between our frontier and the enemy's armies." And he continues in still stronger language, "This pernicious policy had been carried so far that sowing had been forbidden upon a space of four leagues on either bank of the Meuse. It is still unknown by what fatality these atrocious orders were made. The Marquis of Louvois, a man of great intelligence, did not oppose them, and persuaded the King, whose kind nature, nevertheless, I repeat, was undoubted." But though it may be allowed that Louis was naturally kind-hearted and was perhaps over-persuaded by Louvois, the fact remains that the French had not very long before laid waste the

[1] For an interesting account of the effect of this devastation of the Palatinate upon the attitude of the German people towards France, see the Duke de Broglie's, *Frederick the Great and Maria Theresa,* vol. i.

Piedmontese valleys, and that a little later they proposed to destroy Dublin in order to save Ireland. It would seem that the plan of devastating the Palatinate was quite in harmony with their methods of making war.

It would have been well for Louis if he had never sent a French soldier into the Palatinate. In the first place the French failed in their aim and the devastation was useless, for the Germans, more united than ever before, took Mainz and Bonn. Besides, by invading the Electorate, instead of making a movement in a more northerly direction, he had enabled his great rival, William of Orange, to act as he wished and sail for England. That the Revolution of 1688 occurred when it did is due to Louis' excusable though fatal blunder, due to his desire to increase the glory of his house. The whole course of European politics was changed by William's rapid action, which was alone rendered possible by Louis' great mistake. Then, again, the devastation of the Palatinate was another fatal blunder. Just as the invasion had ended his connexion with the English Court, so the devastation destroyed his last hold upon Germany.

The new war in which Louis found himself in 1689, marks an epoch in the history of France. The decline of the monarchy begins. The Revolution of 1688 inaugurates in England a period of constitutional government, of commercial prosperity, of colonial expansion. The success of William III. represents the victory of constitutional over divine right. With the opening of the war of the

League of Augsburg, "The Age of Louis XIV." may be said to be over, just as the Tudor period may be said to end with the defeat of the Spanish Armada. The year 1588 was a turning point in the history of constitutional government and commercial progress in England; it also disclosed to the world the real weakness of Spain and indicated her rapid decline.

The year 1688, again bringing with it the accession of William III. to the English throne, marks an important epoch in the constitutional development of England. It does more, for it sees a revolution in her foreign policy. England comes into line with the members of the League of Augsburg, and in doing so gives a new force to the general European opposition to Louis XIV. The year 1688, too, marks the time when the true character of the French monarchy stands revealed before an indignant Europe. This revolt of Europe against the violent acts of the French monarchy had been gathering force and volume during the last ten years, and was not to be appeased till the treaty of Utrecht had lowered the pretensions of France and allayed the apprehensions of all the Teutonic peoples. From 1688 England and Holland definitely united against the aggressive Catholic monarchy of Louis XIV. The revocation of the Edict of Nantes, and the accession of James II., had brought home to Dutch statesmen the danger from France, and their own helplessness without the alliance of England. That Holland would lose much of her independence by becoming the satellite of England was foreseen

by many Dutchmen; but in 1688—9 the Republic
of the Netherlands had no other course but to co-
operate with William III. From 1688, too, a new
period in the rivalry of England and France begins.
From the Norman Conquest to the reign of Elizabeth, hostility between the two countries was regarded as part of the political creed of each.
Elizabeth and the Stuarts, however, found that a
French alliance was more suited to the circumstances of the time, and even Cromwell very wisely
preferred to ally with Mazarin, than to suspend for a
day the commercial expansion of England at the
expense of Spain.

Had the latter Stuarts acted towards Louis XIV.
with the caution and firmness showed by Cromwell
in his dealings with Mazarin, the preponderance of
France in Europe would not have been dangerous and
the Revolution of 1688 might not have been necessary. But Charles II. and his brother systematically
shut their eyes to the needs of the English nation,
and persistently ignored not only the general interests
of Europe but those of England in order to further
their own personal aims. As the whole tendency of
Louis' policy became apparent, the deep-seated antagonism, religious, commercial, and political, between
the two countries asserted itself. Nothing short of
the Revolution, which destroyed the hopes of the
Catholics and reversed the foreign policy of Charles
II. and his brother, could possibly have restored the
balance of power in Europe. From 1688 England
plunged into a contest at once political, commercial,
colonial, and religious with her ancient enemy

France,—political in that she was opposed to the restoration of James II., to the enslavement or weakening of Germany, and to the extension of the north-east frontier of France,—commercial and colonial, for, apart from the fact that English and French interests clashed in the Mediterranean, France held Canada and that famous scheme for building a line of forts from the Mississippi to the Canadian Lakes to prevent the Anglo-Saxon from developing and spreading his colonies westwards had already been produced,—religious, for it was the fixed belief of Englishmen till the peace of Utrecht that Louis intended to forcibly convert Great Britain to Roman Catholicism. But Englishmen need not have been so apprehensive of an increase in Louis' aggressive policy, for the decadence of France dates from 1688.

This decadence is nowhere so visible as in the change in the character of the art of war. No doubt owing to Vauban, a great improvement showed itself in the attack and defence of strong places, but though the armies had increased in size, the art of war had distinctly declined. There was no scientific commander like Turenne, and though many brilliant victories were won, they were not followed up by decisive results. Luxemburg was the most capable general, but his admirable qualities were marred by indolence and ill health. William III., Louis of Baden, Catinat, and Villeroy were poor substitutes for Gustavus Adolphus, Wallenstein, Turenne, and the great Condé. Signs of decadence were equally visible in the administration. On the death of the

able Seignelay in 1690, the incompetent Pontchartrain
was appointed Minister of the Marine, and Louvois,
who died the following year, was succeeded by
Barbézieux, young and also incapable. Louis as
ever had no conception of the value of the work
done by his capable ministers. " Tell the King of
England," he said the day after Louvois' death,
" that I have lost a good minister, but that his
affairs and mine will go none the worse for that."
But though the value of Louvois' work might
not be appreciated by his master, the debt France
owes to him is immense. The position of Louis
XIV. had never been so threatening to the independence of Europe as it was at the time of William's
landing in England, and had the expectations of the
French Court been realised and a long internecine
struggle taken place, the conflict between France
and Europe might have ended in one more signal
triumph for the French King, which would have
been in great measure the result of Louvois' work
of organisation.

As soon as William III. became master of England and Scotland, the policy of Louis was at once
plain. The accession of William was a blow struck
at the principles to which he attached the most
vital importance. The theory of the Divine Right
of Kings had been rudely attacked and the connection between Catholic and dynastic ideas contempt-
uously ignored.

To Louis' Minister of the Marine, Seignelay, the
Revolution presented itself in a different but no less
forcible manner. He had determined to secure for

LOUVOIS.
(From an old portrait reproduced in Philippson's
Das Zeitalter Ludwigs XIV.)

the French the sovereignty of the Mediterranean, and to gain access to the East Indies through Turkey. The Dutch power was the principal obstacle to the realisation of these schemes. But when in consequence of the Revolution, England and Holland became closely allied, Seignelay recognised that a most serious change in the aspect of affairs had occurred. The measures taken by King and Minister were characteristic of the special aims of both. The royal exiles were received with great magnanimity. James' Queen—the daughter of a niece of Mazarin, whose marriage with James had been brought about by Louis—was conducted from Boulogne by an equerry and received near Versailles by Louis himself, accompanied by his whole court. It is said that a hundred and six coaches were there. There is no doubt that great importance was attached to securing the person of James' son, the heir to the crown, and Louis greeted him first. In his own coach he conducted Queen Mary Beatrice to Saint-Germain. James II. arrived later but did not act with the dignity which his wife had shown. Louis regarded himself as the principal supporter of Catholic and dynastic ideas in the world, he felt bound to support James, and was thus disposed to give Seignelay and Louvois full powers.

As a war with England was inevitable, all the military authorities agreed that a diversion in Ireland would be invaluable. The forces of England and Holland would be drawn off there, and Ireland would in the first stages of the war prove of the utmost service in preventing William from acting vig-

orously in any other quarter, and eventually would
serve as a basis for a more serious undertaking
against England.

In March, 1690, a corps consisting of six regiments, 6300 men under Count Lauzan and several
officers, and supported by a fine train of artillery
and abundant stores of ammunition, was sent to Ireland. The Count of Avaux with a large sum of
money had been in Ireland for some months as
diplomatic representative of the French government. He was a man of considerable acuteness, but
lacked the power of conciliation and took up a position of hostility to all Protestants in Ireland.

Both James and Louis hoped to pacify Ireland
and to give the country a government under which
Protestants could exist. But the anti-English views
of the Catholic Irish were too strong for them and
helped to bring about the chaos which followed the
arrival of James in the country.

To Seignelay it was of the utmost importance
that James II. should be maintained in Ireland.
Cork and Kinsale he regarded as French ports.
Tourville was made Commander-in-chief of the
united French fleet, and was ordered to seek out
the English ships in their harbours, to inflict as much
damage as possible and then to station himself off
the mouth of the Thames to prevent communication between the Dutch and English, and to destroy
the trade between England and the North.

The success of James II. was therefore all-important for the military, naval, and commercial undertakings of the French government. But William III.

was equally conscious of the absolute necessity on the one hand of a loyal, or at any rate, of an Ireland powerless for harm, and on the other of the command of the Channel. The way in which he grappled with the combined forces of France and of Catholic Ireland and the orders given to the English Admiral showed that he was well aware of the peril to which England was exposed from her Celtic dependency, and from the French fleet, when commanded by Tourville and directed by Seignelay.

No sooner had the latter heard of the existence of discontent in England and Scotland and of William's departure for Ireland than he pressed Tourville to attack the English fleet before William had done anything decisive in Ireland.

The English government fully realised the immense importance of preventing France from acquiring the preponderance on the sea. Though the condition of the English fleet was bad, it was necessary to attack Tourville at once, even at the risk of a defeat. Unassailed he could throw men and arms into Scotland and could capture English merchantmen returning from Cadiz. England could not even in those days afford to allow a foreign and hostile fleet to ride unmolested in the channel. Precise orders were sent to Admiral Torrington to unite with the Dutch fleet, and to attack Tourville wherever he could be found. Through Torrington leaving the Dutch unsupported the French won a naval battle off Beachy Head on July 10th, and though severely damaged, Tourville's fleet was still able to keep the sea. The contest for the supremacy of the

18

Channel remained for the moment undecided but the schemes of Louis in Ireland had already suffered an irreparable blow.

James had left France early in 1689. "The best thing," said Louis, on wishing him farewell, "that I can wish for you is that I may never see you again." But the principles which were defended by the greatest monarchy of the age were not destined to take root in Ireland. The political and religious controversy which was being fought out in Europe was to be decided in Ireland in a sense hostile to the wishes and ideas of Louis XIV.

The battle of the Boyne took place on July 1st, and proved decisive. James II. returned at once to France, and all chance of using Ireland as a centre for French expeditions against England passed away. Cork and Kinsale instantly capitulated, and thus the whole south coast of Ireland was lost to the Catholic cause. During the short and last struggle of the Irish in the west under Sarsfield, Louis supplied ammunition, provisions, and money, and St. Ruth, a French general, aided by other French officers, endeavoured to unite and organise the Irish resistance. But St. Ruth was killed on July 12, 1691, and though the Irish, led by one of St. Ruth's officers, General D'Urson, at first made a good stand in Limerick, they gradually realised that they could not expect any efficient help from France. The capitulation of Limerick placed Ireland under Protestant ascendancy, and gave Louis valuable reinforcements in the shape of 12,000 Irish soldiers, who were formed into regiments, and well sustained the cause of France in many a battle-field.

After the battle of the Boyne the antagonism between the united and energetic Catholic monarchy presided over by Louis, and the Protestant Germanic kingdoms of which England was the chief, became more distinct and more clearly defined than ever.

It was evident that while on the one hand, in the great European struggle, England held a leading position, on the other, resistance to Louis was not only an English but also a European necessity.[1]

Ireland being no longer a possible theatre of war, the European contest was narrowed to the war on the continent and to a long-continued struggle between the French and English fleets for the supremacy of the sea and more particularly for the command of the Channel. This rivalry between the English and French fleets is the novel feature in what is always regarded as a dreary list of sieges and battles. The success of the French fleet at Beachy Head had roused to a high pitch the English national feeling against France, whose preponderance at sea was at that moment undoubted. In the Parliament of 1691 it was openly stated that England's power rests upon her fleet alone, and efforts were made to strengthen and render the navy thoroughly efficient. The French realised with equal clearness the importance to them of the mastery at sea.

Louis and his ministers saw that the object for which the war was being waged, viz., the retention of the reunited districts, would never be gained by a war conducted on the mainland alone. If Holland and England were boldly attacked by sea and forced to

---

[1] On England's relations with the Continent see Ranke. *History of England principally in the Seventeenth Century.* (Trans.). Vol. v.

come to terms, the Empire would be compelled to agree to make a peace recognising the acquisition by France of the districts given to her for twenty years at the truce of Ratisbon. Chamlay's assertion with reference to England that "the Romans can only be conquered at Rome" found ready acceptance at the French Court. The Dutch fleet had forced the peace of Breda from the English, why should not the French fleet do likewise? The discontent with William's rule was general in 1691. Not only Catholics and High Churchmen but men who had taken a leading part in the Revolution like Marlborough and Russell were intriguing with James II. The Princess Anne had quarrelled with William, and James had gathered round him a large body of supporters, who held constant communication with his supporters in England. Louis himself had caused enquiries to be made as to the true state of political feeling among Englishmen. In December, 1691, he asked James what success was likely to attend an expedition to England; the latter replied full of hope. Louis himself convinced, and counting on the jealousy of the English and Dutch and on the defection of Russell, the admiral of the fleet, decided that England should be invaded in May of the following year. But the English Government were not so unprepared as it was thought, and Russell did not neglect his duty.

On May 19, 1692, the battle of La Hogue destroyed for the time all Louis' hopes of carrying out his policy by forcing England to make peace. But the English supremacy of the sea was by no means assured, though La Hogue is certainly an important epoch in the history of England's navy, and in 1693 Tourville managed to capture sixty-two English merchantmen in spite of the proximity of a division of the English fleet under George Rooke. For upward of a hundred years the French navy was governed by the regulations drawn up by Seignelay while the value of the merchant service in time of war continued from his time to receive numerous illustrations.

Though a serious blow had been inflicted on Louis' hopes and on James' chances of regaining his crown by the battle of La Hogue, neither Louis nor James regarded their chances of success in a future invasion as hopeless. By Louis' advice James—unlike his son in the later times—agreed to accept very stringent conditions from the English royalists as the price of his return. In 1696, perhaps in consequence of the unsatisfactory results of the campaign just ended in the Netherlands, Louis again determined to support an expedition against England. To ensure success it was absolutely necessary that France should be supreme in the Channel if only for two or three days, and it seemed possible that this might be done early in the year. But though Louis was willing to consider a project for landing in England, he insisted that James' adherents in England should seize a harbour and defend it till the arrival of the French fleet. As soon as—and not before—a harbour had been seized the French fleet would sail. But James' supporters refused to move till the arrival of the French fleet, and so the enterprise was wrecked before any attempt had been made to carry it out, through the lukewarmness of James' adherents and the caution if not sagacity of the French king. Later in the year Louis was ready to take advantage of the famous plot to assassinate William though he refused to be in any way connected with it. James II. hastened to Calais where the French fleet lay prepared. The plot was discovered, James returned to Saint-Germain and the French ministers countermanded their preparations.

Thus the attempts of Louis to secure his ends by obtaining the mastery of the sea and by invading England had by 1696 entirely failed. Similarly on the Continent, though his troops had won several battles, there was small hope that Germany would consent to the permanent loss of the reunited districts. The war was waged on an immense scale, and assumed far greater dimensions than had ever been seen before.

Though France had to defend herself by sea and also on the side of the Pyrenees, the principal theatres of the war were Italy, the Rhine, and the Low Countries. The capture of Mainz in 1689 had indicated to the King and to Louvois the serious nature of the struggle which was coming; and the mode of carrying on the land war which was arranged with consummate skill showed a full appreciation of the gravity of the position. "Louis XIV.," says von Ranke, "arranged France as if she had been a huge fortress in the heart of Europe, as a base of operations and a reserve, if the state of affairs made it desirable for him to take the offensive in any direction, and at the same time as a refuge for the defensive, in case the foes she stirred up might either drive her in, or even in their turn invade her."

In Italy Catinat was fairly successful. William III. had hoped to effect a serious diversion by means of Savoy, who bitterly resented the occupation of Pinerolo and Casale by French garrisons. If the Duke joined the Allies, it might be possible to effect the re-establishment of the Piedmontese Waldenses in their native valleys, and their possible employment, together with the Protestants of southern France against Louis. Similar schemes were projected during the Spanish Succession war and by Alberoni during the Regency of Louis XV.

Louis XIV., fully alive to the seriousness of the crisis, at once summoned Victor Amadeus to give up Verona and the citadel of Turin. The Duke immediately allied himself with Austria and Spain, restored the Waldenses to their valleys, welcomed a body of French Huguenots, and determined to regain Pinerolo and Casale.

But in August, 1690, Catinat won a brilliant victory at Staffarda over Victor Amadeus, and Savoy and Nice and the greater part of Piedmont fell into the hands of the French. During the next year, however, in conjunction with an English plan of invading France from the north, a fine army under Victor Amadeus and Prince Eugène invaded Dauphiné and threatened Casale and Pinerolo. The illness of Victor necessitated a retreat, and Catinat defeated the enemy in October, 1693, at Marsaglia and overran all Piedmont.

On the Rhine after the opening campaign in 1689, the war was mainly defensive. The Empire aided by Russia and Poland was still engaged in the Holy war with the Turks, and though the subjugation of Hungary by Austria had deprived Louis of a useful ally, as long as the war continued the Empire could not employ against Louis its full strength. The campaigns on the Rhine, so fully described by Saint-Simon, are most uninteresting. Lorges, who commanded the French troops, was devoid of military ability, and the long encampments, together with the marchings and countermarches varied by a few skirmishes are quite unimportant.

But it was in the Low Countries that Louis took the greatest personal interest, and there the campaigns, if not very interesting, are at any rate of some importance. In July, 1690, Luxemburg had won a victory over the Prince of Waldeck at Fleurus, but this success was not vigorously followed up, and Louis declared he would have no more battles but would act on the defensive and capture towns in the manner of former days. As usual the arrangements made for the army were excellent, and great attention was bestowed on the commissariat. Early in the spring, Mons, a town which in French hands would be of enormous military importance, was besieged. It fell on April 8th. Louis was present at its capture and returned in triumph to Versailles. He had indeed cause for satisfaction. Though his intervention in Ireland had failed, the French power was preponderant on the sea, and seemed likely was gaining ground in the Netherlands.

The League against him had so far shown no signs of extraordinary activity. It was weakened by the Turkish war, by the continued opposition of the Irish and Scottish Jacobites, by the defeat at Staffarda. But the French cause suffered a heavy loss when Louvois died in 1691, for his successor Barbézieux was young and inexperienced. Very characteristically Louis made himself practically War Minister, and took upon his own shoulders the main burden of the struggle against Europe.

In 1692 Louis left Versailles. Early in May he held a great review of his troops, and at the end of the month he appeared before Namur. With Vauban he arranged the plan of attack with the utmost energy and care. " It is," he writes, " the strongest rampart not only of Brabant, but of the Bishoprick of Liège, of the United Provinces, and of a portion of Lower Germany. Besides securing the communications of all these districts, its situation at the confluence of the Sambre and the Meuse makes it mistress of these two rivers ; it is splendidly placed, either to arrest the action of France, or to facilitate the forward movements of her enemies." He had the satisfaction of seeing its capture at the end of June.

Again the French lost a grand opportunity by not following up their success. Just as Luxemburg should have energetically pursued Waldeck's forces after Fleurus, so now had Louis been a real warrior of even the type of Frederick the Great he could have driven William III. into Holland. But, as the Dutch war of 1672 had amply proved, Louis was not

a real soldier. He had no taste for field warfare.
He had taken one of the strongest fortresses in Europe, and he held its capture to be his most brilliant
military exploit. His personal glory was, he considered, much enhanced by the deed, and he returned
in a triumphant manner to Paris.

The next year, 1693, saw the last appearance of
Louis in person with his armies in the field. In June
he had hoped to take Liège and compel the Dutch
to make peace. William III., however, was very
strongly posted, and now as at Bouchain Louis
declined to give battle and returned to Versailles.
Luxemburg might again defeat William III. at Neerwinden, but it was impossible for the French to
break the power of the League. The years 1694
and 1695 are uninteresting in the annals of the war.
Though Noailles invaded Spain with some success
in the former year, and though in 1695 the Rhine
provinces were again ravaged, it was quite useless
for the French to hope to gain their ends. Luxemburg died early in 1695, and in September of the
same year William III. retook Namur. Though
the war languished on all sides, there still seemed no
hope of peace, till the defection of the Duke of·
Savoy, attesting again Louis' diplomatic skill and
the untrustworthiness of Victor Amadeus, brought
to an issue the question of peace or no peace.

At all hazards Louis was determined to break
the unity of the League formed against him. By
promising Victor, Casale, and Pinerolo, and all
Savoy, and by affiancing his daughter to the Duke
of Burgundy, Louis gained over the Duke and

detached him from the cause of the Allies in 1696. This defection of Savoy seriously affected the League. Louis could now throw 30,000 troops into the Netherlands under Catinat, and the war would be indefinitely prolonged. William III. had long desired peace on the basis of the terms of the treaties of Westphalia and of the Pyrenees, but the defection of Savoy seemed to render such an arrangement impossible. No sooner, however, had Louis shown an unexpected readiness to discuss terms of peace, than negotiations began between France and England under the mediation of Sweden. So moderate were Louis' demands, that when the Congress of Ryswick opened in May, 1697, little difficulty was experienced in settling the terms so far as England was concerned when once Louis had agreed to recognise William as King of England. In September, the first of the treaties which formed the peace of Ryswick was signed with England, Holland, and Spain. Louis recognised William as King of Great Britain and Ireland and promised not to abet any plots against him. He ceded all places taken or claimed since 1678, even Luxemburg, the most prized of all his conquests in the late war, and agreed to the garrisoning of certain strong places in the Spanish Netherlands by the Dutch, such as Ypres, Menin, Namur, which now received the name of *the Barrier*. The Dutch, moreover, obtained an advantageous treaty of commerce, and the policy pursued by Colbert toward the United Provinces was entirely reversed. William III. had some difficulty in persuading the Germans to make peace. But at last they consented very reluctantly, and the second treaty was made in October between France and the Emperor and Empire. Louis ceded all places taken since 1678 except Landau and Strasburg, which to the great grief and rage of the Germans he insisted on keeping. He consented to withdraw from the right bank of the Rhine, but though he gave up Philipsburg, Breisach, and Freiburg, he at once ordered Vauban to furnish plans for the buildings and fortifications of a new Breisach on the left bank of the river. Louis further restored Lorraine, which he had occupied for sixty years, to its young Duke, though Saarlouis remained in French hands. An arrangement was come to about Cologne and the Palatinate, Louis accepting a sum of money in lieu of the claims of " Madame " on the latter, and fore-going his support of a candidate to the electorate of the former.

He undoubtedly expected that one result of the pacification of Ryswick would be that many of the German Princes would return to their old connection with France.

This expectation is very noticeable in Louis' instructions to Villars as ambassador at Vienna in 1698. Louis apparently thought that the German Princes would view with distrust if not alarm the increase of the Imperial power, so successful in Hungary and Translyvania and in the war against the Turks. By his conduct between 1678 and 1688, Louis had destroyed the political edifice built by his predecessors. He now hoped in vain to repair the damage which he had done to one of the most valuable of the traditions of French foreign policy. But the clause in the treaty of Ryswick which stipulated that the religion of the provinces restored by Louis should remain as it was at the time of their restitution had exasperated the Protestant party in Germany, and nullified the effects of any fear on their part of the possible absolutism of Leopold.

The peace of Ryswick was but a truce in the great struggle against the preponderance of Louis XIV. On the most pressing question of the day—the Spanish Succession—not a word was said. Thus left unsolved, the Spanish question was bound to appear shortly on the surface and to tax the skill of all European statesmen.

But though Louis' hope of German alliances was not to be fulfilled, and though he had given up Luxemburg and retired from Barcelona, his diplomacy had again stood him in good stead. The great League was broken up and would not easily be reunited. Lorraine, though nominally independent, was within his grasp, and his position on the north-east was still menacing. In spite of William III.'s pledge to the Emperor, he had kept Strasburg and Alsace. Moreover, he had in no way imperilled his claims to the Spanish Succession, and was in a better and stronger position than any other European power to consider that question whenever it became necessary.

CHAPTER XI.

VERSAILLES AND THE PROVINCES.

1678–1700.

ROM the conclusion of the peace of Nimeguen to the opening of the war of the League of Augsburg is rightly regarded as the period when Louis' greatness reached its height. His reign had so far been remarkably successful; his wars had been uniformly brilliant. The territories of France had been considerably augmented and her influence in Europe was predominant. The French language was used in German Courts and each petty German princeling emulated Louis XIV. and built himself a Versailles. "Louis," says Dean Kitchin,* "stood at the topmost pinnacle of his glory; to see

* Kitchin. *History of France*, vol. iii., p. 211.

how far adulation could go, one must turn to Bayle's *Thoughts on the Comet of 1680*, a treatise which for base and shameless flattery stands unrivalled ; or we must read the obsequious historiographer Pellisson, who called his master 'a visible miracle ;' or watch La Feuillade's mad adoration of the statue he had erected to his king on the Place des Victoires at Paris. Thrice he rode round it at the head of his regiment of guards, with all those protestations which in old times the pagans used before the statues of their Emperors. Nor was this merely the extravagance of eccentric courtiers; it entered into all things. The pencil of Lebrun has left on the walls of Versailles the splendid apotheosis of the monarch; his court poets composed hymns in his glory ; it is recorded that Louis even hummed his own praises with tears in his eyes." But Bossuet's adulation of Louis XIV. in 1685, on the occasion of the death of Le Tellier and a few days after the fatal revocation of the Edict of Nantes had been signed, is perhaps unequalled in servility and inaccuracy : "Our fathers never saw, as we have, an inveterate heresy fall at a stroke ; the deluded flocks returning in crowds, and our churches too small to receive them ; their false pastors abandoning them without even waiting to be ordered off, glad to pretend that they were banished ; perfect calmness maintained in the midst of so vast a movement ; the world amazed at perceiving in so novel an event the most decisive as well as the noblest exercise of authority, and the merits of the sovereign more recognised and revered than even his authority. Touched by so many marvels, let our hearts overflow to the piety of Louis. Let us raise our acclamations to the skies—to this new Constantine, this new Theodosius, this new Marcian, this new Charlemagne."

No opposition existed to Louis' rule. The States-General had not been called since 1614, and after the Fronde the *Parlement* of Paris had no power. In 1673, Louis, by his famous edict, had dealt a final blow at its influence by decreeing that henceforth its courts should no longer be called *sovereign*, but only *supreme*, and that no remonstrances could be made until the royal edicts had been registered.

It would seem as if this period in Louis' reign marked the apotheosis of the French nobility. The gilded saloons of Versailles were filled with magnificently dressed nobles, many of whom had performed brilliant feats of arms in the wars and who now crowded to do homage to their great king. But in reality the French nobility were already ruined. Their excessive luxury, their enormous expenses, their enforced absenteeism from their estates aided, and indeed marked, the triumph of the monarchy over the aristocracy. The measures of Louis and Louvois which had destroyed the influence of the nobility in the country and in the army had completed the subservience and practical overthrow of the great baronial class. On Louis' accession the nobles had considerable authority. Richelieu had devoted the years of his ministry to render the nobility submissive to the crown, and to check their almost independent power in the provinces which they governed. His death had given the signal for

VERSAILLES.

(From an Illustration in Philippson's *Das Zeitalter Ludwigs XIV.*)

a last great revolt against the new governmental system, and it was not till the death of Mazarin that the traditions of the great nobles were finally laid by and their place taken by a political theory which till 1789 dominated France. The decline of the independent authority of the nobles was accompanied by an increased desire on their part to secure dignities and privileges. They became over-anxious about questions of rank and precedence. They vied with the King in scrupulousness about points of etiquette. This tendency had been clearly seen during the second Fronde and marked the last struggles of the decaying nobility. But one characteristic which was common to the great French lords at all periods of their history, and which in the end caused their fall was that they never possessed the hearts of the people to any great extent. In spite of isolated instances to the contrary, the French nobles as a class always showed themselves singularly indifferent to the prosperity as well as to the sufferings of the mass of the nation. The establishment of the absolute power of Louis XIV. was in itself a striking proof of the lack of sympathy between noble and peasant. In the seventeenth century the nobles, in consequence of the neglect of their duties towards their dependents, found themselves helpless before the advancing wave of despotism ; in the eighteenth century, from the same cause, they were mere political ciphers when the Revolution came to sweep them away.

Louis attacked the nobles in various ways. He legitimised his illegitimate children, and he largely

increased the number of the offices by holding which
a man could become ennobled. The nobles were no
longer employed in the royal councils; they had
already ceased to have any power in the provinces.
By attracting them to Versailles and by encouraging
them to prefer an idle life dependent on pensions
and privileges to existence at their châteaux in the
country, Louis had finally destroyed their last chance
of ever offering any effective resistance to the growth
of the monarchy.

Independent then of all restraints, free from all
possible opposition, the monarchy had become the
sole authority. The royal power had done great
things for civilization, and the French had come to
expect everything from the monarchy. In France
it was absolute and centralised. Louis' ministers
chosen from the middle-class families were entirely
dependent on himself, and the chief offices were
kept in ministerial families, such as those of Colbert
and Le Tellier. Louis himself remained as indefatigable a worker as ever. In spite of the flattery and
adoration with which he was surrounded his power
of work was still enormous, and what was more important it was regular and continuous. " Nothing,"
he said himself, " is more dangerous than a king who
generally sleeps but wakes up from time to time."
And so though festivities might follow one another
in rapid succession, and though wars might rage,
the work of the governmental machine never ceased,
and Louis, when he was not with the army, never
failed to preside over its multifarious duties. Under him and in close connection with him worked

the four Secretaries of State. The Chancellor and Controller-General were not necessarily Secretaries of State, though sometimes the Controller-General, as in the case of Colbert, was also Secretary of State. The business of the country was transacted as in Spain by means of Councils. But while in Spain the government was hampered by the mutual jealousies and inertness of its members, in France the Councils worked harmoniously and energetically.

The *Conseil d'État* exercised supreme control over all functions of government and was at once executive, legislative, and judicial. It was divided into six subordinate departments or Councils:—The *Conseil du Roi ou d'en haut*, which consisted of three, four, or five members, all of whom were selected by Louis usually from the legal class. Important matters of internal or foreign policy were managed by it alone. Then came the *Conseil des Dépêches*, which dealt with matters relating to the Interior and in which the Royal Councillors and the Secretaries of State met to transact business; the *Conseil des Finances*, which was supposed to supervise the Controller-General who was Minister of Finance, the Interior, Trade, Public Works, and Agriculture; the *Conseil des Parties* or *Conseil privé*, which was a sort of Court of Appeal; the *Conseil de la Guerre;* which had no regular occupation during time of peace; and the *Conseil du Commerce*, which was not definitely organised till 1700. Gradually the Controller-General with his 32 intendants absorbed into his own hands the whole internal administration and managed all affairs in his own house, and after the King's death the growth of this close bureaucracy became an unmitigated evil. During Louis' reign, however, the constant presence of the King formed a connecting link between the four Secretaries of State and gave a unity to the general policy. But before the end of the seventeenth century the evil effects of this exaggerated centralisation had already become obvious to many of the more enlightened intendants.*

Though the system of Louis XIV. did not break down under the enormous weight of business which it had to carry during his reign, he practically dealt a death-blow to the monarchy during these years by the completion of Versailles. Though Louis' taste for building was as expensive as his taste for war, France is greatly indebted to Louis for the marked improvement in Paris during his reign, for the *Hôtel des Invalides,* for the addition to the Louvre, for the broadening of the streets, and for the laying out of parks. The Languedoc canal and many other works carried out by Colbert also testified to the interest of the King in buildings and improvements.

But Versailles ruined the monarchy. The immense works undertaken by Louis and carried out by Levau and Mansard were begun in 1661, but it was not till 1682 that the residence of the Court was definitely fixed there. Louis never cared for Paris, and he wished to punish the city for its conduct during the Fronde troubles. "Paris," says Martin, "l'importune et lui pese ; il sent sa grandeur à l'etroit dans

* On the subject of the Councils see an appendix to A. de Boislisle's edition of the *Memoirs of Saint-Simon.*

cette cité reine qui ne procède pas de lui et qui l'enveloppe dans sa gigantesques bras ; il hait cette puissance populaire qui a humilié son enfrance, et plus d'une fois terrassé ses prédecesseurs."

Colbert again and again had urged Louis to take more interest in the Louvre and to live in Paris. "Pendant que," he said, " que votre majesté a dépensé des très grandes sommes en cette maison, elle a negligé le Louvre, qui est assurément le plus superbe palais qu'il y ait au monde, et le plus digne de la grandeur de votre majesté." But Colbert was not listened to. Louis was resolved not only not to live in Paris but to make himself a dwelling which should be unique. Fontainebleau, Chambord, and Saint-Germain owed their existence to his predecessors. Versailles and its world were to be his own creation. "Louis," says Martin, "a fait ce qu'il voulait ; il a crée autour de lui un petit univers, où il est le seul être nécessaire, et presque le seul être réel." At Versailles all was Louis' work, all was new, symmetrical, and monotonous ; all was vast and wanting in taste ; all was commonplace and dull. Inside the palace Louis was represented by artists in peace and in war ; his triumphs in love and his victories over his foes were equally celebrated ; he was glorified alike for his care for the arts and for his administration of an Empire.

The King intended to impress the popular imagination with the splendour of his Court, to collect and occupy the nobility round himself, and to form a small world complete in itself. The Court became far too large ; Versailles contained, it is said, some 60,000 who were mostly courtiers, and of these the palace itself could house 10,000. Versailles cost the kingdom about £24,000,000, while the loss of life among the soldiers who were employed to construct the aqueduct of Maintenon was frightful. Immense sums were also spent between 1679 and 1690 on the palace of Marly. Louis' habit was to arrive at Marly on Wednesday and leave it on Saturday, spending Sunday at Versailles. Saint-Simon has left imperishable descriptions of the life both at Versailles and at Marly.

When at Versailles the King was wakened by the first *valet de chambre* at eight o'clock, and then began the King's " *Lever* " or " Rising," which was divided into three parts, each of which was appropriated by a particular class of courtiers. With the valet de chambre, the doctor, surgeon, and the King's old nurse as long as she lived, were admitted. At a quarter past eight the Grand Chamberlain, or in his absence the first gentleman of the bed-chamber, and all those who had the privilege of " grand entry " were admitted. As a rule they only remained a few minutes. Then those who had the " second entry " presented themselves, and a few minutes later the crowd which had remained outside were allowed to enter. As soon as the King was dressed he said his prayers by the side of his bed, and then went into his private room where he issued orders for the day. There he was left alone for a time with his children and people such as Mansard with whom he wished to speak on some particular subject. It was at this time that he discussed his building schemes, and his other

LOUIS XIV.'S BEDROOM AT VERSAILLES.

(From an illustration, based on an old print, in Philippson's *Das Zeitalter Ludwigs XIV*.)

designs for beautifying Versailles. Meanwhile all the Court waited in the gallery till the King went to hear mass. On his way to and from the chapel any one who wished could speak to him. After mass a council was held, except on Thursdays which were devoted to audiences, and on Fridays which were given up to the King's confessor. The King dined at one o'clock, and was waited upon by the first gentleman of the bed-chamber or by the Grand Chamberlain if he was at Versailles. All the courtiers were allowed to be present, and after dinner any one of high rank could have an interview with the King at the door of his room or inside the room if the King bade him enter.

Louis loved the open air and usually after dinner he amused himself with hunting stags, shooting, driving, or walking; and each of these amusements had its own regulations and its own etiquette. After taking exercise the King remained upwards of an hour in his own room and then went to see Madame de Maintenon, speaking to any one who wished to do so on the way. At a quarter past ten he had supper with the Princes and Princesses, the courtiers being allowed to stand round. After supper the King usually spent an hour in his room with his children, he sitting in an arm-chair. His retirement to bed was, like the " Rising," conducted with great ceremony and was divided into three parts.

In the evenings the King often played cards, the stakes being at times very high, or listened to music; sometimes he dined with Madame de Maintenon. For the courtiers the principal occupation of the day was to see the King and if possible to speak to him. It is impossible to describe the fatigue, the dulness, and the insipidity of the life at Versailles. The life at Fontainebleau, at the Grand Trianon, and at Marly was, however, in many respects similar to that of Versailles.

Before he created Versailles and Marly Louis had been very much attached to Fontainebleau. There he frequently had musical water-parties in the evenings. It was there that he fell under the influence of Marie Mancini, it was there that he spent his happiest days with Louise de la Valliére, it was there that Madame de Maintenon first appeared at the councils.* Even after the creation of Marly and Versailles, Louis went once a year with all his Court to Fontainebleau. But after the peace of Nimeguen Louis spent most of his time which was not given up to Versailles in visits to the Grand Trianon or to Marly. In 1687 he built the palace of the Grand Trianon. It was there that, according to Saint-Simon, the famous window scene took place between Louis and Louvois. Till 1700 Louis constantly visited the Grand Trianon. It was at the Grand Trianon that on March 18, 1692, a famous " *appartement*," an evening entertainment which began at seven o'clock and ended at ten, was given in honour of the approaching marriage of the Duke of Maine. Though no dancing but only music, and refreshments was allowed these " appartements " were popular, for etiquette was abolished and each one did as he pleased.

---

* For the life at Fontainebleau see Lair, *Louise de la Valliére et la jeunesse de Louis XIV*.

The King as a rule only appeared for a few minutes, and previous to the "appartement" of 1692 had not been present at one for some years. But on this occasion he stayed a long time and presided at one of the supper tables. After 1700 Louis apparently wearied of the Grand Trianon, and till the end of his life devoted all his attention to Marly. There his building schemes were most costly. Between 1679 and 1715 he must have spent nearly 12,000-000 of francs. To Marly, originally created as a resting-place after the fatigues of Versailles, Louis became each year more and more attached, until at last he divided his time between it and Versailles. When the custom arose for the King and Court to go each week to Marly, the great object of every courtier was "être des Marlys," and it was known that the best way to please Louis was to ask for leave to accompany him on his "voyages de Marly." " Cela s'appelait se présenter pour Marly. Les hommes demandaient le même jour le matin, en disant au roi seulement : 'Sire, Marly !' Les dernières anneées le roi s'en importuna. Un garçon bleu écrivait dans la galerie les noms de ceux qui demandaient et qui y allaient se faire inscrire. Pour les dames, elles continuèrent toujours à se présenter."

These exigencies of Court life were intolerable to certain of the Princesses. The young Duchess of Maine absolutely declined to become a slave to the etiquette of Versailles and Marly, and she was rarely present at the official evening parties, or took part in the "voyages en toilette de gala, et le dînettes dans le carosse du roi." Moreover she

avoided moral conversations with Madame de Maintenon, and gave up her devotional exercises. She
was an able woman and determined not only to
amuse herself but to become of importance and
to secure for her husband, the Duke of Maine, a
recognised position. Clagny had been given the
Duke by his mother Madame de Montespan, but
Clagny was too near Versailles, and the Maines lived
at Châteney till 1699, when they bought Sceaux
which Colbert and his son had made one of the most
beautiful and agreeable houses near Paris. There
the Duchess established herself, and though she tried
to while away the time with her laborious amusements she was nevertheless bored to distraction.
She was more successful in her other aims. While
she lived at Sceaux the Duke went frequently
to Versailles. He followed Louis to Trianon, to
Marly, and to Fontainebleau. He always played the
part of the affectionate and respectful son, who full
of admiration of the glorious majesty of the King,
was never so happy as when basking in the royal
presence. He was equally attentive to Madame
de Maintenon, who repaid his attentions by using
her interest with the King on his behalf. And
he succeeded. He gained places for himself and his
children. He was himself legitimised and became
a peer of France. After the death of the Dukes of
Burgundy and Berry, an edict of July 1714, placed
him and his brother the Count of Toulouse in the
succession to the throne. The Duchess of Maine
had indeed triumphed at Sceaux. But she was
building upon sand. No sooner was Louis dead

than Maine became, after a short struggle, *une quantité negligéable*. The Duchess of Orleans was as alive to the dreariness of the Court life as was the Duchess of Maine, but she quietly endured it. The life at Marly was indeed if possible duller than the routine of Versailles. At Marly Madame de Maintenon was the leading figure and Saint-Simon has fully described her life there.

It was during the years following the peace of Nimeguen that Madame de Maintenon's influence became paramount.* This remarkable woman, the most influential woman, it has been said, in French history, had great influence on Louis' character, though probably her influence on French policy has been exaggerated. " Her position," says Madame de Sévigné, "is unique in the world; there never has been nor ever will be again anything like it." The vivacious Charlotte Elizabeth, Duchess of Orleans, who disliked her, and with Saint-Simon regarded her as the evil principle of French politics, expresses the general views as to her influence. " All the ministers," she writes, " have placed themselves under the heel of this woman." † Madame de Maintenon's work in life was, in her own opinion, to convert the King from evil ways. And there is no doubt that she succeeded. Madame de Montespan was given the Château of Clagny, which cost about

---

* The literature on the subject of Madame de Maintenon is enormous. No one who wishes to form a just estimate of her influence should omit to read : *Madame de Maintenon. D'après des Documents Authentiques.* A. Geffroy, 1887.

† In the *Life and Letters of Charlotte Elizabeth, Princess Palatine,* will be found some severe judgments on Madame de Maintenon.

£12,000, and thither she retired. Madamed de Font-
anges was dead, and the life at Court became gradually
more and more decorous if not austere. As regards
her political influence it would seem that whenever she
was asked for advice and gave it she was usually wrong.
She blamed however the devastation of the Palatinate,
and she probably approved of the acceptance of the
Will of Charles II. of Spain. Her partiality for Villeroi and Chamillart, if, as is always alleged, it had
anything to do with their promotion, was decidedly
injurious to the interests of France. She certainly
advised Louis on the death of James II. to acknowledge the Pretender; from 1709 onwards she was in
favour of making peace at any price. But she only
really cared for matters relating to the Church and her
conscience, and it was in religious questions that her influence on the King was most clearly seen. The year
after her marriage saw the foundation of Saint-Cyr for
the education of the poor daughters of the nobility
who had been ruined by the exigencies of the military
service or by other causes. Mansard was the architect,
and the building, which was begun on May 1st, 1685,
and finished in July, 1686, cost about £56,000. On
July 30th, 1683, the Queen had died declaring that
under God she owed it to Madame de Maintenon that
after twenty years of neglect her husband began to
treat her with kindness. Late in the evening of January 12th, 1684, Madame de Maintenon was privately
married to Louis in the chapel of Versailles in the presence of five persons, Père la Chaise who said mass,
Harlay the Archbishop of Paris who gave the benedic-
tion, Louvois, Montchevreuil, who were witnesses,

MADAME DE MAINTENON.

and Bontemps, the King's first *valet de chambre*, who
prepared the altar.

The marriage itself was never openly acknowledged, though in private with the King's family the
position of Madame de Maintenon was fully recognised. She was addressed as "Madame" by members of the Court, who always spoke of her as
Madame the Marquise de Maintenon. She had a
striking and pleasant appearance. "Her voice" it
was said of her at the time of her marriage, "was
most agreeable, and her manner winning, she had a
bright and open forehead, eyes full of fire, and the
carriage of her figure so graceful and supple that it
eclipsed the best at Court. The first impression she
made was imposing, through a veil of severity; but
the cloud vanished when she spoke, and smiled."

Perhaps nothing illustrates better the change that
came over Louis' life in 1683 and the kind of influence which Madame de Maintenon exerted over
him than the history of the foundation of Saint-Cyr.
Louis was in 1684 at the height of his glory. He
had extended the frontiers of France, he had conquered Strasburg and Casale, and had bombarded
Genoa and Algiers. He had taken Luxemburg, and
threatened to annex the Low Countries. He was the
terror of Europe and the admiration of his subjects.
At this culminating point of his career and reign,
Louis decided to change his whole manner of life and
henceforth to lead a sober if not austere existence.
Both Louis and Louvois at first hesitated when the
plan of Saint-Cyr was laid before them. Louvois
hinted that after the long war the treasury was ex-

hausted. "No queen of France," said Louis, "has ever thought of anything like this." But Madame de Maintenon quietly pleaded her cause. She reminded Louis of his resolution to reform and to convert the whole of his kingdom, and pointed out that such a foundation as she desired would contribute directly towards the end that he had in view. Louis was touched by her arguments and granted her request.

No sooner was the scheme decided upon than Louis took the greatest interest in the welfare of the new foundation, and there exist at the present day some notes which he made with his own hand with reference to the character of the establishment of Saint-Cyr. Up to this time Louis had always been opposed to monastic institutions of any kind, and thought it was for the benefit of his kingdom to reduce the number of priests. He now revised carefully the regulations drawn up by Madame de Maintenon and Madame de Brinon (who was to preside over Saint-Cyr), and had several interviews with the latter in his own room at Versailles. The interest which he began to take in Saint-Cyr must have helped to distract his mind from the painful contemplation of the results of the revocation of the Edict of Nantes and may have tended to allay his anxiety with regard to the League of Augsburg.

On September 7, 1686, Louis paid his first visit to Saint-Cyr on the completion of the building. After a solemn service he entered the garden where three hundred demoiselles sang a hymn in his honour, the music being composed by Lulli.

" Grand Dieu, sauvez le Roi !
Grand Dieu, vengez le Roi !
Vive le Roi !

Qu'à jamais glorieux
Louis victorieux
Voye ses enemis
Toujours soumis.

Grand Dieu, sauvez le Roi !
Grand Dieu, vengez le Roi !
Vive le Roi ! " *

At the beginning of 1689 Louis was present at a performance of *Esther*, and was so delighted that he came several times, on each occasion bringing a number of visitors. On the fourth representation a brilliant company was present, including James II., the dethroned King of England. But after a representation of *Athalie* in April, 1691, Madame de Maintenon awoke to the fact carefully impressed upon her by the clergy, that dramatic performances of this sort were not suitable for an institution such as Saint-Cyr. With characteristic energy she revolutionised the whole method of life and instruction in her convent. The writings of Fénélon, who had introduced the new mysticism, were removed, changes were made in the management, and Madame de Maintenon herself began a course of the strictest possible supervision over the lives of the pupils. She hoped indeed with Louis that Saint-Cyr as a school of morals and piety would in time leaven all France. But on behalf of religion Ma-

---

* Th. Lavallée, *Madame de Maintenon et le Maison Royale de Saint-Cyr*, p. 76.

dame de Maintenon was willing that greater works should be undertaken than even the building of Saint-Cyr. She was as anxious as Louis to bring about unity in religious matters, and she always opposed the Protestants, the Molinists, and the Jansenists. Louis regarded the very existence of Protestants in France as a danger to his rule, and he moreover desired to secure for himself the glory of effecting their conversion. Madame de Maintenon asserts that she pleaded in vain with the King for some mitigation of the proceedings; nevertheless, she held that the forced conversion of the Huguenots was incumbent upon a Christian monarch. Her influence was throughout on the side of intolerance. She stirred up and fanned theological hatreds; her religious animosities were most persistent. The banishment of Fénélon was a disgrace to the monarchy, the attacks on the Protestants and the Jansenists were most prejudicial to the nation. She was intimately connected with all these blunders. It was indeed very unlikely that Louis in 1685 of all years would allow himself to be restrained in what he considered to be the final blow to religious independence within France. Ever since 1661 he had shown uneasiness at the presence of the rival authority of the Pope, and several times he had made it clear that he viewed with great dissatisfaction the existence of a power which claimed jurisdiction over his subjects. In the affair of Créqui he had won a victory over the temporal power of the Papacy; in that of the *regale* he attacked the Pope in his spiritual capacity; in 1682 he had successfully asserted his claim to be supreme in the Church as well as in the State.

The *regale* or King's right to receive the revenues of vacant bishoprics and to appoint to all living within the diocese during the vacancy was recognised all over France except in Guienne, Languedoc, Dauphiné, and Province. Louis determined to extend his right over these provinces, and in 1673 and 1675 declarations of his right were published. Nicholas Pavillon, Bishop of Alet, and Caulet, Bishop of Pamiers, who were Jansenists, protested and appealed to the Pope; Innocent XI. took up their cause, and when the two bishops died forbade Louis to put his views into effect in the diocese of Pamiers.

But Louis, rigidly orthodox as he was, breathed defiance at the Pope and called the famous council of 1682 which under the direction of Bossuet laid down four propositions :

(1) That the Pope has no authority over the temporal power.

(2) That the spiritual authority of the Popes should be regulated by General Councils.

(3) That the exercise of Papal authority should be in accordance with the usages of the Gallican Church ; and

(4) Papal decisions in matters of faith are not valid till they have received the consent of the Church.

The clergy and nation supported Louis in this contest from patriotic motives. They regarded the Papacy as a foreign power, and it seemed likely

at one time that Louis would play the part of
Henry VIII. and supported by a coalition of the
bishops of the Court party, like Harlay, with the
bishops who held extreme Gallican views, declared
the national Church independent. Thus did Louis
attempt to establish his supremacy in spiritual,
as he had already done in temporal matters. Innocent XI. refused to accept the decision of the
council and the revocation of the Edict of Nantes
did not mollify him. He supported the League of
Augsburg; he opposed Louis' schemes with regard
to the Archbishopric of Cologne; and he desired
the success of William of Orange. On his death
Madame de Maintenon helped to bring about an
understanding between Louis and Alexander VIII.
Though Madame de Maintenon cannot be described
as the author of the revocation of the Edict of
Nantes she longed for the conversion of all France.
The Court, the clergy, and the *Parlements* were all
eager for the extirpation of heresy. Argument,
bribery, and violence were the three methods employed in turn. " M. Pelisson," wrote Madame de
Maintenon, "works wonders; he may not be so
learned as M. Bossuet, but he is more persuasive."
To reunite the sects of the Catholic Church and to
stamp out the Protestant schism was to her, as it
was to Bossuet, one of the principal aims of her life.
Neither indeed can Louis be severely blamed for
attempting the conversion of the Protestants. " If
Louis XIV. was mistaken in his policy, the mistake
was shared by all his ministers, by all the great men
of his age, and by all the public bodies of his king-

dom. The error was the error of the whole of France." It is impossible to overlook the extreme bitterness with which the French Catholics regarded their Protestant fellow-subjects. When the Chancellor Le Tellier died in 1685, he thought he had seen the accomplishment of his dearest wish—the religious unity of France.

Religious unity, as Louis understood it, was impossible in France, but his improved life only increased his determination to extirpate heresy, and made him more intolerant than ever of any deviation from the beaten track. Hardly had the Huguenots been suppressed when his methodical mind received a severe shock from the appearance in France of the religious system known as Quietism. Harlay, the profligate Archbishop of Paris, took up a very pronounced attitude of hostility towards all who espoused these mystic opinions, and was supported by the King. Bossuet, who had just concluded his controversies with the Protestants, was himself involved in a struggle which resolved itself into a duel between him and Fénélon, the tutor of the Duke of Burgundy, and in 1695 the Archbishop of Cambrai. Fénélon had refused to agree to a formal condemnation of the opinions of Madame Guyon whose writings had attracted considerable attention, and had found himself confronted by Bossuet. The contest between the two was " a spectacle which for three years engrossed the attention of the whole of Europe." During the struggle Fénélon published his *Explication des Maximes des Saints* (1697), a vindication of himself and his opinions which still further exasperated his ene-

mies. But closely connected with the theological
causes of dispute between Bossuet and Fénélon were
probably certain political considerations. Each of
the men may have hoped on the death of Louis to
play the part of a Mazarin or of a Richelieu. Bossuet the tutor of the Dauphin, Fénélon the tutor
of the Duke of Burgundy, had each good reason for
their political ambitions. From 1695 to 1697 the
struggle between these two prelates raged. Bossuet,
a man of action, disliked intensely the views of the
mystics and dreaded the effect of their propagation
in France.

From the first Louis, instigated by Madame de
Maintenon and Bossuet, had determined to crush
Fénélon. Fénélon may or may not have hoped to
become the first minister of the Duke of Burgundy
whenever the latter became king, but it is very
doubtful if Louis' suspicions roused by the *Maximes* were justified. Great pressure was brought to
bear on Innocent XII. and at length Fénélon's views
were condemned at Rome. Innocent had only been
gained with difficulty. The Jesuits at Rome had
defended Fénélon, and it was only when Louis'
complaints and remonstrances grew into menaces
that the Pope yielded so far as to condemn by a
brief of March 12, 1699, twenty-three propositions
taken from the *Maximes des Saints*, without, however, declaring them heretical or sentencing the
book to the flames. This victory was, however,
sufficient for Louis, Fénélon was banished from the
French Court, and Madame de Guyon, whose mysti-
cal writings had been the origin of the whole de-

FÉNELON.

(From an illustration, based on an old print, in Philippson's
Das Zeitalter Ludwigs XIV.)

bate, was with the full approbation of Madame de
Maintenon and Bossuet incarcerated at Vincennes.
" No wrath like a woman's " remarked an Italian
prelate with reference to Madame de Maintenon's
open partisanship.

But while Louis was creating Versailles and
Trianon, Marly and Saint-Cyr, while the laborious
amusements of Sceaux were in full progress, and
while he was at an enormous sacrifice securing an
appearance of religious unity, France was suffering
unspeakable misery. The Dutch war of 1672 was
the first event that upset Colbert's plans and calculations. The necessity of raising money forced him
to adopt measures which he abhorred. Loans, new
taxes, the sale of public offices, were expedients
the disastrous nature of which he was fully aware.
But he had no other course open to him. The
Dutch war cost more than fifty millions of livres,
and the money had to be found. After the Peace of
Nimeguen Louis while proceeding with his *Réunion*
policy never paused in his magnificent works at
Versailles, Trianon, and Marly, though Colbert
urged economy and described the sufferings of the
people. Le Peletier, who succeeded Colbert as Controller-General—and who held that office till 1689,
was a well-meaning man, but he was quite unable to
resist the extravagant tastes of Louis.

In 1684 the weight of the taxes led to riots in the
provinces, which reappeared from time to time
throughout Le Peletier's ministry. The many ex-
emptions from taxation rendered the lot of the
roturier particularly hard and aroused a bitter feel-

ing towards the rich, who not unfrequently paid
little or nothing. Moreover the collection of the
taxes was often accompanied by corruption and
fraud and violence, and many unfortunate men were
thrown into horrible prisons from which they rarely
emerged alive. But the year 1685 was destined to
bring more troubles upon the French nation. As if
existing exactions and the inequalities of taxation
were not sufficient evils, the revocation of the Edict
of Nantes added fresh difficulties. Before the end of
1685 many of the intendants recognised the import
of this blow struck at commerce and industry. But
though Louis was aware of the disastrous effects of
his act he actually contemplated expelling the Jews
from France at this crisis. On May 6, 1688, Le
Peletier wrote to the intendant of the *Generalité*
of Bordeaux : " The King desires you to examine
the design which he has in his mind of expelling
the Jews from the kingdom. But this step should
only be taken after much consideration, lest the interest of commerce which has already been damaged
by the exodus of the Huguenots should fall into
utter ruin."

Fortunately for France this project was never
carried out. But the disasters caused by the revocation did not interrupt Louis' building schemes. In
1688 nine millions of livres had been spent on the
gigantic works for bringing water from the Eure to
Versailles, works which were interrupted by the war
with the League of Augsburg and were never taken in
hand again. It was a very difficult matter to raise
money for this new war. An appeal was made to

the large towns and promises given that no efforts
would be spared to bring about a firm, sure, and
lasting peace.   On this assurance Paris gave 400,000
livres, Toulouse 300,000, and other towns in
somewhat similar proportions.   The provinces were
also called upon to provide additional troops, the
result being that the number of the French troops
was greater than had ever been seen in the service
of a single country.   Moreover some towns received
permission to borrow, others to repudiate their
debts.   Additional offices were created and sold and
the public debt was largely increased.

Le Peletier, not knowing how to raise more
money, pleaded ill-health, retired, and was succeeded
by Pontchartrain, who became Controller-General in
1689.   He simply followed the policy of his predecessor in an aggravated degree.   He was obliged,
says a French historian, to have recourse to " des
expédients mesquins :—Vente des lettres de noblesse,
creation de charges inutiles, enregistrement des
armoires."   No minister ever displayed so much
ingenuity in the creation of new offices, and he bequeathed to France thousands of privileged func-
tionaries—a useless and most pernicious legacy.

The misery of the provinces during all these years
was extreme.   In many parts the peasants were reduced to living on boiled herbs alone ; in 1691 the
Prince of Condé, Governor of Burgundy, wrote to
Pontchartrain that in all the villages which he passed
through in a journey which he had just taken in Burgundy he had not seen a single inhabitant who had
not begged from him.   Want and destitution were

universal and they gained ground steadily. And all
the while the French armies were gaining brilliant
victories at Staffarda, at Fleurus, and Neerwinden.
" The people," wrote Villani, " perished of want to
the sound of the Te Deum."

From the year 1692 the starving population became dangerous. Desperate men demanding bread
infested the country and threatened all who had
property or who were known to have money. The
forests became the hiding-places of bands of armed
and ferocious peasants who issued out only to rob
and to kill. " France," said Fénélon in 1693, " is only
" a large hospital desolate and without food." The
peace of Ryswick checked to some extent the dis-
tress, and France breathed again. But before she
had time to recover her strength she was plunged
into the Spanish Succession war and all the evils of
the previous twenty years reappeared with terrible
force.

But taxation, absenteeism, and centralisation were
not the only evils from which the provinces suffered.
Tenant-right existed over Picardy, the Île de France,
Vermandois, Champagne, and Artois. Towards the
close of the seventeenth century many nobles who
had been ruined by the crushing weight of the
military service, or who had exhausted their finances
at Versailles and had become impoverished, attempted
to raise their rents or to sell their land. Then there
arose bitter opposition from the farmers and though
the government sided with the provincial and impoverished nobles, legislation failed to stamp out
tenant-right. In 1679 and in 1707 and again in 1714

royal edicts, such as only a despotic government
could enforce, and increasing on each occasion in
severity, attempted to deal with this new difficulty.
But though the landlords were backed up by all the
weapons of the government of the *Grand Siècle*,
they failed to assert their so-called rights against the
stern resistance of the farmer and peasant.

The contrast between the life at Versailles and the
life in the provinces during these years is striking.
Still more striking was the continued devotion of the
French people to the King. In their misery the mass
of the French lower orders accused the ministers and
their agents of being responsible for their calamities,
The towns when making grants for the war expenses
were moved as much by patriotism as by fear. Even
while a foreign war was eating away all their resources the inhabitants of a town would willingly
and joyfully raise statues and various monuments in
honour of Louis XIV. and his victories.

In 1685 statues were erected in almost every part of
the kingdom. In 1689, Marseilles put up one of Louis
on horseback ; in 1691 Tours erected to the glory of
Louis a triumphal arch ; and in 1692 the town of
Issoire in Auvergne employed the sculptor James
Suirot to erect a statue of the King. Undoubtedly
there existed throughout France, at any rate down
to the Spanish Succession war, a widespread admiration for and appreciation of the grandeur of Louis'
reign. In 1699, the Moorish envoy, gazing at the
Seine from a window in the Louvre, only expressed
the general feeling when he declared that if those
waters were ink they would not suffice to describe

adequately the grandeur and magnificence of Louis XIV.

The French people had desired military glory, and Louis' reign since Mazarin's death had indeed been glorious. The King had not only satisfied all the aspirations of his subjects; he had gained for his country in Europe a well earned prestige which it never entirely lost.

CHAPTER XII.

THE SPANISH SUCCESSION QUESTION.

1697–1700.

THERE are many problems in Louis' long reign which still await solution. Opinions are even now at variance as to the real motives which prompted the King in the full tide of victory to consent in 1668 to the treaty of Aix-la-Chapelle. Till quite lately opinions have been equally divided as to Louis' reasons for making the peace of Ryswick. He knew there was a strong party both in Holland and England in favour of peace, and that it was well-nigh impossible for William III., in the teeth of a bitter opposition, to carry on war much longer. He was fully aware that the Duke of Bavaria was dissatisfied with his alliance with the Emperor. He

315

had just detached the Duke of Savoy from the
Coalition and he could now in consequence expect
fresh and startling successes on the north-east frontier. Spain was not in a condition to defend the
Netherlands, and could not even ward off attacks on
her northern frontier. During the war France had
demonstrated to Europe her enormous strength.
Such immense armies had never before been seen in
Europe: William III. himself declared that the
army with which Condé won Senef would in this last
war have been a mere division. The armies of
France were the best in Europe.

Being in such a comparatively strong position it is
somewhat surprising that Louis should not only have
made peace, but should have given the allies such
advantageous terms. As it stands, the treaty of
Ryswick seemed a decided blow to the pretensions
of France. Her influence in Poland had just received
a check in the election to that throne of Augustus of
Saxony and the defeat of the candidature of Condé.
She had already retired from that commanding position in Italy which she owed to the genius and determination of Richelieu. She had abrogated the
four articles of 1682, had made her peace with Rome,
and had restored Avignon. But the peace of Ryswick
still further curtailed her powers and lessened her
prestige. By it she withdrew from her claim to convert the truce of Ratisbon into a definite peace and
so to annex to France the " reunited " districts.

Moreover, the policy with which Louis had set
out in 1661 had not been carried out. Though
France was the first power in Europe on land, she

had failed to secure the command of the sea, and the Mediterranean had not been turned into a French lake. Though Vauban had fortified her north-east frontier, she had not as yet annexed the Spanish Netherlands and she had been forced to withdraw from the Rhine frontier. Any hope Louis may have had of securing the Imperial dignity for himself or for the Dauphin had by the end of the century completely disappeared.

Under these circumstances it has puzzled historians to explain Louis' consent to the peace of Ryswick, and the moderation of his tone just when it seemed that by the continuance of the struggle for a year or two he might have secured far more favourable terms. Even in the harangue pronounced on February 16, 1699 at Versailles, by Ben Aïcha, the envoy of Muley Ismael, Emperor of Morocco, allusion was made to Louis' unheard of moderation in sacrificing his own gains to the glory of giving peace to so many vanquished nations.

The general conclusion now arrived at is that just as Louis in 1668 consented to a treaty in the expectation of gaining the whole of the Spanish Netherlands on the death of Charles II. of Spain, which he regarded as imminent, so in 1697 he again consented to make peace in order to have his hands free when the death of Charles II. should take place. That event could not be postponed much longer, and when it should occur Louis was certain to secure a great addition of territory and power. As long as war continued there was always the possibility that in accordance with the wish of the Dutch and English, the Archduke Charles would occupy Catalonia, then full of German troops.

As the Archduke was a candidate for the throne of Spain, it would obviously be most disastrous to French interests were he in Spain when Charles II. died. In the face of so much jealousy of France in Europe, it was of vital importance to Louis that no armed coalition should be in existence when the death of the king of Spain took place ; it was equally important he should have leisure to arrange his plans.

Louis' diplomacy and knowledge of foreign politics and the inner history of foreign courts was always remarkable. But while the Spanish Succession war affords ample illustrations of his well-reasoned policy, the history of the period between the conclusion of the peace of Ryswick and the acceptance of the Will enables us best to appreciate the very unusual sagacity shown by him in his choice of instruments, his close knowledge and clear views of the questions at issue, and the ability with which he kept the main object of his policy in view.

Never was a diplomatic game played with more consummate skill, and, as it turned out, with more success. Louis' previous relations with Spain had not been such as would inspire any confidence that the Spaniards would easily recognise in him a friend and an upholder of their interests. He had injured them in the Devolution war, and his success against the Dutch in the next war would have been followed by the annexation of the Spanish Netherlands. At Nimèguen Spain was again the principal sufferer.

During the war, however, a revolution had taken place at Madrid. The Queen Regent, who was a sister of the Emperor Leopold, was in 1676 overthrown by the nobles and Don John, a natural son of Philip IV., was received at Madrid with enthusiasm. He was a great admirer of Louis XIV., and as soon as the peace of Nimeguen was made, he hastened to propose to Louis that Charles II. should marry Louise of Orleans, one of the royal nieces. The marriage was at first popular in Spain, and Louis hoped, if Louise had no children, to get, through her influence, the right of the Dauphin to the Spanish Succession recognised. In any case he trusted to form a party in Spain capable of sustaining his pretensions. Unfortunately, in September, 1679, Don John died before Louise even arrived. Another revolution took place, and the Queen-Mother's anti-French influence was again paramount. Louis did not despair, and succeeded in forming the nucleus of a French party in Spain, which survived the war of the League of Augsburg, and reappeared after the conclusion of the peace of Ryswick ready to support the French cause. In order to increase and strengthen this party, and to provide for all contingencies, Louis determined to send Harcourt to Madrid. His arrival there in February, 1698, constitutes an epoch in French, if not in European, history. For it was mainly due to Harcourt's skill that the Spaniards gradually contracted so great a hatred of the Austrians, that in 1700 it seemed quite natural that the Spanish Empire should be left to Louis' grandson, and that Louis should accept the Will.

In his labours Harcourt was aided by the acute difference existing between the views of Europe and those of every Spaniard, whose one object was to prevent any partition.

The decline of Spain rendering the development of France possible was so obvious, and the Spanish Empire was so enormous, including the Spanish Netherlands, Sicily, Naples, the Tuscan Ports, Milan, and the dominions in the New World, that Europe was interested in the Succession question and meant to have a voice in the disposal of such vast and disconnected territories.

Two attempts had already been made to settle the future government of the Spanish Empire. In 1668, by the Partition treaty between France and Austria, it was settled that on Charles II.'s death Louis should take Franche-Comté, the whole of Belgium or the Spanish Netherlands, and certain territories in the north of Spain, while the Emperor Leopold was to take Spain and most of her foreign possessions. In 1689 again, William III., filled with an exaggerated fear of Louis XIV.'s schemes, guaranteed to the Emperor Leopold the entire Spanish Succession—an arrangement marked by about the same amount of wisdom as was the determination of the Whigs after the death of the Emperor Joseph I. to reconstruct the empire of Charles V. for the benefit of Charles VI.

But at the time of the peace of Ryswick neither of the above arrangements held good, and Europe prepared to consider the whole subject *de novo*. Of the three candidates for the Spanish Succession the Dauphin had a good claim if the renunciations of his mother and grandmother were invalid. Louis claimed the Spanish heritage for the Dauphin as the son of Maria Theresa, the eldest daughter of Philip IV., and insisted that the renunciations of Maria Theresa were invalid on the following grounds. In the first place one of the clauses of the marriage contract stated that the renunciation was worthless unless the dowry of Maria Theresa was paid at the time agreed. This dowry had never been paid. Secondly, Louis urged that neither the Cortes nor the *Parlement* of Paris had ever ratified the renunciation, that Maria Theresa being a minor had no power to deprive herself of her rights, and further that it was desirable in the interests of Spain that a prince should succeed capable of maintaining the unity of the Spanish Empire. With his large army, his powerful fleet, his excellent generals and clever diplomatists, it seemed that Louis' arguments had a greater chance of success than the claim of the Emperor Leopold.

Leopold claimed by reason of the right (1) of his mother who was a sister of Philip IV., and (2) of his first wife Margeret Theresa, a younger daughter of Philip IV. Neither his mother nor wife had ever signed a renunciation. As his daughter Maria, married to the Elector of Bavaria, had renounced her claims, Leopold regarded his position as unassailable, and was willing to give Spain to his son by a second marriage, the Archduke Charles. The Court of Spain had regarded his candidature with satisfaction. For many years the two branches of the House of

Hapsburg had been closely connected, and the feeling in Spain was in favour of the House of Austria, especially since France was regarded as the natural enemy of Spain.

The third candidate was the son of the Elector of Bavaria, the Electoral Prince. And till his death he was the favourite candidate. His claims were probably best from a legal point of view, and Charles II. had rightly refused to recognise as valid the renunciations which Leopold had extorted from his daughter, the mother of the Electoral Prince. And moreover the succession of the Electoral Prince would not disturb the "balance of power" so dear to all European statesmen. As King of Spain he would not endanger the tranquillity or the independence of the rest of Europe. But the Emperor refused to regard the Electoral Prince as a formidable candidate. He caused a will made by Charles II. in his favour, to be annulled, and pressed forward the claims of his son the Archduke Charles.

The question was obviously in all its aspects so thorny, and so likely to lead to a European war that shortly after the peace of Ryswick negotiations were opened between France, England, and Holland to effect by means of a partition an amicable arrangement of the difficult question. The relations between England and France after the treaty of Ryswick had remained very unsettled. Though Louis had recognised William as King he had not recognised the succession. James II. still lived at Saint-Germain, and Louis declared to Portland, the English envoy, that he had no intention of removing

GENEALOGICAL TABLE OF THE CLAIMANTS OF THE CROWN OF SPAIN, 1698–1700.

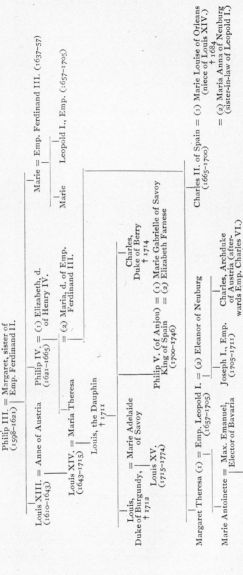

him. But having once declared his views on the question of the expulsion of the Stuarts, Louis became most gracious and made friendly overtures to William. In April, 1698, Tallard was sent to London, negotiations were opened, and Louis told Portland at a hunting party how pleased he was at the overtures made by William. In his extreme anxiety to secure the Spanish kingdom for his grandson, Philip, Duke of Anjou, Louis was quite willing to provide against the possible union of the French and Spanish crowns in the future, and it was only after long and obstinate negotiations that he agreed to the substitution of the Electoral Prince for one of his grandsons. By the First Partition treaty (October 11, 1698), the Electoral Prince was to have Spain, the Spanish Netherlands, and the Spanish possessions in the New World, the Archduke Charles received Milan, and the Duke of Anjou the two Sicilies, the Tuscan Ports (Porto Ercole, Porto San Stephano, Orbitello, Piombino, Telamone, Porto Longone in Elba), Finale, and Guipuscoa.

The news of the treaty, as had been expected, filled the Spaniards with rage. Charles II. made a will leaving all the Spanish possessions to the Electoral Prince, and the Spanish patriotic party were satisfied. William III. and Heinsius were equally pleased, for the Electoral Prince, with no navy, could not endanger the commerce of England and Holland. Both the Emperor and Louis were discontented, but the latter agreed with William that the treaty was to be carried out. In January, 1699, the Electoral Prince died. Louis heard of the death of

the Prince at midday on the 8th of February. In
the evening he spoke a good deal about it and
sympathised with his father the Elector. He had
already, however, with his accustomed energy, dictated two despatches, one for Harcourt, and one for
Tallard ordering him to sound William as to a new
treaty. On the 13th he drew up a most elaborate
scheme for a fresh partition of the Spanish Empire
and sent it to Tallard, and again on the 23rd he wrote
another long letter to his envoy on the same subject.
It was evident from the first that grave difficulties
had arisen in arranging a fresh Partition treaty.

Louis' despatch of the 13th is a masterpiece for
lucidity and ability. The death of one of the claimants left the Spanish Empire to be divided between
the remaining two. " I know," he writes, " how
alarmed Europe would be to see my power raised to
a greater height than that of Austria." With this
recognition of the worship of the idea of the balance
of power, he proceeds : " But the Emperor's power is
also so greatly increased by the submission of the
princes of the Empire and by the advantageous
peace which he has just concluded with the Porte
(Treaty of Carlowitz), that it is in the general interest,
if he becomes stronger, that my power also should
be sufficient to counterbalance that of the Emperor."
Louis then pointed out that he would propose to
add Milan to the share allotted to the Dauphin by
the First Partition treaty, and that the Archduke
should have Spain, the Indies, the African possessions, the islands of Sardinia, Majorca, Minorca,
Ivica, and the Philippines.

WILLIAM III. OF ENGLAND.
(From an old print, and reproduced in Philippson's
Das Zeitalter Ludwigs XIV.)

Should the Archduke receive such a share, it is of vital importance that Milan should not be in Hapsburg hands. The Milanese serve as an easy communication between the two branches of the House of Austria, and in Hapsburg hands would go far to raise the power of that house to the prejudice of the interests of the rest of Europe.

" I foresee," he continued, " great difficulties in the way of obtaining the consent of the King of England to the addition of the Milanese to my son's portion. Should you see that it is impossible to overcome the objections raised, you can make a suggestion for bringing to a satisfactory conclusion this important matter."

The suggestion was nothing less than that Lorraine should be united to France in exchange for the Milanese, which was to be handed over to the Duke. A new power would thus be formed in Italy, and France would have added little to her strength, for, as Louis truly said, Lorraine was so surrounded by French possessions that it was practically already in the power of the French monarchy.

But his next suggestion shows how strongly his mind was set on making France invulnerable. " I would promise," he said, " to give to the Duke of Savoy the kingdoms of Naples and Sicily ; he could also have the Tuscan ports and Finale on condition that he ceded to me the Duchy of Savoy, the principality of Piedmont, and the county of Nice, and his possessions in Montferrat ; which last I would hand over to the Duke of Milan."

Another scheme which he hinted at was to give

the Duke of Savoy the portion allotted above to the
Archduke, to hand over to the latter the kingdoms
of Naples and Sicily, to place the Duke of Lorraine
in Milan with Savoy's possessions of Montferrat, and
to leave in the hands of France the remainder of the
estate of Savoy with Lorraine and Guipuscoa.

One important question was left to the end of the
despatch—that of the Spanish Netherlands. And
with regard to this debateable land, Louis showed
considerable knowledge of the feelings of Europe.
" The King of England and the States-General," he
said, " would be equally irritated at seeing them in
my hands, or in those of the Emperor."

In dealing with this delicate question Louis fore-
bore to make any definite proposal, but threw out
four alternatives which Tallard might lay before
William.

The first suggestion was to form the Low Countries into a republic which should be closely united
by treaty with Holland, while the second was to
hand them over to the queen of Spain after the death
of Charles II. The third project would be, Louis
thought, not acceptable to the taste of William. It
consisted in renewing the treaty made in 1635 by
Louis XIII. with the States-General, for the partition of the Low Countries between France and
Holland. The fourth suggestion—and this was the
one perhaps the most popular with Louis—was to
give the provinces as an independent sovereignty to
the Elector of Bavaria.

But great difficulties were at once experienced.
The pretensions of the French had increased ; and

the proposal that the Spanish Netherlands should be made into a separate principality and given to Bavaria was not well received by William. Louis had in fact proposed that France should be rounded off by securing Lorraine, Savoy, and Nice, and that she should gain a predominant influence in the Netherlands. The maritime powers at once refused to consider the possibility of the formation of the Spanish Netherlands into an independent state, though they were not opposed to the transfer of Lorraine to France. The Court of Vienna was strongly opposed to the suggested arrangements. The Austrians were looking to the establishment of their power in Italy, and had already in their own minds anticipated the settlement effected at Utrecht.

These lengthy negotiations occupied Louis' full attention. He examined article by article the propositions made by the English. With keen foresight he pointed out the dangers attendant on the Spanish throne being given to the Archduke. "The Spaniards are," he rightly declared, "jealous of any attempt to dismember their empire, which they wish to preserve entire. I shall be obliged to take up arms and conquer that portion of the Spanish dominions assigned to my son." No detail escaped his vigilant eye, and he prepared for all eventualities. After four months of incessant labour Louis agreed to the terms of the Second Partition treaty. But the effects of the death of the Electoral Prince were never entirely removed, and it was only after great difficulty that Holland was induced to agree to the treaty, Louis and William were building upon sand.

The Emperor would not accept the treaty, and in England its unpopularity was universal.

It was not till May, 1700, that the Second Partition treaty was finally ratified. By it the Duke of Anjou secured the Two Sicilies, the Tuscan ports, Guipuscoa, and the Milanese, but the latter was to be exchanged for Lorraine. The Archduke Charles was to receive Spain, the Spanish Netherlands, and the Spanish possessions in America. The news of the Second Partition enraged the Spaniards beyond all bounds. The Queen broke all the furniture in her room, and Charles II. was equally angry. England and Holland were regarded as the originators of the treaty, and Charles, alarmed at the idea of the influence of Protestant powers being felt possibly in his American possessions, and completely influenced by the French faction supported by Portocarrero, was gradually persuaded to forego his natural inclination to leave his dominions to the Austrian House. Innocent XII. advocated the continuance of the union of all the Spanish dominions, and it was held in Madrid that a descendant of the great representative of Catholicism in Europe would be the best sovereign for Spain.

On October 7th Charles signed a will leaving his dominions to the Duke of Anjou and his successors; failing them, to the Duke of Berry. On November 1st he died, and thus terminated one of the most melancholy existences recorded in history.*

---

* A full account of the diplomacy bearing on the Partition treaties will be found in A. Legrelle's *La Diplomatie Française et la Succession d'Espagne.*

Louis' motives in agreeing to these treaties are hard to follow, and have given rise to much controversy. He knew that the question of the succession was still a very open one, and that his supporters in Spain could not be depended upon. And he may have thought that at any rate he had secured substantial gains. Had the terms of either Partition treaty been carried out, the Mediterranean would in all probability have become a French lake, and it was the appreciation of the damage which such a state of things would bring to English trade that caused so much opposition to the treaties in England. Though apprehensions with regard to the balance of power in the Mediterranean were as yet somewhat inarticulate, English merchants were fully alive to the importance of their interests in the Levant and generally to the value of their ever extending intercourse with the Mediterranean countries. Though the causes which have made England a Mediterranean power have been at work for centuries, the Spanish Succession war proved an important epoch in the history of the English influence and of the European equilibrium in the Mediterranean. Louis was himself fully alive to the importance of securing French influence over at any rate the western basin of the Mediterranean. But in his correspondence he explained his agreement with the partition schemes on general grounds. In writing to Tallard he declared that he had consented to the First Partition treaty in order to ensure the peace of Europe. " After I have sacrificed so much to give my subjects repose," he wrote, " no interest is more important than to preserve the tranquillity which they now enjoy." He was no doubt anxious for a permanent peace, but he only relinquished his grandson's claim to Spain with regret. " I can," he wrote to Tallard, "enforce my grandson's rights, but my desire for tranquillity leads me to make terms with England."

At the same time it must be remembered that though he sent Tallard to arrange about a subdivisión of the spoil, Louis was well aware of the effect which would be produced upon the minds of the Spaniards when once they heard of a Partition treaty. Historians have therefore been inclined to believe that " the Partition Scheme was a blind," and that both " Partition treaties were in fact part of a game played skilfully by the French King to quiet and delude England and Holland, to paralyse the Emperor, and to incline the Spaniards through fear towards the French interests." It is difficult, however, to suppose that all Louis' voluminous correspondence was dishonest, and that he was playing false during the three years following the treaty of Ryswick. He had most solemnly protested over and over again that he would keep the conditions of the treaty of Partition. Early in 1700, the Emperor had agreed to the Second Partition treaty, the Archduke might have entered Spain as its future sovereign, and if he had done so the war of the Spanish Succession would never have taken place. Harcourt, convinced that a Bourbon prince had no chance of becoming king of Spain, had left Madrid in May. And as late as June of the same year

Louis informed William that the Spanish Council were strongly disposed in favour of the succession going to his grandson, but he asserted : " Neither the offer of the Emperor, nor other offers still more advantageous, will ever lead me to violate the engagements which I have taken."

Twelve days before Charles' death Louis ordered Tallard to insist that England and Holland should hasten their military preparations so that the treaty of Partition could be carried out. " I cannot believe," he wrote, " that they [England and Holland] will fail in executing agreements so formal and so precise, when the time shall arrive to carry them out."

Such words make it wellnigh incredible that Louis should have again and again urged Tallard to hasten the military preparations of England and Holland if he had seriously contemplated taking a step which would bring him into immediate collision with both those powers.

He had been for some time busy trying to modify the terms of the treaty so that France should obtain Savoy and Piedmont in place of Naples and Sicily, which were to form a kingdom for Victor Amadeus, and up to the death of Charles II. he was negotiating on this subject. There seems then little ground for ascribing to Louis a policy of diabolical ingenuity which would have justified the popular opinion of him held in England. Until the death of Charles Louis acted towards the maritime powers in perfect good faith, and fully intended to carry out the partition.

On November 1st Charles II. of Spain died, leaving the Spanish Empire to the Duke of Anjou.

CHAPTER XIII.

THE SPANISH SUCCESSION WAR.

1702–1713.

HE most momentous question of Louis' reign now awaited decision. Should he accept the Will of Charles II.? There is no reason for thinking that Louis' hesitation was assumed. While on the one hand he saw that the acceptance of the Will would bring to the House of Bourbon a dominion rivalling that of Charles V., on the other it was patent that Europe would not stand by and quietly acquiesce in a political revolution which would gravely affect the equilibrium of the European states-system. Advancing years too no doubt contributed to Louis' hesitation. He was no longer served by the Lionnes, the Colberts, and the Louvois of his more prosperous

CAROLUS II D.G. HISPANIARUM, ET INDIARUM REX CATHOLICUS.

CHARLES II. OF SPAIN.

(From an illustration, based on an old print, in Erdmannsdörfer's
Deutsche Geschichte von 1648–1740.)

days. While his own views had begun to lack firmness and clearness, his councillors themselves showed that they were incapable of executing a policy which would have tried the capacities of Louis' most able ministers.

The acceptance of the Will too meant a very considerable change in his foreign policy. France would have to forego the gradual annexation of the Spanish Netherlands and the extension of her influence in Italy,—a policy which had hitherto been carefully adhered to. Louis' intention of establishing a great French Empire dominating Europe would also have to be modified.

The study of the two weeks succeeding the death of Charles II. is of the deepest psychological interest. Some light is thrown upon the considerations which weighed most with Louis by closely following the historical sequence of events. Tallard had arrived at Fontainebleau on November 2d, and had already heard of the arrival of couriers from Spain bringing news of the Will of Charles II., and of the formation of a strong party at Court in favour of the acceptance of the Will. He had an audience of the King at which Madame de Maintenon and Torcy were present. Tallard expressed himself in favour of adhering to the Partition treaty,* and painted in strong colours the European opposition which would be aroused if Louis accepted the Will. Torcy, Tallard declares, supported him to such an extent that on the next day, the 4th, Louis wrote

---

* All allusions to the Partition treaty refer of course to the Second Partition treaty.

to Briord, the French ambassador in Holland, ordering him to tell Heinsius that he would keep to the
treaty of Partition.

On November 9th the news of the death of Charles
II. reached Barbézieux at Fontainebleau, and he had
the honour of informing Louis of the fact. The
King at once put off his hunting expedition, and
issued orders that during the winter no comedies or
festivities should take place. An opportunity was
thus suddenly offered him of carrying out one of his
most cherished hopes, one of his most important
political ideas. An enormous increase of the power
of his country and of his own prestige would result
from the union of the two countries under Bourbon
rulers. And not only would the dynastic interests
of his house be served ; the interests of religion
would also be advanced. The prospect was opened
before him of placing the destinies of a great empire
under his own most Christian influence. His engagements with England and Holland caused a natural
hesitation, and it was only after a sharp struggle with
himself that he decided in favour of the Will.

His hesitation was reflected in the attitude of his
leading advisers. To a solemn council summoned
on the 10th of November to discuss the Will of
Charles, only three ministers were bidden, Torcy,
Pontchartrain, and Beauvilliers, his habitual councillors.

The Chancellor Pontchartrain had no decided
opinion. He contented himself with weighing the
pros and the cons, and to the end refused to make any
decision. He occupied a middle position between

Beauvilliers, the President of the Council of France, and Torcy, the Minister of Foreign Affairs. The former held that Louis should adhere to the plan of Partition, that the acceptance of the Will would be followed by war, and that war would cause the ruin of France ; the latter, on the contrary, strongly urged the immediate acceptance of the Will. To him the accession of the Duke of Anjou to the crown of Spain was of the utmost importance to French interests. He had no doubts, no misgivings, and in the coming years devoted much time and energy to the cause of Philip V.

What advice Louis received from Madame de Maintenon is not known. She and the Dauphin were present at this memorable council, but she said nothing during its session, and never seems, at any rate publicly, to have expressed a decided opinion. Monseigneur on the other hand was from the first openly and strongly in favour of the acceptance of the Will.

It is not surprising that when face to face with one of the most difficult of modern problems, Louis' advisers should have shown great perplexity. The crisis was short but acute, and the pressure of external circumstances proved too strong for the King. Pressing appeals came from Spain, strong representations from his own Court ; while neither Portugal nor Savoy liked the arrangements made by the treaty of Partition. The affairs in the Peninsula required a prompt and decisive reply. It would seem that Louis' mind was made up on Thursday, November 11th, though the Court did not know in which direction. The courtiers only realised that the period of uncertainty had passed away. On Friday, the 12th, a despatch, couched in dignified terms, was sent through Blécourt to the Queen of Spain at Madrid, conveying Louis' acceptance of the Will. At the same time a long memoir was sent to William III., containing a full description of the cruel dilemma in which, owing to the patriotism of the Spaniards, he had been placed, and the reasons which had induced him to throw over the treaty and accept the Will. In this memoir, which is of peculiar interest, Louis begins by pointing out that up to the death of Charles neither he nor his ministers paid any attention to the general wish of the Spanish nation to place a French prince on their throne : " Cette inclination générale des peuples que leur véritable intérêt leur inspirait n'a point été cultivée par les ministres de sa majesté." He then adduces the reasons which have brought about his decision to accept the Will. In the first place the wishes of Charles II., if carried out, would entirely prevent the union of France and Spain, and so the jealousy of European powers on that score need not be feared. Secondly, the great object of the Partition treaty was to secure the peace of Europe by obtaining the consent of the Emperor to the arrangements made by it. This consent had not been obtained, and consequently war was certain, even if the Partition scheme was carried out. The Archduke on the Spanish throne will naturally oppose any partition of his dominions, and it will be necessary to enforce the execution of the treaty by dint of arms. A long war will ensue, and such a war is

contrary to the spirit of the Partition treaty. Then
Louis pointed out, thirdly, that the acceptance of the
Will was by far the lesser of two evils. France and
Spain will remain separate, as they always have been.
France will not secure any territory on the Spanish
frontier, she will not receive Lorraine nor the kingdoms of Naples and Sicily. Thus France will literally be far weaker than if the Partition treaty was
executed.

The Spanish ambassador was told of Louis' decision the same day, though the secret was kept till
the following week. On Saturday, the 13th, after
supper in his own room, Louis playfully asked
"Madame" and the Princess of Conti what they
thought of the Spanish difficulty. Both said that
they would send the Duke of Anjou to Spain. " I
am sure," replied Louis, "that whatever I do will be
blamed by a good many people." On the following
Monday, November 15th, Louis and the Court proceeded from Fontainebleau to Versailles, arriving
there at four o'clock. He had arranged to make a
public declaration of his policy the following morning. On Tuesday, November 16, 1700, Louis
therefore introduced his grandson to the Court as
Philip V. of Spain. Saint-Simon's description of
this impressive scene is well known. After Louis
had received a visit from Castel dos Rios, the Spanish ambassador, and had told him that he could salute
the Duke of Anjou, who was present, as King of
Spain, he ordered the folding doors of his room to
be thrown open, and directed that all should enter.
After having gazed majestically on the crowd of

courtiers before him, Louis said, pointing to the Duke of Anjou: "Gentlemen, there is the King of Spain. The Spanish crown is his by the right of birth, by the Will of the late King, and by the unanimous wish of the entire nation. This is the will of God, and I yield to it with pleasure." Then turning to Anjou, he continued: "Be a good Spaniard, it is now your first duty, but remember that you were born a Frenchman, and preserve the union of the two nations; by this means you will render both happy and will give Europe peace." Then Castel dos Rios approached with his son and exclaimed: "Quelle joie! Il n'y a plus de Pyrénées; elles sont abîmées, et nous ne sommes plus qu'un." After Louis had given an audience to Sinzendorf, he proceeded to the Chapel, the Duke of Anjou walking on his right hand.

It is of little avail to attempt to justify the cancelling of solemn engagements, or to endeavour to explain away obvious facts. But there is still less reason for ascribing to Louis any peculiar malignity in thus disregarding his previous engagements. He simply acted in strict accordance with the political morality of the age. Treaties were in both the XVIIth and XVIIIth centuries viewed with remarkable indifference, and many instances might be cited to show that France had not the monopoly of bad faith at that period. Nay, more, it may be urged that Louis' action was beneficial to Spain and Europe generally. Under the Archduke's rule it is certain that though the downward career of Spain might have been checked, that remarkable recovery which she owed to the invigorating, revivifying, Bourbon initiative would never have taken place. She would have remained waterlogged under a dull Hapsburg régime. And Europe would not have gained any advantage. The increased Hapsburg influence in Europe would have been disastrous to the growth of civilisation, and the balance of power would not have been placed on any more satisfactory basis. Louis' decision was undoubtedly beneficial to Christendom, and the war that followed was not due to that decision, but to an extraordinary misapprehension on his own part and on that of his advisers of the real current of European opinion.

The accession of the Archduke to the Spanish throne would have been followed by the revival of an empire on the model of that of Charles V. This result could not have been foreseen at the time, but in those days of sudden deaths it was in 1700 not at all improbable.

To avert such a possibility, to prevent the return of the days of Francis I. and Charles V., any means might be considered by a Bourbon king as justifiable.

To Louis it seemed that no matter what decision he might come to, a European war was absolutely certain. The maritime powers had no love for him, Europe was sluggish and inert. Supposing he clung to the Partition treaty, was it likely that the contracting powers would support him in carrying it out? Would England or Holland deliberately take up arms in order to rob the Emperor or Spain of the kingdom of the Two Sicilies, the Tuscan Ports, Savoy, Nice, and Lorraine, in order to place them

in the hands of France? It has been well said that
if Louis had allowed the Archduke to succeed to the
throne of Spain after Charles II. had made a will in
favour of Anjou, he would have deserved to be
canonised as a saint, but he would have lost all claim
to be a statesman.

The character of Philip was not likely to inspire
great confidence among those who, like Madame de
Maintenon, the Duchess of Orleans, and the Duc de
Beauvilliers, knew him best. His piety, his love of
justice, his natural straightforwardness and affection
for those around him, were counterbalanced by in-
decision, an uncertain temper, and a distrust of his
own powers. He was moreover slow of speech and
his voice was disagreeable. He had been brought
up with his brothers the Dukes of Burgundy and
Berry in severe isolation. They had undoubtedly
suffered from over anxiety on the part of their
tutors and governors. " I am miserable," the young
Duke of Berry is reported to have said on hearing of
Philip's accession to the crown of Spain. " I have
no hope of being a king like my brothers, and by
the departure of my brother, the Duke of Anjou, all
the governors and sub-governors will fall upon me,
and I already have too much of those that I have.
What will it be then when I have the rest ? It is to
be hoped that they will make me infallible." Had
Philip remained some ten years more under the immediate care of a few wise people who understood
his faults, and at the same time appreciated and knew
how to develop his good traits, had he become a man
before he was made a king, it is quite possible he

might have gone down to posterity as a wise ruler, instead of being merely known as the husband of Elizabeth Farnese. " Madame," the Duchess of Orleans, probably understood him best. She had loved him from childhood and preferred him to the Duke of Burgundy. She recognised that under his extreme timidity were concealed some excellent qualities. Her influence over him was great, and her letters when in Spain show that she appreciated thoroughly the childlike, easy-going nature of the young sovereign, who was never intended by nature to be a king.

Beauvilliers had no confidence in his capacity; the Marquis of Louville, who had known him for years, and who accompanied him and watched over him in Spain, said of him : "C'est un roi qui ne règne pas, et qui ne règnera jamais." On his arrival, however, at Madrid Philip shewed unwonted energy, rising early, being present in council with his ministers, and expressing his opinions on all matters. But this energetic fit soon passed away. He retired to rest from one to three A.M. ; he rose late. He had no memory, not even for important affairs of state, and he soon contracted a great dislike for work of all sorts. Nay, more, he hated amusements and took no delight in anything. He hardly ever spoke in public, and spent all his time in bewailing his departure from France, and grieving over his absence from his brothers. In six months all his popularity had disappeared, and the publication of caricatures showed plainly the opinion held of him by the mass of his subjects.

Philip had bidden his brothers farewell on January 22, 1701, at Saint-Jean de Luz. The parting scenes were very affecting, and not again on this earth were the three brothers to meet. A more difficult task than governing Spain could not be imagined. The Spanish monarchy was a despotism in which the clerical influence was preponderant. The existence of local assemblies, of local customs, of social privileges checked all attempts of the central power to assert itself in the provinces. At the time of the death of Charles II. the central power itself was hopelessly lethargic and inert, and revolved round the person of the King. Provincial independence and disunion prevented the growth of any national feeling, and in proportion as the central power grew more ineffective, more subservient to official oligarchy, and more and more incapable of creating among the Spanish people the idea of public good, so provincialism increased in intensity. The system of government by a number of councils—a system tried in France on Louis XIV.'s death with no chance of success—was admirably adapted for preventing all chance of reform, while the privileges of the nobles, accompanied by idleness, pride, selfishness and intrigues, presented a formidable bar to all hopes of regenerating Spain. National unity and civil equality were indispensable for any real improvement. The extraordinary decadence of Spain was now to be followed by an equally extraordinary resurrection.

The French monarchy was very different. The public administration founded by Richelieu, Colbert, and Louvois had no counterpart in Spain. A centralised government and a powerful bureaucracy had seriously diminished provincial liberties and individual powers of resistance. This system, carefully organised and well administered—like the legal system of Henry II. of England—controlled the despotic tendencies of the King. It had become well-nigh impossible for a French sovereign to over-ride the limits imposed on him by the laws. The subordination of all interests to the public good, the diminution of provincial independence, and of social privileges, the establishment of a central administration sufficiently powerful to command obedience throughout the length and breadth of the land, such reforms, it was thought, would introduce new life into Spain, would save her from all danger of a disastrous civil war, and would launch her on a career of prosperity.

In the introduction of French influence and of French ideas of administration, lay the only hope of the Spanish monarchy. Spain lay like a waterlogged vessel by the side of her active and well-equipped ally. The Spanish grandee naturally was opposed to all ideas of reform. Refusing to take any share in the government of his country, he was keenly susceptible to, and ready to resist any governmental influence whatever. Living most of the year in Madrid, and occupied mainly with pleasure and intrigue, the Spanish noble was none the less an important obstacle to any attempt by King or Council to govern the country. A more serious difficulty was the provincial spirit, which saw in any increase of centralisation the curtailment of its liberties and privileges. The whole force of France under Napoleon was some hundred years later to retire foiled in its attempt to cope with the independence of the Spanish provinces. During the Spanish Succession war Louis' first attempt to govern Spain in French fashion were similarly doomed to failure, and for some years the waves of reform and centralisation dashed harmlessly against the walls of that provincialism, which was never stronger or more aggressive than at the time of the accession of Philip V. This provincial temper was clearly illustrated in 1705, when a disastrous civil war broke out, which continued till after the peace of Utrecht. Not recognising the immense and almost insuperable obstacles in his way, Louis determined, on his grandson's accession, to govern Spain through Philip, and by directing his policy to restore Spanish finances and make Spain a useful ally in the coming European struggle.

To all Spaniards in whom a real love of their country outweighed every other consideration local and personal, the very idea of a close union with France opened up a new vista of immense possibilities. To them Louis XIV. appeared as the " incarnation of active royalty, active, just, and benevolent." He was to them a sort of god who could on the one hand in a few months re-establish order in the finances and honesty in the administration, and on the other give strength to the army and navy, and introduce a universal system of equal justice for poor and rich alike. Louis himself was prepared to direct the Spanish policy and to inaugurate reforms. He had in fact little choice. Philip had arrived in Madrid on February 18, 1701, and before the year was over it was evident that a European war was on the verge of breaking out. In 1701 the Emperor had begun hostilities in Italy, and on May 4, 1702, war was formally declared against France and Spain in London, Vienna, and at The Hague.

This war Louis had to a great extent brought on himself. The mere acceptance of the Will would not have led to any serious hostilities. Neither England nor Holland would have taken up arms, and without their assistance the Emperor was powerless. Louis had been right in his conjecture that England would not quarrel with him about the acceptance of the Will. The Second Partition treaty was, like its predecessor, intensely disliked in England, and on the same grounds. And the reasons of the English dislike are not difficult to understand. By the treaty France would become mistress of the Mediterranean, and the English trade in the Levant would be ruined. The possession of Guipuscoa would enable her to secure trade with the West Indies and South America. France would not only make the Mediterranean into a French lake ; she would gain the command of the sea, and with it universal monarchy. The balance of power founded by the peace of Westphalia and confirmed at Nimeguen and Ryswick would be endangered if not entirely overthrown.

In England men would have preferred war to the treaty, but they preferred the Will to both. Louis' decision to accept the Will was received in England and in Holland with resignation if not satisfaction.

The Will provided that the Spanish monarchy was to remain independent, and the execution of the Will would not, it was thought, compromise the existing equilibrium of European forces. But Louis made an undoubted mistake in the month of December, 1700, when he reserved the rights of Philip to the French throne. Public opinion was at that time so extremely sensitive on the question of the possible union of the crowns of France and Spain, *i. e.*, of a universal Bourbon monarchy in the West, that a man usually as keenly alive to the necessity of putting himself in the right as Louis was, ought to have deferred to the general feeling. Louis' motives indeed were probably easily explained. The Duke of Berry had shown no signs of capacity, and Louis may have thought that in the event of the death of the Duke of Burgundy, Philip might be called to the French throne, and Berry sent to govern Spain. Moreover, there were numerous precedents for reserving rights in similar cases. Henry III., the elected king of Poland, had reserved his rights to the French throne. But whatever may be urged in justification of Louis' action in reserving the rights of Philip, the fact remains that Louis blundered. Europe demanded in 1700 what it demanded and obtained some eleven years later, a solemn guarantee before Europe that the two crowns should be forever separated. The fatal declaration of Louis placed then a formidable weapon in the hands of his religious and political adversaries.

This error, serious as it was, might not, however, have led to war had not Louis followed it up by, if possible, graver mistakes. Though Philip V. had been recognised by William III., by the States-General, and by many of the lesser princes of Europe, such as Savoy, Bavaria, Brunswick-Wolfenbüttel, and others, Tallard had been for some time convinced that the acceptance of the Will would be followed by war, and the same conclusion appears to have been forced upon and definitely accepted by Louis. He was advised that his true policy was to seize all he could before the inevitable war began. To this extraordinary and fatal want of appreciation of the real feeling of the English and Dutch peoples at this critical moment, the war was probably due, though many writers aver that his imprudent action, so unlike the sagacity which marked his conduct from the peace of Ryswick to the death of Charles II., was due to the reappearance of his former ambitious policy and to his conviction that he could now dictate the law to Europe. Certainly his seizure early in 1701 of the line of Spanish fortresses known as the Dutch Barrier, altered the whole complexion of affairs, while his contemptuous release of the captured Dutch garrisons recalled his similar blunder in 1672. This line of fortresses, including, as it did, Luxemburg, Namur, Mons, and the seaports of Nieuport and Ostend, were of the utmost importance to Holland. If they remained in French hands there was no security that Holland would not herself be conquered. The Dutch were infuriated; public opinion in England was roused, and William III. was enabled on September 7th to lay the foundation of the Grand Alliance in the Triple League between England, the Emperor, and Holland. By the terms of the Grand Alliance the kingdoms of France and Spain were never to be united or governed by the same person, and a reasonable satisfaction was to be given to the Emperor and the English King. The three powers further agreed to recover the Spanish Netherlands as a barrier for the protection of the United Provinces from the French, to protect Dutch and English commerce, and to compel the cession of the Milanese, and the Italian dominions of the Spanish crown for the Emperor. It was quite possible that even then England might have refused to engage in a European war had Louis acted with prudence and moderation, and restored the barrier fortresses. Instead of doing so, however, and moved perhaps by female influence, certainly by a misplaced feeling of chivalry, and an injudicious zeal for the Church, he recognised the Pretender, James III., as King of England. He thus not only broke his engagements solemnly entered into at Ryswick, but he alienated the English nation. The effects of this mistake were most disastrous upon France. Public opinion in England rose to fever heat. Indignation at the insult was followed by alarm at the prospect of further aggrandisement by Louis. Universal dominion and the establishment of Catholicism all over Europe were supposed to be the objects of his policy.

It is, while impossible to extenuate, extremely difficult to explain Louis' entire misapprehension of the condition of public feeling in England. The English had no wish for war, and the dismissal of the Dutch guards, the reduction in the army and navy, and the recognition of Philip V. as King of Spain by William, ought to have convinced Louis that if he only walked warily he could carry out his own solution of the problem which had been puzzling Europe for half a century.

But French statesmen have rarely at a great crisis interpreted aright the temper of England, and Louis, in spite of the fact that he had the best information of any European monarch, was no exception to the rule. He never had understood English political life, and his failure to appreciate the real position of affairs in England in 1701, combined with his over-weening ambition and confidence in his own powers, brought with it a heavy penalty.

War being upon him, it was absolutely necessary to take immediate action. Practically all Europe was opposed to him. Spain, therefore, must be turned into a useful ally. France and Spain re-organised by French methods would, closely allied, be supreme in southern Europe and command the Mediterranean. The Turk would thus be controlled and Louis would occupy a paramount position in southern Christendom. It was therefore at once necessary to direct the policy of Spain, and to re-organise her administration. For this work a man was required. Louis decided with characteristic decision that he was the man. From 1701 to 1709, in answer to the Spanish Junta which begged him to assume the direction of affairs, he took charge of the Spanish monarchy and carried on the administration of the Spanish government. All attempts at reform, however, failed, owing to intrigue and dissensions at the Spanish Court, till the intelligence of the ambassador Amelot triumphed over all difficulties, and for the moment it seemed as if the governmental machine of France would be introduced into Spain. But the disasters of the war endangered the throne of Philip V. and the security even of that of Louis XIV. Amelot's policy was interrupted. Louis was compelled to relinquish his schemes for the complete regeneration of Spain and to look to the safety of his own throne.

Till 1709, however, Louis endeavoured to carry out the superhuman task of warring against united Europe while organising in the smallest details an internal revolution in Spain. He was not only content to direct the life of the King and Queen of Spain, he took an active part in supervising the whole administration. That such interference would arouse discontent among the Spaniards was recognised by Louis, but he hoped that in consideration for the benefits gained by Spain from the French alliance, Spain would acquiesce in his supremacy, and in his unremitting intervention. France had placed at the disposal of Spain her armies, fleets, and resources. In return it seemed a small thing to insist upon the recognition of French influence in the Spanish councils.

It was obvious that unless thorough and sweeping reforms were at once carried out, the close union of the two countries would only result in the ruin of France. Certainly as long as the war lasted, exceptional measures were necessary, and Louis, who saw clearly the advantages to Spain of a reorganisation of the government in every particular, naturally expected the hearty co-operation of the Spanish nation. No time was lost in further considerations, and Louis promptly began his attempt to guide the destinies of Spain.

He advised the immediate creation of a Supreme Council, known as the *Despacho*, and composed of four persons. By means of a strong executive Louis hoped that the necessary reforms might be carried out. In order that Spain should be able to be an efficient ally, her finances must be reorganised. Louis therefore appointed to this task Orri, a laborious administrator, full of expedients and bent on destroying the abuses which disgraced the financial system of Spain. A hard and insolent reformer, Orri became at once unpopular. Nevertheless he began the work of reform, which was continued till the outbreak of the French Revolution by a series of skilful administrators. Similar reforms were to be carried out in the army, navy, and all departments of state. Over this stupendous work the French ambassador was to preside. He was to guide the King, reorganise the Court, supervise the reforms, and be present at the meetings of the *Despacho*. He was to be in frequent communication with Louis, who himself issued directions on every subject. Never, perhaps, was Louis' love of the details of administration so clearly illustrated. He knew all about the *personnel* of the Spanish government; and not an appointment nor a dismissal took place without his authorisation. To govern

Spain from Paris was a herculean task, but Louis
did not shrink from it.

While Philip was in Italy from February to December, 1702, Louis not only directed the government of Spain, but also carefully organised the
details of Philip's expedition.   During 1702, therefore, Louis managed the affairs of France, Spain,
and Italy.   But Spain occupied most of his attention.   For the work which he had in hand the choice
of efficient agents was obviously of the utmost importance.   Harcourt, most unfortunately for the
success of Louis' policy, fell dangerously ill at this
critical moment, and the Comte de Marsin was
appointed ambassador with instructions not to interfere directly in the government of Spain, but merely
to offer advice.   Louville was given to Philip as a
councillor and private friend, and Anne Marie de la
Trémoille, Princesse des Ursins, was appointed
attendant of the young Queen Louise of Savoy.

For many years the Court of Spain lived in entire
and well-nigh abject dependence upon Louis.   This
subordination, however, of Spain to France was
never popular among the Spaniards themselves.
People do not like being reformed and organised by
force, and the Spaniards of all people required very
delicate handling.   Full of pride, their suscepti-
bilities were very easily wounded.   All Louis' attempts to unite the Spanish and French aristocracy
by an exchange of honours and decorations failed to
prevent continual bickerings and feuds.   As early as
the end of 1702, before the reverses to the French
and Spanish armies had interfered with Louis'

plans, a strong opposition to his policy had showed itself, and many Spaniards, already weary of the French domination, spoke of the Archduke as a possible King of Spain. This public discontent was far harder to grapple with than the attempts of either Philip or his Queen to secure a small modicum of independence. Early in 1703 a palace intrigue, fomented by the ambitious Princesse des Ursins, resulted in the temporary overthrow of the *Despacho*, and the retirement of Porto-Carrero. This insubordination was at once checked by Louis. Portocarrero was recalled, the *Despacho* re-established, and the Court of Madrid was never so submissive to that of Versailles as during the rest of the year 1703.

In matters of Spanish foreign policy, Louis was equally all powerful. He promised Guelders and Limbourg to the Elector of Bavaria with the title of hereditary governor of the Low Countries. No question of importance was settled in Spain without his advice being asked, and on the occurrence of the disaster of Vigo Bay a letter arrived from Louis to Philip in which he gave directions with reference to the remnant of the treasure, which had arrived in Spain.

The years 1703 and 1704 formed a critical period in the history of Louis' relations with Spain. The allegiance of even Castille to Philip was not assured, that of the other provinces was more than doubtful. Nor was Louis fortunate in the choice of his representatives at Madrid. Marsin had given way to the Cardinal d'Estrées, whom Louis considered to be a most capable envoy, and whom Saint-Simon describes as being " vif, ardent, bouillant, haut à la main, accoutumé à décider, souvent trop de feu en se traitant les affaires." But his sojourn in Spain was short, and his successor, the Abbé d'Estrées, after nearly a year's residence in Madrid, gave way to the Duc de Gramont, whose embassy ended in the spring of 1705.

This task of administering the Spanish Empire from Paris would have taxed all the energies of Louis and his ministers in peaceful times ; as it was one can only wonder at the temerity with which such a task was undertaken during a European war. By the end of 1702 Louis knew all the details of the personal administration of Spain, and no appointment was made, and no dismissal was effected, without his sanction. The nomination to the archbishopric of Seville was approved by him, he drew up a list of the Gentlemen of the King's Bedchamber, he fixed upon the President of the Council of Finances. The saying of the French envoy in Spain accurately represents the position of affairs: " We wait," says he, " for the decision of the King on all points."

During these years palace intrigues and dissensions between Louville, the Princesse des Ursins, the Cardinal, and Abbé d'Estrées went far to compromise the work begun by Louis XIV. The violence of the Cardinal and Louville, though for a time successful, made the French influence very unpopular. The recall of the Cardinal in October, 1703, followed by that of Louville three months later, and the brief exile of the Princesse des Ursins early in 1704, brought about by the Abbé d'Estrées, only increased the discord at the Spanish Court. The recall of the Abbé d'Estrées, who had become hateful to Philip and his Queen, owing to the part he had taken in the opposition to the exiled princess, was followed by further intrigues. The Duc de Gramont was distinctly not the man for the crisis. "Il avoit pour lui," says Saint-Simon, "son nom, sa dignité, et une figure avantageuse, mas rien de plus." He plunged into the labyrinth of palace intrigues, formed a cabal, the object of which was to ruin the Queen's influence, opposed the return of the Princesse des Ursins, and openly declared that Louis governed Spain from Paris. All the ambassador's plans failed; Louis allowed the Princesse des Ursins to return, and agreed to the wishes of Philip and the Queen. He moreover disavowed any intention of openly governing Spain from Paris. De Gramont, finding he was not supported by his sovereign, had no option but to ask for his recall.

With the arrival of his successor, Amelot, Marquis de Gournay, a man of very different calibre to that of his predecessors, begins a period of some four years when the plans of the French King with regard to Spain on the whole received a successful trial. Though hampered by disasters in the field, the policy of Louis, as carried out by Amelot, was not only extremely valuable at the time, but ensured for Spain immense benefits in the future. Amelot's embassy brought with it such startling changes that it might almost be said that the work of reform in Spain was never seriously taken in hand till his arrival at Madrid in 1705.

Before, however, Amelot had arrived, Louis had already realised that the war was likely to prove far more serious for France than any previous one. When the war broke out it might at first sight have appeared likely that France would at least hold her own. She had all the resources of Spain at her back, she could rely on the support of Portugal and Savoy, and above all among her allies were numbered the Electors of Cologne and Bavaria. The value of the alliance of Bavaria could not be over-rated. By it Germany was divided and the road to Vienna lay open. With such allies the French cause, to judge from previous European contests, might appear to possess the elements of success.

But the war had hardly passed through its initial stages when it was seen that the conditions of this new contest were dissimilar from those of previous wars, and that the supremacy of France was likely to be, if not entirely effaced, at any rate seriously diminished.

The true causes of those disasters to France which left her at the Peace of Utrecht shattered and launched on that downward course which saw her influence in Europe destroyed in 1763 and her monarchy overthrown in 1792, are not far to seek. In the first place the England of Queen Anne was very different from the England of the Stuarts or even from the England of William III. Strong and united, with Scotland no longer a danger, and Ireland at her feet, the England of Marlborough, Godolphin, and Somers was a formidable foe. And if England was growing in strength, her rival was beginning to feel the effects of a long period of despotic rule, characterised by some fatal mistakes. At this tremendous crisis France felt keenly the loss of the finest elements of her national life, of which she had been deprived by the revocation of the Edict of Nantes. Moreover, at the very outset of the war, the disorganisation of the state was very apparent. At a time when great statesmen and able administrators were required, the principal offices of the government were held by a Court favourite. Louis' ministers and generals, though in many cases capable men, could not compare in ability with Colbert, Louvois, Lionne, Condé, and Turenne. Of his four Ministers of State, Saint-Aignan, Duke of Beauvilliers, was the President of the Council of Finance. The son-in-law of Colbert and the friend of Madame de Maintenon, Beauvilliers had gained the confidence of the King, and indeed that of all who knew him, by his high character, his devotion to his duties, and his modesty. He had advised Louis not to accept the Will, and he was strongly opposed to the ill-timed recognition of the Pretender. Phelypeaux, Count of Pontchartrain, the Chancellor of France and Minister for the Marine had been named Controller-General in 1689, and on the death of Seignelay he was also given the post of Minister of the Marine and Minister of the King's Palace. In 1699 Louis had relieved him of all his offices and made him Chancellor. He was a man of great independence of character, and in order to defend the liberties of the Gallican Church had even resisted the

bribes of Madame de Maintenon. A hard-working,
well-informed man, he was for those days remarkably
honest, and had a conciliatory manner which made
him popular. Saint-Simon, whose friend he was,
describes his character in flattering terms. Jean
Baptiste Colbert, Marquis of Torcy, the Minister of
Foreign Affairs, had seen much of Europe, having
been ambassador in England, Denmark, and Portugal. Of all Louis' ministers he was the most capable, and showed during his ministry so much zeal
for the welfare of France, and so much ability in
discharging the duties of his office, that on Louis'
death, the Duke of Orleans, who had always disliked
him, made him a member of the Council of Regency.
The fourth minister, Chamillard, of all Louis' ministers, was, it has been said, the most modest and the
least capable. In 1699 he had succeeded Pontchartrain as Controller-General, and in 1700, on the death
of Pomponne, had been made a Minister of State.
In 1701, on the death of Barbézieux, he added the
duties of Minister of War to his other functions.
The friend of Madame de Maintenon and Beauvilliers, he had never desired the honours that were
forced upon him. Saint-Simon, who liked him,
speaks highly of his personal qualities, and there is
no doubt that the much-abused Chamillard was fully
alive to his unfitness for the posts of Controller-
General and Minister of War. When the unfortunate minister, who possessed no statesmanlike
qualities, shrank from the responsibility of filling
the two most difficult offices in the Government,
Louis, unconscious of the gravity of the situation,

assured Chamillard of his support. "Je vous seconderai," he graciously said.

Louis had for so many years been assured by Louvois, that he had himself conducted, often from Versailles, the campaigns of his armies, that he seems not to have realised the immense value of the services of his late Minister of War. And further Louis does not seem to have recognised that his greatest military successes were won when he was himself young, strong, active, and aided by the advice of the greatest military organiser of the century. In 1701, all was changed, though he alone failed apparently to appreciate the fact that any change had taken place. His personal efforts, backed by his long experience, were but poorly seconded by the incapable and timid Chamillard, though the latter was aided by Chamlay, who had been trained by Louvois. "All the wheels of the machine existed but the principal spring was more than half broken." Louis had undertaken an impossible task, and the colossal struggles of France were unavailing. Even if Louvois had been alive, and the French armies had been led by Turenne or Condé, it would have taxed all the efforts of the French monarchy to combat the European Coalition of 1701, led by Marlborough and Eugène. As it was Catinat and Boufflers were old, and Vendôme, Villars, Berwick, Noailles, and Tessé were practically untried men. Though before long Villars, Vendôme, and Berwick showed that they were great commanders, and the art of war received some brilliant illustrations from these French generals, their efforts were from the first checked and hampered by the elevation of men like Villeroy to the supreme command, by the lack of military resources, and by the meddling and inefficient war administration. The state of things in many points anticipated the position of affairs in 1870. From Versailles the movements of the armies were directed and the most contradicting orders were given. At Versailles, too, the knowledge of the geography of Germany was of a very elementary character. As might be expected, the most serious mishaps to the French arms were the inevitable result of this mischievous system. Villars found himself in 1702 ordered to march across the Rhine with an army, the ranks of which were half empty, insufficiently officered, and the men badly supplied with arms and even clothing. The movements of 1704 were ruined through the delay caused by the chiefs writing for orders from Versailles and through Villeroy being unable to understand the drift of the contradictory directions which he received. In 1707 Tessé complained that for seven or eight days bread and water had been the only food supplied to his troops, and that the officers could not be provided with any horses. Under conditions such as these, which augured ill for the success of the French, Louis had begun his herculean task of defying all Europe.

Armies had to be provided and kept up in Italy and Flanders, on the Rhine and in Spain. In Flanders Boufflers, who had distinguished himself by seizing the Barrier towns early in 1701, had, after some slight successes in 1701 and 1703, suffered severe reverses at the hands of Marlborough, who,

VILLEROY.
(From an illustration, after an old engraving, in Erdmannsdörfer's
Deutsche Geschichte von 1648–1740.)

by the end of 1703, had driven the French out of the
Electorate of Cologne, and had captured Liège,
Bonn, and Luxemberg, and had occupied all Spanish
Guelders. But these reverses were not entirely due
to the presence of Villeroy, who shared the chief
command with Boufflers in the Netherlands in 1703,
or to the superior generalship of Marlborough.

It had been decided at Versailles that decisive
blows were to be struck in Germany and in Italy.
The commanders in Flanders were ordered to remain
on the defensive, and many of their troups were sent
to reinforce the army in Alsace under Catinat. The
integrity of the French monarchy had just received
a blow in the loss of Landau, and the Elector of
Bavaria was in a precarious position, exposed to the
attacks of the Imperialists. Catinat had become
timid and irresolute at a moment when it was absolutely necessary to take the offensive, and by a bold
invasion of Germany to drive back the Germans and
confirm the Bavarian alliance. Villars, whose skill
and audacity were well known, was put in command
of an expeditionary force, and passing the Rhine he
inflicted a disastrous defeat upon the Imperialists at
Friedlingen on October 14, 1702. The equivocal
conduct of the irresolute Elector of Bavaria, who,
instead of effecting a junction with Villars, fell back
towards Ingolstadt, compelled the retirement of the
French into Alsace. The next year saw an attempt
to carry into execution one of the most brilliant
conceptions devised during the war. Like Turenne
in 1645, and like Napoleon, in 1809, Villars planned
nothing less than a march on Vienna. This design,

audacious as it was at first sight, was quite feasible in 1703, and had it not been for the conduct of the Elector, the campaign of 1809 might have been anticipated by a series of movements as successful and as brilliant as those executed by the Emperor. At the beginning of 1703 Villars besieged and took Kehl (March 12th), and having, in spite of the murmurings at Versailles at his delay, made very careful preparations, he crossed the Rhine again on April 5th, and effected a junction with the Elector at Villingen on May 6th. No time could have been more opportune for a march in Vienna. Before the year was out the Hungarians were in fierce rebellion. In Italy the Austrian troops were fully occupied, while Louis of Baden was held in check by Tallard from Alsace. Villars and the Elector with an army of 40,000 men were now in the centre of Germany, and ready to strike at the heart of the Empire. But jealousies and animosities at once sprang up and interfered with the successful execution of any plan of operations.

Villars' project can best be learned from his own words. " He resolved," he tells us in his memoirs, " in order to conceal his purpose as long as possible, to extend his men in quarters as far as Ulm, as though his principal object had been to enable his wearied cavalry to recover their strength. It was then settled that the Elector should pass some days at Munich, that the Bavarian army should spread itself along the Danube from Ulm to Regensburg, and that about June 1st the infantry of the Elector, and a considerable detachment from the French army, should embark in boats . . . and should descend on Passau, meeting some of the Elector's troops on the Inn, and all the necessary artillery which was at Braunau, a fortified place on the Inn. By carrying out this project Passau would certainly be taken within three days : Linz, as weak a place, would fall, and Vienna could be quickly reached." Villers, who had himself lived in Vienna for three years, was convinced that its capture would be an easy matter, and like Turenne and Napoleon he had grasped the importance of the upper valley of the Danube and realised that its occupation practically placed Vienna at his mercy.

Eugène years later himself allowed that Villars' magnificent project could have been carried out. " The Emperor Leopold thought Vienna was so certain to fall that he was about to leave it. . . . The only troops available to defend the city were a few recruits on the way to join their regiments."

But unfortunately, after much hesitation, the Elector had made up his mind to adopt another plan. He proposed to effect a junction with Vendôme's troops and then to penetrate into Austria by way of the Tyrol. In June, Villars being left to protect Bavaria, the Elector marched to join Vendôme at Brixen. But the latter never got further than Trent, and the Elector was checked by the rising of the Tyrolese. The defection of the Duke of Savoy compelled Vendôme to make a hurried retreat and Maximilian found that any attempt to advance through the Tyrol would result in the loss of all his army. Meanwhile, though the position of

Villars on the Danube had become perilous in the extreme, with his accustomed daring he still hoped to carry out his great project. Though threatened by the forces of Louis of Baden and Count Styrum, he proposed to the Elector to take advantage of the Hungarian revolt and to march on Vienna. " Let us make two armies," was his advice to Maximilian, " it is possible to defend Bavaria with one ; let the other march into the Austrian dominions. You will meet 30,000 Hungarians in rebellion. An army of the enemy must be directed to defend Austria ; and meanwhile the Duke of Burgundy who has taken Brisach and has no foe in his front, will invade the Empire."

But not receiving any reinforcements from Tallard (who served under Burgundy) or any co-operation from the Elector, Villars was left to extricate himself from his position between an enemy in his front and one in his rear. On September 20th he completely defeated Count Styrum at Hochstädt, and shortly afterwards he resigned his command and returned to Versailles and was succeeded by Marsin. There is little doubt that had Villars been properly supported from Versailles, had he been ably seconded by Vendôme and Tallard, and had his plans not been frustrated by the Elector of Bavaria, the war which terminated in 1714 might have ended in 1703. No doubt Villars' inability to secure the hearty co-operation of the incapable and vacillating Maximilian was due in some measure to his own impatient temper and want of tact. Still, in spite of Villars' shortcomings, his conception of a decisive march on

Vienna was admirable, and France lost in 1703 a grand opportunity of compelling the Emperor to sue for peace.

The events of 1704 demonstrated clearly the value of the services of Villars and proved the turning-point in the war.   An advance on Vienna was again meditated, but Marsin was probably incapable of carrying out a great design, and he was as usual hampered by want of soldiers, of money, and of munitions of war.   The allies, however, had by this time realised the serious results which might flow from these unchecked operations on the Danube.   Marlborough's famous march to the Danube was followed by the devastation of Bavaria and the battle of Blenheim. The defeat of the French saved the Empire and Vienna from French invasion, and placed Bavaria in subjection to the Emperor.   Tallard was taken prisoner, Landau was recaptured by Baden, and Trarbach and Trèves were reduced by Marlborough and the Emperor.   Leopold erected a statue on the field of battle with the inscription : *Agnoscat tandem Ludovicus XIV. neminem debere, ante obitum, aut felicem, aut magnum vocari.*

Early in 1705 Amelot arrived in Spain, but the condition of affairs both there and in Europe generally, were extremely unpropitious for the inauguration of his master's system.   Louis' anxieties, heavy enough already owing to the defections of Savoy and Portugal in 1703, the landing of the Archduke in Spain, the rising in the Cevennes, and the loss of Gibraltar in 1704 had been greatly increased by the defeat at Blenheim and the necessity of defending the Rhine frontier. Though Vendôme to some extent restored the French cause in Italy by the battle of Cassano in August, 1705, and though Villars' successful campaign on the frontier of Lorraine had frustrated the hopes of the allies and had produced an excellent effect, the gravity of the situation was such that it was very remarkable that Louis should have continued to carry out with calmness and firmness his schemes for the reorganisation of Spain.

Within Spain itself there seemed less chance of carrying through a successful reform policy in 1705 than in 1701.

By 1705 the scandalous intrigues of the French at Madrid had alienated a large number of Spaniards, who forgot the great advantages which Spain derived from Louis' assistance in arms and money. The enthusiasm with which the accession of Philip V. had been greeted had subsided, and the partisans of the House of Austria were encouraged. A strong anti-French party was openly formed and grew upon the discontent caused by the loss of Gibraltar, the increasing disbelief in the power of Louis XIV., and the discord in the Court.

All the more credit is then due to Louis and Amelot, the former for encouraging, the latter for carrying out a work which bestowed immense benefits on Spain. Amelot's indomitable courage surmounted all difficulties, and in spite of the continued failure of the French and Spanish armies, and of the fierce opposition within Spain itself, he accomplished so many real reforms that it may be said that modern Spain dates from his period of office. Under his influence Spain began to be rapidly transformed. The industries, letters, arts, and to some extent the institutions of France were introduced, and it has been truly asserted that had it not been for the terrible disasters experienced by the Spanish and French armies, which led to his recall, and in part to a modification, and in part to a postponement of all his schemes of reform, Amelot would have proved himself the Colbert of Spain.

He was recognised by Saint-Simon as a man of honour, of sense, possessed of considerable enlightenment, and endowed with great power of work. He had had a legal education, and owed his advancement to merit alone. His modesty and natural urbanity did not prevent him from adhering firmly to any resolution which an unerring instinct showed him was right. His simplicity, sagacity, straightforwardness, and trustworthiness had enabled him to succeed, in spite of his want of family connection, in whatever he had undertaken. His residence in Spain afforded fresh proof of the success which had ever attended his efforts, and was marked by the inauguration of reforms which were continued by Alberoni and the statesmen who came after him.

During the preceding four years Louis XIV.'s views regarding Spain had undergone considerable modifications. He had learned much of the temper of the inhabitants and of the methods of the government, which was new to him. He had, moreover, gauged to some extent the character of Philip V. and the capacities of his various councillors. He had made many false steps. He had formed not a few erroneous opinions. His schemes for the thorough reorganisation of Spain on French lines had obviously failed. It was necessary to acknowledge that failure. And in 1705 it was more than ever necessary to look facts in the face, and to recognise boldly that the situation in Spain was most critical. Its revenues had not increased since the death of Charles II., its leading governmental departments remained in a state of chaos. Had the Archduke Charles made a bold bid for the throne of Spain in the spring of 1705, it is difficult to see how Philip could have resisted the attempt. None of the haughty Spanish grandees who surrounded their king were remarkable for statesmanlike qualities. It was clear that the country could not be saved by the men who formed the Spanish Court. It was therefore necessary to inaugurate a new political system in accordance with which Philip should ostensibly govern Spain, while increased powers should be given to the French ambassador, who should be practically the First Minister of the Spanish monarchy.

Louis had, moreover, recognised that it was not possible for him to carry out his policy without the assistance of the Princesse des Ursins. She was indispensable to the success of his schemes. The appointment of Amelot was approved by her, and in her hands was practically left the composition of the new Spanish ministry. Henceforward by means of the Princess and of Amelot, Louis proposed to govern Spain. The Princess solemnly promised Louis to act in perfect harmony with Amelot, and she returned to Spain in August, 1705.

It was a bold experiment, but its success justified Louis' decision. The King, it was stated in Amelot's instructions, was so satisfied with the solid qualities of the Princess and her knowledge of Spanish affairs, that he thought he could not do better than send her back to Madrid at once. Having decided that the Princess and Amelot were to be the organs of the French government in Madrid, the work of reforming and reorganising the whole governmental machine was promptly taken in hand. A new *Despacho* was formed, consisting of five members, but practically controlled by Amelot; a French Jesuit, Père Robinet, succeeded Daubenton as Philip's confessor, and changes were made in almost all departments which were calculated to insure efficiency in the Spanish state system. The moving spirit was, however, Amelot, acting in accordance with the views of the Princesse des Ursins, which she had previously expressed to Louis. "La Princesse des Ursins," wrote Louis to his embassador in June, 1705, "a proposé ce que je vous écris." *

The programme of the new government was ambitious enough even for peaceful times. It consisted of nothing short of the introduction of the French system of government into Spain. For the establishment of this system three things were necessary: the humiliation of the nobles and of the religious orders, and their complete subordination to the central authority, and the destruction of the provincial

---

* For an excellent account of Louis' policy to Spain see A. Baudrillart, *Philippe V. et la Cour de France*, Vol. I.

liberties of the non-Castilian portion of Spain. The nobles feared the introduction of the French monarchical spirit, and viewed any attempt at change with great suspicion. Louis' directions to Amelot fully justified these suspicions, and are interesting as throwing light on his own fatal policy to the French nobility. "You must," he wrote, "preserve all the external prerogatives of their dignity, and at the same time exclude them from all matters on which their knowledge would tend to increase their reputation."

To prevent the Spanish nobles taking any part in state affairs, to destroy all union between them, and to leave them a useless and harmless appendage of the Court was the definite aim of Louis' representative in Spain. The opposition of the nobles to the introduction of the French monarchical system, and that of the religious orders to any attempt to force upon them the position of the Gallican clergy, was, however, as nothing compared with the difficulties to be apprehended from any attempt to change the provincial institutions and liberties. But during the course of a long and terrible war it is impossible to inaugurate changes of a sweeping character, and the military disasters of 1706 interfered largely with Louis' hopes of carrying out fully his schemes for Spanish reform. Philip's failure to regain Barcelona in May was the beginning of a series of disasters. On May 11th, the day on which the siege of Barcelona had been raised, a total eclipse of the sun took place. As the sun in his glory was Louis' favourite emblem, the eclipse was thought to portend further disasters to the French cause. The Anglo-Portuguese army, after taking Salamanca, pushed on, and the Archduke was proclaimed king of Spain in Madrid on June 25th. All reforms were thrown to the winds, and the abolition of the privileges of the Catalans was indefinitely postponed. Aragon inclined towards the side of the Archduke, Catalonia and Valencia openly declared for him. Philip showed unexpected courage and energy, and was warmly praised by his grandfather. News of the failure of Philip at Barcelona, and of the disaster of Ramillies, had reached the French King on the same day. But Louis was always seen at his best in the hour of adversity. He surveyed the position of affairs with dignity and calmness, and urged Philip to guard against capture by his enemies. " All depends," he wrote, " upon the preservation of your person." " We have not," he added, " been successful in Flanders ; it is necessary to submit to the judgment of Providence."

The Spanish monarchy seemed at its last gasp, and the wildest expectations of the allies likely to be realised. Madrid was in the hands of the Archduke, and Philip and his Queen were fugitives. The fidelity of the Spanish grandees was shaken, and many of them hastened to recognise the Archduke as king of Spain. Even the aged Porto-Carrero gave his allegiance to Charles. But Philip showed unexpected energy, and the loyalty of the Castilian people never wavered. The fury of the Madrid populace was indeed such that the Archduke and his army could barely get the necessaries of life, and the occupation of Madrid by the foreigner was of very short duration.

But the disasters of 1706 had convinced Louis of the necessity of peace. One French army under Villeroy had been defeated in May at Ramillies, and another under Orleans and Marsin had been overthrown in September at Turin. The Netherlands were lost, and the French cause in Italy was ruined. Madrid had been occupied by the Archduke, and Berwick had been driven back into the west from Portugal. These successive disasters seemed likely to overwhelm France, and to bring about a speedy close of the war. Villars alone had gained successes, and had not only driven the Germans beyond the Rhine, but had even contemplated taking the aggressive. But in spite of this gleam of success it seemed impossible for France, crippled as she was, to continue the war. Louis had justification when he wrote in October that the government could no longer carry on hostilities, and that he had proposed to the English and Dutch that negotiations for peace should be opened. But no treaty could be signed unless Philip was prepared to sacrifice a portion of his dominions. However, the allies refused to treat, and nothing was left to Louis but to carry on warlike operations with vigour. The allies paid dearly for their error. Flushed with success, they had missed an excellent opportunity of securing more than their just share of the spoils of war. The fortunes of France and Spain were at their lowest ebb in 1706.

With the year 1707 matters began to mend, and

though Louis experienced disasters, he was never reduced to the position of 1706. The King and ministers made prodigious efforts. Though exhausted and badly administered, France had still immense resources, and thousand of recruits joined the armies. In April, 1707, the victory of Almanza, with which the name of Berwick will ever be associated, proved even more decisive than Blenheim. It assured the throne of Spain to the House of Bourbon, and enabled the interrupted reforms of Amelot to be continued. Aragon and Valencia returned to their allegiance to Philip, and many of their privileges were suppressed. A great step was taken towards that centralisation of powers at Madrid which Louis had always advocated, and which Amelot was enabled in part to carry out. The constitution of Castile was solemnly promulgated in Valencia and at Saragossa, and was henceforth accepted in the kingdom of Spain. Thus the political results of Almanza were of vast importance to Spain and in their later effects proved the wisdom of Louis' views with regard to the necessary reforms in that country. But though success had begun to attend the efforts of Louis in the Spanish peninsula, he was not deterrred from carrying out a new policy with regard to Italy. It had become quite apparent to the French king that it was impossible for him to carry on war successfully at four different centres. The foreign policy of both Richelieu and Mazarin had been marred by a similar attempt, and very wisely in 1706 Louis had determined to withdraw from Italy, and to employ the released troops on

his exposed north-eastern frontier and in Spain. He
fully realised that before peace could be made
Philip would be compelled to consent to some partition of his dominions. The evacuation of Italy
would no doubt leave that country in the hands of
Austria, but Spain would be preserved to Philip, and
France would be saved a vast expenditure of money
and the sacrifice of a large number of soldiers.

The evacuation of Italy, arranged in March, 1707,
by the convention of Milan—so justly attacked by
English writers as an act of treachery on the part of
the Emperor, was undoubtedly a wise action on
the part of Louis, though Philip himself naturally
resented the unopposed occupation of north Italy
by the Austrians and the inevitable seizure of
Naples. Philip's worst fears were soon realised.
The retirement of the French from Italy was followed in August not only by the loss of Milan, but
by the further loss of Naples, while the Duke of
Savoy invaded Provence and besieged Toulon. The
Whigs, too, delighted at the victory of Ramillies,
took up a more hostile attitude than ever towards
Louis, and in October passed their celebrated resolution that no peace " can be safe or honourable for
her Majesty and her allies, if Spain and the Spanish
West Indies be suffered to continue in the power of
the House of Bourbon."

But on the whole the year 1707 was favourable to
the French. The inroad into Provence and the
attack on Toulon failed, owing to the resistance of
Tessé and to a quarrel between Amadeus and
Eugène. The allies retired discomfited behind the

Alps, and the English fleet failed to supply the
Camisards with arms. Moreover, a great French
army in the Low Countries had, under the skilful
leadership of Vendôme, kept invasion back, and
even advanced to the Sambre, and Villars on the
Rhine successfully assailed the lines constructed
from Stolhofen to Kehl and the Black Forest, and
invaded Germany with the object of combining his
operations with those of Charles XII., or at any rate
of aiding the revolted Hungarians. He levied con-
tributions in Swabia and Würtemberg, and filled the
coffers of the army. If Charles XII. had effected
the desired junction at Nuremberg, Vienna would
have fallen, and the Swedish King would have been
master of the Empire. But the influence of Marlborough turned Charles from the French alliance,
and Villars' hopes were again disappointed. If he
had to fall back across the Rhine on the approach
of a strong force under the Elector of Hanover, his
campaigns had inspired his troops with fresh
courage.

Though the Spanish monarchy had lost Milan
through the retirement of the French, and in August
of the same year Naples, the loss of which was hastened by the hostility of Clement XI. to the Bourbon
Church policy, Philip V. found himself at the end
more secure in his possession of the Spanish throne
than he was at the beginning of 1707. On his
reiterated requests, Louis agreed, in 1708, to recon-
sider the question of interfering actively in Italy.
There the overbearing conduct of the Emperor had
produced deep discontent among the Italian states.

But Louis was unwilling to risk men and money unless he could be sure that the Italians had thrown off their habitual lethargy. Tessé was sent to report on the condition of the Italian peninsula, where he found everywhere divisions, uncertainty, and general want of energy. The Emperor had ordered a considerable army to march into Italy to consolidate his conquests, and unless Louis did the same the Italians would naturally side with the Imperial cause. Louis did not send troops, and adhered to the policy inaugurated by the convention of Milan. Clement XI. was compelled to recognise the Archduke as king of Spain. The year 1708 was indeed not only marked by political failure, but also by military disasters. The carefully prepared expedition to Scotland on behalf of James Edward failed through the sudden indisposition of that prince, and the complete supremacy of England on the sea, while the campaign in Flanders ended in the defeat of Oudenarde, the capture of Lille, and the invasion of France. These continued disasters again brought forward the question of peace. Louis was anxious to bring the war to a close ; he was prepared to agree to the partition of the Spanish Empire ; he was ready to accept as Philip's share Naples, Sicily, Sardinia, and the Tuscan presidencies.

On one occasion, when some one spoke of founding another Saint-Cyr, Madame de Maintenon said that there were other things much more urgent, " to secure peace, and relieve the poor people of their burdens." "Yes," added Louis, "that is what a king should aim at : peace in his kingdom, and relief

THE EMPEROR JOSEPH I.

(From a print reproduced in Philippson's *Das Zeitalter Ludwigs XIV.*)

of his people. But to obtain these advantages for them we are forced against our will to oppress them. We want peace, but a good peace, and I ask it of God continually, who alone can change the hearts of those who oppose it."

There is no doubt that Louis was sincerely anxious for peace. The terrible winter of 1708–9 only confirmed him in his pacific views. The Court was the scene of cabals and intrigues. The ministers Beauvilliers, Torcy, Pontchartrain and Chamillard were opposed by the Duke of Maine, Boufflers, Huxelles, Harcourt, and Villeroy. There was even a division of opinion among the ministers themselves. Chamillard desired peace at any price. Spain he regarded as a useless encumbrance, and he desired to break off the close alliance between her and France. The state of the finances was appalling. A Colbert would have despaired of ever bringing order into the existing chaos. To raise money with which to pay the soldiers, Chamillard had created privileges and posts of all sorts and kinds, the sale of which produced large sums. New taxes had been levied even on marriages and baptisms. Lotteries had been established. After every possible device had been adopted for raising money, the condition of the finances was such that it was obviously impossible for France to continue the war. Chamillard had for some time been anxious to retire from his office, and told Louis that the burden was too heavy for him, and would kill him. "Well," said the old King, "let us die together." But at last Louis agreed to defer to public opinion, and the device so frequently

adopted in the years immediately preceding the
Revolution was tried, Chamillard being succeeded
by Desmarets, a nephew of Colbert. The public
credit was for a moment restored, and new supplies
were raised on loan. The change, however, brought
little real improvement. The south of France had
not recovered from the Camisard struggle ; in Paris
Jansenism had again raised its head, and the Archbishop and the royal power were in opposition. The
frightful winter brought with it famine and insurrections. The price of the absolute necessaries of life
was almost prohibitive, and under the very windows
of the King's rooms the people clamoured for bread.
Revolutionary placards were posted up, anonymous
letters spoke of Ravaillac and Brutus ; Madame de
Maintenon and Chamillard were directly attacked.
The hospitals were crowded and overflowing, corpses
of peasants who had died of hunger were frequently
seen in the woods. The French nation had suddenly
found itself pauperised and in danger of bankruptcy.
To any one who understood the financial condition
of the country peace seemed absolutely indispensable.
No one grasped the position of things better than
did Louis XIV. Though seventy years old, in intelligence and in courage he was superior to any of his
ministers. He worked each day as regularly as he
did when he took up the cares of government upon
Mazarin's death. His knowledge of the details of
the administration was more profound than ever.
He had such a lively appreciation of the evils under
which France was suffering that after the winter of
1708–9 he determined to subordinate all considera-

tions to the one object of bettering the condition of France.

In this self-imposed task Louis was aided by Madame de Maintenon. Ever since the opening of the war she had been obliged against her wish to take some part in political affairs. She held conferences with the ministers; she gained the confidence of Villars; her letters to the Princesse des Ursins prove the enormous interest which she took in Spanish affairs. Her solicitude for the King led her to keep from him many events of a vexatious character. Her principal care was for him, and she knew no other will than that of her husband. Her many submissions, self-sacrifices, and losses of friends for his sake only augmented her desire for rest and peace. The troubles of the end of the reign were not attributable to her, for her advice was rarely taken. But her work in caring for the King is beyond all praise. Throughout his troubles she acted the part of a faithful and loving wife, for whom Louis showed the greatest regard. The King would often come into her room and lock the door. Then " sometimes he sheds tears, which he cannot control. Presently a minister comes, bringing bad news. If my presence is required I am called; if not I retire in some corner and pray. Sometimes I hear that all is going wrong; then my heart beats, and I cannot sleep at nights."

In 1707 Louis had realised the necessity of withdrawing from Italy, and the convention of Milan had signified to the world the reality of his conviction of the need of lessening the area of the struggle. Early in 1709 he decided to give up his attempt to govern Spain through his envoy and the Princesse des Ursins, in other words to relinquish all active attempts to establish firmly a Bourbon on the throne of Spain, and to leave Spain to defend itself. This new decision, this important modification of the policy of 1701, was signified to Europe by the recall of Amelot in April, 1709.

But though Louis might decide to abandon Spain, though he might recall his ambassador, he could not undo the work of the last four years. The period of Amelot's embassy saw a silent revolution effected in Spain. Since his arrival an army had been created, well equipped and regularly paid. The finances had been placed on a better footing than in any previous reign, and all signs of poverty in the royal household had passed away.

Moreover, excellent changes had been quietly carried out in the government. The royal authority had been firmly established, the power of the councils had been regulated, the independence of the nobles curbed, and the Church forced to contribute to the necessities of the State. Though the provincial liberties had been to some extent suppressed, the provinces were on the whole loyal; anarchy had given way to a central authority which endeavoured to mete out equal justice to rich and poor alike.

The allies were so convinced of the uselessness of attempting to conquer Spain that, content with holding their own in Catalonia, they devoted all their efforts to force Spain to yield to their wishes by victories gained over France in the Netherlands. With every prospect of success, their tone when

Louis demanded peace in 1709 was haughty and overbearing.

Louis sincerely desired peace. He was convinced of the hopelessness of any further attempts against the combined forces of the allies. He was prepared to cede Spain and the Indies to the Archduke, and to reserve Naples and Sicily to Philip. He was ready to restore Strasburg to its position as a free Imperial city. He was, in fact, prepared to propose terms which one would have thought even the rapacious Dutch would have accepted. But Philip, as in 1706, resolved to throw himself upon the patriotism of his subjects. And in 1709 he was in a far stronger position than in 1706. In 1706 he relied mainly upon the people of Castille, while many of the nobles declared for the Archduke. In 1709, well-nigh the whole of Spain was prepared to support him, and the nobles were among the foremost to oppose any partition of the Spanish Empire.

In arranging terms of peace with the allies, it was obvious that Louis could not now speak for his grandson. This new complication was not lost sight of by the English, Imperial, and Dutch plenipotentiaries. They had no intention of continuing a war with Spain while France was enjoying the blessings of peace. They therefore insisted that Louis should be responsible for the renunciation by Philip of his crown within two months, and that, failing the latter's assent, Louis was to aid the allies in compelling him to agree to the treaty. But the preliminaries of The Hague were not destined to be accepted. Louis' soul revolted against the humiliating conditions. He recalled his envoy in May, and broke off negotiations. "If I must continue the war," he said, "I will contend against my enemies rather than against my own family." The whole of France shared his indignation, and when the proposals of the allies were read to them by the King's order, the troops of Villars demanded with fury to be led against the foe. In a circular published by the advice of Torcy and sent to each province, Louis appealed to the French nation to support him in his endeavour to secure reasonable terms. He showed the unreasonableness of the allies, and expatiated on their insincerity and intolerable proposals. "Seeing, then," he said "that our enemies in their pretence to negotiate are palpably insincere, we have only to consider how to defend ourselves, and show them that France united can resist the united powers of Europe in their attempts, by fair means or by foul, to ruin her. All the ordinary sources of revenue are exhausted. I come before you for your counsel and assistance, at a time when our very safety as a nation is at stake; let us show our enemies that we are still not sunk so low, but that we can force upon them such a peace as shall consist with our honour and with the good of Europe." The effect of this appeal was at once seen. The war from being dynastic became national, from being a war for the interests of the Bourbons it became a war for the preservation of the French kingdom, if not for the very existence of the French nation. The enthusiasm of his subjects gave Louis an army larger than any which he had yet been able to put into the field, and the command was given to Villars. The campaign which saw the battle of Malplaquet was at once opened, but none the less Louis was as firmly convinced as ever of the absolute necessity of peace.

CHAPTER XIV.

PEACE.

1709–1713.

O keep French troops in Spain was to make peace impossible. To show his enemies then how sincerely desirous he was to end the disastrous war, Louis determined to order the withdrawal of his troops from Spain. The carrying out of this resolution was a necessary complement to his intention to lessen, if not wholly abandon, his political influence in that country. The political and military abandonment of Spain were simultaneous. With difficulty Louis was persuaded to allow the French troops to remain in Spain till August, 1709; at the beginning of September Blécourt succeeded Amelot, but with very different functions. Amelot had combined the functions of Prime Minister with those of French ambassador.

Blécourt was to be a mere envoy and to confine his
duties to observing closely all that went on, and by
working cordially with the Princesse des Ursins, to
keep Louis informed as to the exact position of
things in Spain. His position though a modified
was still a delicate one. The hatred felt against
the French was now universal, and the popular feeling was encouraged by the Spanish ministers.

This hostility was regarded by Louis with equa-
nimity. Torcy and all his ministers were convinced
that no peace could be made unless Philip V. was
dethroned, or the allies could be persuaded that no
political union based upon a formal treaty existed
between France and Spain. The battle of Malplaquet, fought on September 11th, was a glorious defeat for the French. It restored the nation's respect
for itself ; it saved France from invasion.

The difficulties which Villars had to contend
against during the campaign only served to bring
out his military genius. His army was at the outset
without proper food or clothing, inferior to the opposing forces in point of numbers, and deeply dis-
couraged. Within a short time the great French
Marshal succeeded in converting his dispirited troops
into a fine army, well found and well fed. He acted
at first strictly on the defensive, but after one of his
lieutenants, Artagnan, had taken Warneton, a small
town on the Lys, and 1600 prisoners, he hoped
to be able to save Tournay. But the town fell on
July 27th and the citadel capitulated on September
2nd. The victorious allies under Marlborough and
Eugène then marched upon Mons, the capital of

Hainault, and Villars was ordered to try and save it. Boufflers, old and decrepit, willingly consented to serve under his young and illustrious colleague, and refused the latter's invitation to share the command.

Though too late to prevent the investment of Mons, Villars advanced to Malplaquet, a village situated on the top of a ridge a few miles to the southwest of Mons, and during the night and day after his arrival, took up a strong position. On either side were woods, that of Lanière lying on the east and that of Taisnière on the west. From the highroad, which Villars skilfully fortified, the ground falls away in ravines towards the plain of Mons. On September 11th the allied troops attacked Villars' fortifications, and one of the bloodiest battles of the war took place. Boufflers commanded the right wing, and was opposed to Tilly and the Prince of Nassau, nephew of William III. Villars himself fought, on the left, which was threatened in front by Eugène, and on the extreme right of the allies by Withers. At first the allies were driven back with great loss, but when Withers threatened to outflank the French left, Villars was compelled to withdraw troops from the centre. Marlborough, with his unfailing judgment, seized the opportunity and hurled upon the weakened centre English and Dutch troops under Tilly and Cadogan. Villars had been wounded and carried off the ground, and Boufflers was compelled to retire. With consummate skill the old warrior succeeded in drawing back in good order, leaving the allied forces in possession of the ground.

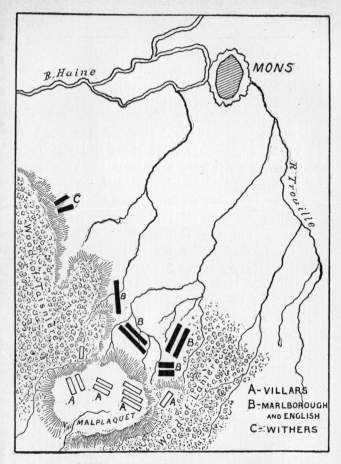

BATTLE OF MALPLAQUET.   SEPT. 11, 1709.

The country between the Rivers Haine and Trouille is broken by
forests and pierced by narrow valleys.   Between the woods of Taisnière
and Lanière is the Trouée, an open gap through which Mons can be
approached from the south and west.   Villars, attempting to raise the siege
of Mons, fortified himself on the high ground near Malplaquet.   The
allies took the offensive, but it was not till Villars had to send reinforcements to hold the wood of Taisnière, against Withers, that Marlborough
pierced the weakened French centre.

387

It was a dearly bought victory; the French lost
about 12,000 men, while the allies did not lose less
than 20,000. Though Mons fell, the campaign did
much to restore the spirit of the troops and the confidence of the nation. Villars had shown that the
dreaded Marlborough could be faced and fought,
and Louis rightly interpreted the popular feeling
when he made Artagnan a marshal, and showered
favours upon the wounded general. The King
still desired to come to terms with his foes. But
for a time his hopes for peace were frustrated.
The answer of the Dutch in February, 1710,
to his expressed desire for peace was more insolent than ever. Philip was to be dethroned
by Louis, and then only would peace be possible.
And Philip himself had successfully opposed his
grandfather's wishes. The deliberate inaction of
Bezons, the commander of the French troops in
Spain, had in September destroyed any hope of
Spanish success in the latter months of 1709, and
Philip firmly declined to consent to the transference
of Luxemburg, Mons, Namur, Charleroi, and Nieuport to the Elector of Bavaria. English writers assert that Louis' object was really to hand over the
Spanish Netherlands to the Dutch as a bribe to
induce them to desert the Grand Alliance. In any
case the project failed. Philip refused to yield a
single town and the English made with the Dutch a
Barrier treaty which cemented their alliance still
more closely.

In the spring of 1710 Louis again signified his will-
ingness to enter into negotiations. Opinion at the

Court lay strongly in the direction of peace, though different views were held as to the best means to bring about a settlement. Madame de Maintenon since 1706 had openly and frequently declared in favor of an immediate peace. She was willing, if necessary, to turn the French arms against Philip, and to carry out the wishes of the allies. Clearly realising the lamentable condition of France, and convinced that God wished to punish her country for the undue extension of its limits and for its insolence and pride, Madame de Maintenon declared in her letters that it was of no avail to struggle against the hand of God. She was much perturbed at Louis' conversion to a moral life being almost coincident with the beginning of a series of misfortunes, which increased as the end of his life drew nigh. " The designs of God," she wrote at the time, " are incomprehensible. Three Christian kings—namely, Louis, the Pretender, James Edward, and Philip V.—appear to be abandoned, and heresy and injustice triumph. Let us hope that it will not be for long."

For the sake of securing peace to her own country she was ready to sacrifice Philip. Though her views were clear and decided, and though they were based on religious conviction, they fortunately did not prevail with Louis.

The Grand Dauphin, the father of Philip, naturally supported his son. It was only when France seemed to be on the brink of destruction that, yielding to the unanimous opinion of the members of the Council, he agreed that France should give a subsidy to the allies.

The Duke of Berry sided with his father. He deplored Louis' intention of abandoning Philip and applauded the latter's determination to fight to the last. The Duke of Burgundy, after the disasters of 1709, had become a strong advocate of peace. He recognised the necessity of abandoning Spain, but, like Louis, he refused to consider the possibility of fighting against Philip. The Duke of Orleans, labouring under suspicion of plotting to succeed Philip in case the latter was dispossessed, had little influence.

Of the ministers, while Desmarets, Pontchartrain, and Torcy were inclined to peace at any price, and were thus more or less in sympathy with the views of Madame de Maintenon, Beauvilliers and Voysin sided with Louis and the Princes.

All were, however, agreed upon the necessity of peace, and negotiations were opened at Gertruyden-berg in March. Louis' offers were far more considerable than those which were afterwards accepted at Utrecht. But the real point at issue was the dethronement of Philip by French troops. At long sittings of the Council, on May 11th and June 1st, the matter was fully discussed in all its bearings. Finally it was decided to recognise the necessity of a partition of the Spanish monarchy. Sicily and Sardinia were to be reserved for Philip, and France was to pay the allies a subsidy during the continuance of the war. A chain of barrier fortresses was to be set up to satisfy the Dutch, and the whole of Alsace was to be ceded to the Empire. These with other concessions made the terms offered by Louis well worthy of acceptance by the coalition. The allies, however, most unwisely insisted that France must aid in the dethronement of Philip, and declined to make peace on any other terms. Louis, as a last resort, offered, if the allies would retire from their position, not to ask for any compensation for Philip. The allies, however, refused to consider the question, and on July 25th the French envoys set off for Paris. There was great joy in Spain at the news of the rupture of the negotiations at Gertruydenberg. The Duke of Medina Celi had fallen on April 15th, and French influence, guided as ever by the Princesse des Ursins, had now still further triumphed. Louis renewed his close connection with Spain, placed Vendôme at the head of the army in the Peninsula, and thought of sending Amelot back to Madrid. But the disasters of Almenara in June, and of Saragossa in August, followed by the entry of Charles into Madrid, checked for a time the rising hopes of the supporters of Philip at Versailles. The peace party raised their heads, and Louis for a moment feared that any further effort would be useless. He determined to persuade Philip to abdicate quietly, and the Duc de Noailles was sent to Spain to make this proposal. The year 1710 thus marks the complete desertion of the policy adopted in 1701. The condition of Spain seemed fully to justify the fears of Louis XIV. It had been denuded of French troops, and its government no longer directed from Versailles, had fallen into the hands of men hostile to the French system. France had moreover offered to the allies a subsidy to enable them to expel Philip, and Louis had attempted to persuade his grandson to abdicate voluntarily.

But from 1710 the light began to dawn both in Spain and France. The change of government in England marked a weariness of the war throughout that country, and a deep distrust of the war policy of the Whigs. In Spain the victories of Brihuega and Villa Viciosa (Dec. 8th and 10th) destroyed the hopes of the Archduke Charles and replaced Philip on the throne. In spite of the embassy of Noailles the King had firmly refused to abdicate, and he was fully justified. The Spanish nation devoted to Philip's cause was more determined than ever to adhere to the sovereign of their choice. Lastly Louis on hearing Noailles' report and delighted with the victory of Villa Viciosa changed his whole attitude and wrote encouraging letters to his grandson. The year 1711 opened most hopefully, and before the end of January Vendome's successes in Catalonia still further damaged the fortunes of the allies in Spain. In April, the death of the Emperor Joseph I. brought fresh hopes to the House of Bourbon. An express was sent by Louis to Philip with the news. Surely, it was now argued, if the Spanish Empire was partitioned and forever separated from the French monarchy, the balance of power in Europe would be less endangered than by the union of the Spanish and Imperial crowns under Charles VI.

Though Louis' endeavours to make some arrangement with Austria failed, the English Tory statesmen were now willing to consider terms of peace on the basis of the continued possession by Philip of Spain and the Indies. Philip himself strongly opposed any partition of his dominions and resented extremely the loss of Gibraltar to the English. To his complaints Louis wrote letters of moderation and good sense. "There are occasions," he said, "when it is necessary to know how to lose." But Philip was governed by his wife and the Princesse des Ursins, and both ladies were opposed to concessions. Without any clear policy, devoid of counsels of vigour or energy, Philip took no advantage of the victory of Villa Viciosa and things were allowed to drift. Nothing could be expected from a Court influenced by women and incapables, honeycombed by intrigue, and dominated by indolence. At this crisis, as at every crisis during the war, the initiative had to come from France. A capable envoy must be sent at once to obtain the adhesion of the Court of Spain to a reasonable partition of the Spanish Empire. Taught by experience Louis now recognised that a first minister was absolutely necessary if order was to be restored and wise counsels were to have the upper hand in Spain. It was obviously inconvenient to place the French ambassador in such a position, and a Spaniard would naturally refuse to carry out a policy of partition. An Italian then must be found, and Torcy wrote suggesting three Italian cardinals. But the Court of Spain offered a strenuous resistance.

The Princesse des Ursins replied that Philip would have no first minister. Louis was in a difficult position. The Spaniards detested the French influence, the suspicions of the allies would be at once aroused if they noticed any tendency towards the union of the two kingdoms such as Amelot's residence in Spain had seemed to imply. Louis' solution was a wise one. From 1711 in clear and emphatic terms he renounced the policy of governing Spain from Versailles or of uniting the two monarchies under one head. This new definite policy carried out during the embassy of the Marquis of Bonnac to Spain in 1711 was embodied in the famous renunciations which publicly recognised the separation of the two monarchies of France and Spain.

Henceforward France may influence but not govern. The two nations may be united in a friendly alliance and the reigning houses by ties of blood. But Spain must be left to work out her own fortunes. She must appear before Europe a power as independent as that of France or of England. Whatever Louis' wishes and hopes had been in the earlier phases of the war, events had proved too strong for him. The independent spirit of the Spaniards was a revelation which he slowly was compelled to recognise, and though the accession to the Imperial throne of the Archduke Charles enabled the English Tory Government to modify the policy of the Whigs and to permit a Bourbon to sit on the throne of Spain, public opinion in England insisted on the renunciations.

Probably no task was ever undertaken by Louis more difficult than that of persuading the Spaniards to consent to a partition of their dominions. His envoy Bonnac was observant, sagacious, and faithful, and he fulfilled the expectations formed of him in carrying out his most delicate mission with infinite success. He immediately grasped the political situation. He saw that Philip V. was without any power of

decision, and was governed absolutely by the Queen,
who, embittered by her misfortunes, was strongly
averse to any concessions, and that the Princesse des
Ursins was alone capable of influencing the Queen,
but very sensitive of any attempt to lessen her
authority at the Court. To manage such a trio
required tact, and Bonnac advised Louis to assert no
authority over the King and Queen, and when writing to them to seemingly allow them full independence. Four days after his arrival Philip signified to
his grandfather his assent to the loss of Gibraltar and
Port Mahon, and his adhesion to the Assiento treaty.

At the close of 1711 France seemed to be still in
a most perilous situation. Marlborough certainly
had fallen in disgrace, but the enemies of France
were apparently still united in desiring her ruin.
France was only saved by the victory of Denain,
and by the policy of Harley and St. John.

In his interview with Villars before the latter's
departure for Flanders, the aged monarch spoke of
the possible advance of the allies to Paris, and told
the Marshal that he had resolved, should such an
advance be made, to collect as many troops as he
could, and die in a last attempt to save his country,
and his crown. The English commander, Ormond,
on July 16th, 1712, proclaimed a suspenion of arms
with the French, and Villars, with whom Ormond
was in constant correspondence, published a like proclamation with regard to the English. Weakened by
the withdrawal of the British army, the allies suffered
a series of disasters. Eugène had left Albemarle
with eight thousand men in an entrenched camp at

Denain. This camp Villars determined to storm.
On July 24th the attack was made, the principal
obstacle being a deep ditch in front of the entrench-
ment. Villars, recognising the importance of rapidity of movement, refused to spend any time in filling
the ditch with fascines. "Our fascines," he said,
"shall be the bodies of the first fallen." After a
stubborn defence the allied forces fled in panic, and
a large number perished in the Scheldt.

"Villars," said the great Napoleon in after days,
"saved France at Denain." The Marshal had again
given evidence of the quickness of eye for which he
was well known, and of his unconquerable energy
and dash. Before the end of the year the reduction
of many towns had established a strong barrier, and
France was safe. It is impossible to overestimate
the political importance of Denain. Louis XIV. at
once recognised the real meaning of the victory. On
July 29th he wrote to Villars: "I cannot speak too
highly of the way in which you formed the design
in concert with the Marshal Montesquieu, the secrecy
which you preserved, and the means you took to
execute it. Nothing is more likely to advance
favourable negotiations of peace than the re-establishment of that superiority of our arms which has been
so unfortunately lost for many years. . . . The
powers now in deliberation will be much more tract-
able when they see the disappearance of all Prince
Eugène's hopes of the invasion of my kingdom.
This is the result which I hope to gain (*c'est le fruit
que j'espère retirer*) from the very important service
which you have just rendered me."

MARSHAL VILLARS.
(From Courcy's *Coalition of 1701*.)

Louis was not deceived in the estimate which he had formed of the importance of Denain. The capture of Marchiennes, Saint-Armand, Mortagne, Douai, and Bouchain restored the prestige of the French arms, and, with the defections of the English placed to the Dutch and the Imperialists in great measure at Louis' mercy. The allies, furious at the failure of their plan of securing ascendancy at the conference, for a time suspended all negotiations. But Louis' anxiety for peace was not only equalled but surpassed by that felt by the English ministry. Bolingbroke determined if necessary to make a separate treaty with France, and visited Paris early in August. Ten days' personal negotiation with Torcy adjusted the principal points of difficulty, and smoothed the way for a satisfactory settlement of all the matters at issue between the two countries. Before his departure Bolingbroke had an interview with Louis at Fontainebleau.

There he found the Court in high spirits at the successes of Villars. Even Louis, on hearing of the capture of Marchiennes, had thanked the courtiers for their congratulations. In his interview with Bolingbroke, the aged King, speaking rapidly and indistinctly, acknowledged his obligations to the Queen of England and avowed his earnest desire for peace.

On Bolingbroke's arrival in London a suspension of arms with France for four months was proclaimed in London.

The congress of Utrecht was opened on January 12, 1712, but before many weeks were over both

Bourbon Courts had been thrown into inexorable grief and consternation at the successive deaths of the Duchess and Duke of Burgundy, followed by that of their eldest child the Duke of Brittany. In both Paris and Madrid it was believed that the Duke of Orleans was sweeping away the royal family in order to secure the throne for himself, and it was asserted that neither the lives of Louis XIV. or Philip V. were safe. But these domestic afflictions only increased the determination of the allies to force from Philip an absolute renunciation of all claims to the French throne. To this the Court of Spain offered an obstinate resistance, and during a great part of 1712 Louis had to employ alternately persuasion and menaces to induce Philip to accede to his demands. On July 8th the Spanish nation was informed in a proclamation that their King had renounced all claim to the French throne, and in December these renunciations of Philip were ratified by the Spanish Cortes. Somewhat naturally the English ministers desired that the States-General should ratify the French renunciations. But Louis regarded such a request as a personal insult, and Torcy wrote to Bolingbroke that " the Estates in France have nothing to do with questions regarding the succession to the Crown, they have not the power either to make or to abrogate the laws." It was indeed true that practically the States-General could hardly be said to exist. The sovereignty in France resided in the King alone, and all that Louis would concede was that the *Parlement* of Paris should register the renunciations. In March, 1713,

the renunciations of the Dukes of Berry and Orleans
were solemnly registered by the *Parlement*. The
Spanish ambassador in France was, however, firmly
convinced that all these renunciations were worthless, and that in the event of the death of the
Dauphin, Philip V. would return to France.

The question, too, of Bavaria required delicate
handling. The ally of Louis, the Elector had lost
his territories after Blenheim, and, after Malplaquet,
he had been compelled to leave his government of
the Spanish Netherlands and to fly into France. Restored in 1711, he was recognised by Philip V. in
1712 as hereditary sovereign of the Low Countries.
Maximilian's chances of being restored to Bavaria
seemed indeed remote. He had been put to the ban
of the Empire, and even Louis thought the recovery
of Bavaria from Austria was impossible. But the
Elector owed his eventual restoration to the determination of the Dutch not to allow any ally of Louis
to reign over the Spanish Netherlands.

Eventually, after much negotiation, the best
solution of a difficult matter was found to lie in
the restoration of Maximilian to his hereditary
dominions.

In February, 1714, a close alliance was formed between France and Bavaria, which remained unbroken
for many years, and which resulted in the accession
of Charles of Bavaria to the Imperial throne as
Charles VII., in 1742.

On April 11, 1713, the Peace of Utrecht was finally
signed. To England France yielded Newfoundland,
Acadia, and Hudson's Bay, though she reserved Cape

Breton and her share in the fisheries of the coast. She also promised to dismantle Dunkirk and to recognise the Protestant Succession in England. She was forced to see the firm establishment of England as a Mediterranean power, and her dreams of domination over Southern Europe dispelled. At the time of the Partition treaties, and again when he accepted the Will, Louis had definitely aimed at making the Mediterranean into a Bourbon lake.

But the English interests in the Mediterranean Sea were very considerable. And not the least important results of the Spanish Succession war were that England, obtained ample securities for the interests which she had already acquired in the Mediterranean, and that Louis was compelled to relinquish schemes which Napoleon a century later again attempted in vain to realise. With regard to Holland, France agreed to the establishment of a Barrier, and to the cession of the Spanish Netherlands to Austria. She managed, however, to regain Lille, Aire, Bethune, and Saint-Venant. With Prussia there was little to settle. France recognised the royal title of the Elector, his rights over Neufchâtel, and his possession of Upper Guelderland. The King of Prussia on his part renounced all his claims on the principality of Orange, and on the lordships of Châlon and Châtel-Berlin in Franche-Comté. France further recognised the claims of the Duke of Savoy to Sicily with the title of King. She restored to him Savoy and Nice, and it was agreed that if Philip's line failed, the House of Savoy should reign in Spain. Louis made no concealment of his delight at the conclusion of peace.

Writing to Philip, he congratulates him on the fact
that he was now recognised, even by his enemies, as
King of Spain, and declares that at one time he had
never hoped for such a happy result of the war.
France had suffered severe defeats and had been
forced to make cessions to England, but these cessions were mainly in America, and as a compensation
she could look to the establishment of a Bourbon
dynasty at Madrid. Far different were the feelings
of Philip. Spain had lost heavily by the peace.
Her possessions in Italy and the Netherlands were
handed over to the Emperor and to the Duke of
Savoy, while England secured Gibraltar and Minorca, and the Assiento or grant of the slave trade
with America. She was now shut out as it were from
the general life of Europe, and remained isolated
behind the Pyrenees. This feeling of rage and dis-
appointment explains Philip's delay in signing the
treaties of peace with England, Savoy, and Holland,
and his deep-seated determination to reconquer on
the first opportunity his lost possessions in Italy.
But Spain was at this moment helpless, and Louis,
determined to obtain peace, could always secure
Philip's obedience by threatening as a last resource
to withdraw the French troops from Spain. Though
the Emperor stood out, he could do nothing without
his allies. Villars proved too strong for Eugène,
took Landau and Freiburg, and on March 6, 1714,
the Peace of Rastadt between France and Austria
was made, followed by that of Baden between France
and the Empire. Writing in February to Madame
de Maintenon, about the signature of the Peace of

Rastadt, Louis had said : " I thought you would not be sorry to hear this good news a few hours before the rest of the world, but say nothing about it, only that Prince Eugène has returned to Rastadt, and that the conferences are going on again. I am sure of peace and rejoice at it with you. Let us thank God with all our hearts."

By the treaties with the Emperor and Empire, Louis secured the replacement of the Electors of Bavaria and Cologne in their territories ; he kept Alsace and Strasburg, and the terms in the Peace of Ryswick with regard to the re-establishment of the Roman Catholic faith in all his dominions were retained. The Emperor, on his part, agreed to accept the conclusions come to at Utrecht with regard to his possessions of Naples, Sardinia, Milan, the Tuscan Ports and the Spanish Netherlands. He further agreed to the formation of a Barrier, and Louis recognised the erection of Hanover as an Electorate.

Spain was not included in the above arrangements, and Philip felt deeply hurt that his grandfather should have made peace with the Emperor without compelling him to renounce the title of King of Spain. Till the death of Louis XIV. the relations between France and Spain were strained. The reforms of Amelot and Orri admirable though they were in many respects, had been accompanied by the appearance of a vast number of French financiers and contractors in Spain. Extortion had increased under the French system, and taxation had become heavier. The French agents of Louis had begun the work of financial and commercial re-

organisation, but much remained to be done. The
French were unpopular at Madrid, and the death of
Philip's brave Queen, Maria Louisa of Savoy, in
February, 1714, followed by that of the Duke of
Berry on May 11th, only increased the hostile feeling
against the French. The remaining surviving son of
the Duke of Burgundy, a child of four, alone stood
between Orleans and the succession, and it seemed
quite possible that round him might rage, in the near
future, a struggle between the two branches of the
Bourbon family.

Philip himself was determined to break through
his renunciations and, though not to unite France
and Spain under the same head, to place them in
the hands of the same branch of the House of Bourbon. Suspicious of Orleans, he demanded that the
Dauphin should be put under his own care, and that
in the event of Louis' death the Regency should be
confided to him. But Louis absolutely refused to
listen to Philip's schemes for the abrogation of the
renunciations. The death of Anne had thrown the
government of England into the hands of the Whigs,
who, as Louis believed, desired an excuse for re-
opening the struggle. Apart from a question of
policy, Torcy assures us that Louis was sincere in
his determination not to break pledges solemnly
given. But an event soon occurred which ended for
a time the influence of France upon Spain. The
marriage of Philip to Elizabeth Farnese brought with
it the fall of the Princesse des Ursins in December,
1714, and gave an intimation to the world that Spain
was prepared to act independently of France. As

the Princesse des Ursins " passed the mountains,"
writes Mr. Armstrong, in his *Life of Elizabeth
Farnese*, " the Pyrenees recovered their existence,
and Spain and France were separate." Whatever had
been her faults, the Princesse had on the whole used
her talents in the service of France. It is not too
much to say it was greatly due to her agency that
the influence of the *Grand Monarque* was exercised
in varying degrees in Spain for some fifteen years.
She was seen at her best when working with Amelot,
whose wisdom and discretion held her quick and
jealous temper in check. Always governed by ambition, always jealous of any diminution of her
power, she fell from a position almost unique in the
history of modern European monarchies through
want of tact and loss of temper. Louis was unusually fortunate in his agents, but he rarely was
served with greater ability than by the celebrated
Princesse des Ursins.[1]

Her return to Versailles proved to be only the
prelude of her exile. The celebrated friendship between her and Madame de Maintenon had long since
cooled, and moreover she and the Duke of Orleans
were mortal foes. When the latter heard of her
probable arrival, he proposed at once to go to Paris,
since, as he himself declared, he would not answer for
himself should they meet. Madame de Maintenon
promptly recognised the necessity of getting rid of
her former friend. After a short stay at Versailles

---

[1] Mr. Armstrong in his *Life of Elizabeth Farnese* gives a graphic
description of the condition of Spain at the end of the Spanish
Succession War.

and several interviews with the king at Marly, it was clearly intimated to the unfortunate and heart-broken woman that though Louis would grant her a pension, she would do well to reside in Italy. After remaining in Genoa some years, she established herself in Rome, and there spent the rest of her life among strangers far away from the France that she loved and had served so well. To her constant watchfulness and untiring energy the Bourbons owed their possession of Spain.

After the peace of Utrecht was signed, Louis devoted himself to the completion of the policy which since 1711 he had set himself to carry out—the political union and the dynastic separation of the crowns of France and Spain. And this policy was one which after the stormy scenes of the Regency commended itself to statesmen in both countries and influenced the destinies of two nations down to the Revolution.

A close union between France and Spain—Louis had said—was necessary for the benefit of both. Each kingdom should, however, govern itself according to its usages and customs, and remain independent of foreign intervention. Thus the jealousy of hostile Europe would be unable to find any ground for asserting that Spain was the creature of France. But Louis had not before his death secured even the partial adhesion of Spain to this policy without experiencing grave difficulties, and the political union between the two countries was in danger of shipwreck during the meeting of the Congress of Utrecht. Louis desired peace. He was old, and France was exhausted. He was convinced that she could not withstand another European attack. He was anxious to hand down to his successors France at peace and with her borders extended. And no sooner had the Peace of Utrecht been made than his desire to keep that peace became overwhelmingly strong. Honour forbade that the renunciations should be broken. The close union of France and Spain depended on the strict adhesion to the terms of peace.

Philip on the other hand was young. He owed his throne to the national feeling in Spain against the dismemberment of the monarchy. He was the founder of a new dynasty. How could he, then, be expected, before he had been on the throne of his adopted country twelve years, to consent to a serious and disgraceful partition? He had during the long war been almost miraculously saved time after time from absolute ruin. Would he not be justified in trusting to Providence to cover the plans of his enemies with confusion? Spain had actually suffered less than France. She was less exhausted, less denuded of men, less impoverished. As to the renunciations, Philip regarded them as only extorted by force and only made to be broken. The authority of Louis XIV. alone compelled the unwilling agreement of Philip to the partitions and to the denunciations. No sooner was Louis dead than the schemes of Alberoni and Elizabeth Farnese expressed the real wishes of the Spanish King, and for a time checked that union between the two monarchies which it had been the object of Louis XIV. to bring about.

The history of the last fifteen years of the reign of Louis XIV. must ever be regarded as the most remarkable in his life, so far as he himself is concerned. At no period did Louis show more energy and vitality; at no period was his influence more strongly felt, at no period was his personality more generally recognised.

During the years from 1702 to 1708 and from 1712 to 1715, the Court life proceeded pretty much on its old lines. The young Duchess of Burgundy did her best to direct the gaieties of the courtiers. She took part in the hunting and riding expeditions, in the comedies and fêtes. And at the end of 1707 we find the Court assembled at Marly and the Duchess arranging entertainments to divert the King and Queen of England. The victory of Almanza gave, perhaps, some justification for these festivities. But the King, old and austere, took little part in any Court gaieties, and though Madame de Maintenon sometimes arranged comedies to amuse him, and though at the beginning of 1708 he appeared at some masques, it was always difficult to distract him from serious considerations. From 1708 to 1712 the Court became sombre and saddened. These were the years of disasters abroad, followed by attempts on the part of the allies to make peace on terms humiliating to France; these were the years when famine and misery stalked through the country, and when death visited the royal family. The gaiety of the Duchess of Burgundy came suddenly to an end when her husband, blamed for his share in the disastrous campaign of 1708, returned to be attacked by a

malignant and badly informed public opinion. In
the spring of 1711 the death of the Dauphin filled
the whole Court with dismay, which gave way to
absolute despair when the Duchess of Burgundy,
her husband, and her eldest son, the Duke of Brittany, were carried off early in 1712. The whole of
France was dazed and overwhelmed with grief. The
hopes of " the Burgundy party," which on the death
of the Dauphin had turned their eyes towards Cambrai, in anticipation of the accession of the young
Duke of Burgundy, were dashed to the ground. The
political life of Fénelon was finished, and with the
death of Burgundy passed away the best chance ever
offered to the House of Bourbon of preventing a
future revolution by strengthening their hold on
their people by wise and timely reforms. " We have
no longer a Court," wrote Madame de Maintenon ;
" all those who were its ornaments have disappeared."
During these years of terrible disasters abroad and
of heartrending misfortunes within his own family,
Louis showed a marvellous control over himself.
He felt his afflictions, says Saint-Simon, and could
not restrain his tears before his ministers and once
before Villars. But he showed undoubted courage in
the calm and dignified way in which he faced misfortune. He preserved, as a rule, the same impassive
exterior when good news, such as the success of the
negotiations for peace, had been conveyed to him.
This self-control, which he first learnt to exercise
during the struggle with Condé and the Fronde,
never left him, and continued to the end of his
life.

Saint-Simon's description of Louis' courage under adversity is well known. Overwhelmed with his country's misfortunes and his domestic griefs, the old King showed throughout a constancy and a strength of will which surprised all who knew him. His constant trust that the future would bring him good fortune, his unshaken courage, his wisdom—it was such qualities as these, says the Court historian, which gained for him the admiration of Europe and for which he deserved the name of Great.

It was not till 1712 that the Court shook off its gloom. Peace was in sight and Villars' victory at Denain in July, 1711 had saved France from invasion and had retrieved the national honour. Peace restored many nobles to Versailles, and till the death of Louis the Court became again brilliant and gay. After four years of restraint a reaction naturally set in, and the last three years of Louis' reign form a prelude, so far as the Court was concerned, to the days of the Regency.

Just as at the Restoration of Charles II. so in 1712 disasters and a period of constraint were succeeded by an outburst of immorality. Gambling increased, scandals multiplied. Madame de Maintenon was fully alive to this state of things, but was quite unable to check it. Her position was indeed assured, and the troops of place hunters still believed that her authority was paramount. She interviewed the ministers and to some extent guided their counsels; she was treated as Queen by the King's regiment; it was said that Louis had appointed her to be Regent on his death. But she was too fully occupied with

guarding Louis from all trouble and annoyance to
be able to exert an energetic influence in favour of a
reformation of morals.

Though Louis was rapidly approaching his end
his political activity was still remarkable. He was
determined before his death to carry out the terms
of the peace of Utrecht with regard to the Spanish
monarchy, and by careful arrangements with reference to the Regency on his death to leave France
and Spain at peace. In accordance with these reso-
lutions Louis sent Berwick to Catalonia to aid Philip
in reducing Barcelona, and in spite of the sympathy
shown to the revolted Catalans by the Emperor and
by England Louis carried out his intention. The
fall of Barcelona on September 13, 1714, marked the
end of the Catalan revolt. Philip was anxious to
proceed to severities, but Louis urged moderation
and clemency. He was willing that the walls of
Barcelona should be razed to the ground, and that
the whole country should be forced to accept the
laws of Castille, but he strongly advised that the
Catalans should be allowed to enjoy their municipal
privileges, and that a courageous people should not
be treated with useless inhumanity. Majorca and
Ivica were conquered in the following spring, and
Louis could rest satisfied that, in spite of the obstacles
placed in his way by the Austrians and English, the
Emperor had lost all influence in Catalonia and in
the Balearic Islands, and that Philip was master of
his dominions. His next task was to leave the two
branches of the Bourbon House in amity, and to
provide for the succession. To effect this Philip and

Orleans must be reconciled. The suspicion that
Orleans had aimed at succeeding Philip, if the latter
was dethroned, had never been removed, and it required much tact and correspondence to bring about
a reconciliation. But Philip never wavered in his
resolve to secure control over the Dauphin, and, if he
died, the eventual succession to France. And this
determination ran counter to Louis' dispositions. In
July, 1714, he had given Maine and Toulouse the
position of Princes of the Blood, and a little later he
had left the Regency to Orleans in conformity with
his rights of birth and the spirit of the late treaties.
The education of the young Louis was to be placed
in the hands of Fleury, Bishop of Frèjus, while the
Duke of Maine was to be his guardian, Villeroy his
governor, and Le Tellier his confessor.

In this manner had Louis by the time of his death
settled the important political questions which required immediate solution. But the intrigues of the
Spanish party made it quite clear that on Louis'
death the Regent would have grave difficulties with
Spain. Louis' own predilections were in favour of
the Duke of Maine, and it is to his credit that he did
not permit himself to make grave political blunders
in order to satisfy his own personal wishes.

France could, on the whole, look back on the war
of the Spanish Succession, and on the settlement of
Utrecht with satisfaction. The system established
by the peace of Westphalia would, in the opinion of
Europe, have been overthrown had the crown of
Spain been united to that of France or Austria. And
it was that conviction which was answerable for the

war of eleven years. The coalition of 1701 and the preliminaries of peace signed in London in 1711 (October) averted these two dangers. French blood had been spilt in Germany and on the banks of the Rhine from 1702 to 1708, in Italy and Provence from 1701 to 1707, in the Low Countries from 1701 to 1712, and in Spain from 1701 to 1714. In spite of her disasters, the position of France was very different in 1714 from what it had been in 1648. No one then could have foreseen her steady development and consistent territorial aggrandisement. She had secured by the treaty of the Pyrenees Artois and Roussillon and many other important places, by the treaty of Aix-la-Chapelle a portion of Flanders, by the treaty of Nimeguen Franche-Comté, by the treaty of Ryswick the rest of Alsace and Strasburg.

The system inaugurated at Münster and Osnabrück in 1648 had proved successful. The theory of the balance of power had been kept diligently before their eyes by all statesmen, and the pacification at Utrecht was the triumph of that theory.

While Spain was left entirely independent, her territories in Italy and Flanders were given to the Emperor and to Savoy. Austria herself was checked by the two rising powers of Savoy and Prussia, the latter of whom was destined to succeed France in the position of defender of the German liberties.

Louis' error in attempting to enrich himself at the expense of the Empire had resulted in the enhancement of the power and prestige of the Emperor. At one time, when the allies refused to make peace at the Hague and Gertruydenberg, it had seemed likely that the European equilibrium would be endangered if not destroyed by the partial annihilation of the French power. Europe was saved from this calamity by the heroism of Louis himself, by his regard for the honour and welfare of his people, by his keen sense of what was expected from the royal power. His indomitable energy during misfortune was backed up by the devoted zeal of his ministers, by the skill of his ambassadors, and especially by the prudence of Torcy. The fall of the Whigs in 1710, followed by the dismissal of Marlborough and the death of Joseph I., each in its turn contributed to bring the leading European ministers to take a statesmanlike view of the situation. The untiring efforts of Louis during these last days of the war were admirably seconded by the brilliant successes of Villars. At Utrecht, Louis received the reward of his labours. He obtained terms far more favourable than those offered at Gertruydenberg, and he had the satisfaction of feeling that he had preserved not only the integrity of his kingdom, but French nationality itself. During these years the intimate connection subsisting between the Monarch and the people receives ample illustration, while the general conviction that the sovereign was the incarnation of his subjects was of vital importance, and its thorough acceptance by the French nation colours and explains their attitude during the whole of the Spanish Succession war. Had France been governed in that critical year of 1709 by any other than a monarchical system, she would have suffered serious territorial loss, and would have been left humiliated, dismembered, and ruined.

From that fate Louis had saved her, and at the end
of the war he had added a page to her history which,
if in many respects an overwhelmingly pathetic and
painful one, will at any rate be remembered among
the most glorious in her history.

CHAPTER XV.

THE END.

1714–1715.

FRANCE after the conclusion of the peace of Utrecht was, compared with most European countries, in a strong position. She had undoubtedly suffered enormously from the calamities of the war, and was much exhausted.

By the terms of the treaty of Utrecht, she had lost considerably, especially in the colonies. Tournai, Menin, Ypres, and Furnes had been ceded in the North, Exiles and Fenestrelles in the Alps. But Artois, Roussillon, Franche-Comté, Alsace, and Flanders remained to her, and Lorraine was almost within her grasp. Compared with her position in 1643, she had achieved an enormous territorial extension.

Her prestige was little if at all diminished ; she had again shown herself invincible. She had defended herself against a terrible Teutonic onslaught, during which struggle the question of the Spanish Succession had lost itself in the reappearance of the old rivalry between the French Bourbons and the Austrian Hapsburgs. Though the balance of power in the Mediterranean was preserved, France had succeeded in carrying out the principal aim of her policy. She had placed a Bourbon on the Spanish throne and had kept him there.

No doubt the allies were perfectly justified, in 1701, in attacking France and Spain by land and by sea. Though French historians delight in pointing out that as Philip remained on the Spanish throne the desolating war of 1701–1712 was useless, it must be remembered that the political condition of Europe in 1712 was very different from what it was in 1701. In 1701 Louis XIV.'s power was not only still unbroken, and his schemes of aggrandisement still vast, but Philip was his nominee and instrument. In 1712 Louis' power had been brought very low, he had relinquished all schemes of aggression, and Philip had shown himself independent of his grandfather. His renunciations, and his adoption of an independent attitude towards France, coincided with the accession of Charles VI. to the Imperial throne and with the failure of the allies in Spain.

The Spanish power had been destroyed in Italy, and the Low Countries had been handed over to Austria. "Bourbonism" had received a check and its power of aggression was for the time minimised.

The Grand Alliance, in its earlier stages, was perfectly justifiable, but from 1707, the date of the celebrated Whig Resolution, the allies began to deviate
from the path which they had chosen in 1701. Like
the coalition of 1793 their object from 1707 was to
reduce France to the rank of a second rate power.
Each of the allies was bent on territorial acquisitions
though the balance of power continued to be the
pretext of hostility. It was not till the Tories under
Bolingbroke and Harley came into office in 1710,
that the new policy inaugurated by the Whigs was
repudiated. The treaty of Utrecht was then made.
The new European position taken up by England in
1688, and the extraordinary growth of her power
and resources, had been one of the main causes of
the disasters to the French armies; the retirement
of England from the war was the principal cause of
the French success at Denain, her victories against
the Emperor, and the maintenance of her position
in Europe in 1715. And the results of the war,
while they satisfied the honour of France, were invaluable to Spain and to England.

France owed her safety not a little to Spain herself. The allies had found it impossible to succeed
in face of the patriotism of the Castilians, and after
Almanza and Villa Viciosa the Spanish resistance
was of the utmost value to France. Henceforward,
Spain having passed through the fire of adversity,
had to be reckoned with as a European power. The
great qualities of the Spanish race had shown themselves ; Spain gained by losing her outlying provinces, and a veritable renaissance took place under

27

the Alberonis, Ripperdas, and others, culminating in the reign of Charles III. In saving Spain from the House of Hapsburg, Louis XIV. had done much for the balance of power. Though "Bourbonism" became the terror of misguided English statesmen, there was surely something to be said for an alliance between the Bourbons of France, Spain, and Italy, as a counterpoise on the one hand to the Teutonic peoples, and on the other to the growing Slav influence. There was never any real danger of the Pyrenees ceasing to exist, and Louis' solution of the greatest international puzzle of the seventeenth century was, after the war of the Spanish Succession, recognised to be the only possible one. If there was any real danger of a universal monarchy, that danger in the early years of the eighteenth century came rather from Vienna than from Paris.

France too owed a deep debt to her own people. In spite of the unpatriotic conduct of the inhabitants of the Cevennes, in spite of the complaints of Fénélon and of Vauban, the nation as a whole had loyally supported the government. After Malplaquet Villars had not suffered any reproaches, but was allowed to persevere and to win victories at Denain and Landau. France lastly owed much of her success to her able diplomatists, who had watched her interests with extraordinary skill and success.

But though Louis bequeathed the tradition of a brilliant and successful foreign policy to his successors, he left to succeeding generations in France a religious legacy, which proved the source of much

trouble and confusion. The revocation of the Edict
of Nantes had been carried out and the reduction of
the Cevennes during the latter war had removed
any further danger from the Huguenots. But the
Jansenists remained a strong party, including, as they
did, many of the clergy and magistrates and well-to-
do *bourgeois.* Jansenism it had been said reached
even to the throne of the King. This division in
the Gallican Church between Jesuitism and Jansenism was regarded by the government with disfavour
on account of the political side of Jansenism. Every
opponent of the existing state of things naturally
sided with that party which professed independence
of thought, and opposition to extreme centralisation.
Louis had always regarded the Jansenists with suspicion. He knew they did not see the necessity of
absolute union in both religion and politics, he suspected that they desired provincial liberties, the freedom of the Church from state control, and more
power for the aristocracy. He was himself considerably influenced in religious matters by Le Tellier,
the successor of Père La Chaise, and Le Tellier was
a hard intolerant Jesuit.

There is no doubt that the Jesuits took advantage
of the King's dislike of any tendency to divide the
nation into two hostile camps ; they exaggerated
the independence of the Jansenist opinions and their
factious designs ; they accused them of being the
enemies of all authority whether residing in the Pope
or in Bishops or even in Kings ; they accused them,
moreover, of trying to secure for Orleans the succession to the throne. Louis was thoroughly alarmed.

He probably thought that the Jansenists and Huguenots were equally heretics, and he believed that unless
severe measures were at once taken his successor
would find on his accession that a civil war was on
the point of breaking out.

Madame de Maintenon, many of whose friends
were Jansenists, was distracted by her fears and
doubts. De Noailles, the Archbishop of Paris, was
himself a moderate Jansenist, and had seen much of
Madame de Maintenon. But the Jesuit faction was
unrelenting. In 1705 a Bull from Clement XI. destroyed the Peace of Clement IX. (1668) and proclaimed the heretical nature of the Jansenist
opinions; in 1710 Louis ordered the destruction of
Port Royal, which was rased to the ground. Not
content with this success, his advisers determined to
obtain a condemnation of the doctrines contained
in Quesnel's *Reflexions morales sur le Nouveau Testa-
ment*, a book published in 1695, strongly recommended by De Noailles and other bishops, and very
popular in France.

In 1713 Clement XI. was induced by the Jesuits
to issue the famous Bull *Unigenitus* in which he ex-
plicitly condemned 101 propositions taken from
Quesnel's book. To accomplish this result pressure
of the most illegitimate kind had been brought to
bear on the Pope. When the French envoy asked
Clement later why he had condemned such an odd
number, the latter replied, seizing his arm and burst-
ing into tears : " O ! M. Amelot, M. Amelot, what
would you have had me to do ? I strove hard to cur-
tail the list, but Father Le Tellier had pledged him-

self to the King that the book contained more
than a hundred errors, and with his foot on my
throat he compelled me to prove him right. I have
condemned only one more." [1]

Not even at Rome had theological hatred been
carried to a like extent, and the blame for these proceedings must be shared by Louis, Madame de
Maintenon, and Le Tellier. The effects of this Bull
were most disastrous. De Noailles and eight
bishops refused to accept it, and were supported by
the *Parlement* of Paris and many of the most intelligent of Frenchmen. Louis refused to yield or to
adopt a neutral attitude, and insisted on regarding
the opposition to the Bull as opposition to his
own authority. A cruel persecution of the well-to-
do and orderly classes at once took place, 30,000 of
whom are said to have suffered, and the result of
perhaps the saddest episode in the lives of Louis and
of Madame de Maintenon was that up to the Revolution the nation remained divided into two hostile
camps.

In passing judgment on the general character of
Louis' rule and its effects upon France, it must
always be remembered that his rule was popular.
France had from the beginning of her history shown
a strong inclination for a monarchial form of government, and just as she had welcomed the rule of
Henry IV. as a relief from the civil wars, so she
gladly preferred the despotism of Louis XIV. to any
further ruinous attempts to secure a semi-constitu-

---

[1] For an impartial account of the struggle between the Jesuits and
Jansenists, see Rocquain, *L'esprit Revolutionaire Avant la Revolution.*

tional régime. In a long reign such as was that of
Louis, it is an easy matter to find subjects for
criticism.

Perhaps, however, the portion of his life for which
the least allowance will be made, is the period between his mother's death in 1667 and his marriage
to Madame de Maintenon. In these years the most
successful and, from a military point of view, the
most glorious of his reign, his private life, unlike
that of Justinian, was often open to severe criticism.
He seems to have thought he could fly in the face
of even the low moral standard of the day, and not
only emulate, but surpass the conduct of Charles II.
of England. Freed from his mother's control, Louis
plunged into a course of life which continued till the
death of Maria Theresa. In 1671 he appeared in
public driving with Madame de Montespan and
Louise de la Vallière. Such conduct on the part of
one who held a prominent position in Europe had
very evil effects, and before long every German
princeling had his Versailles and his mistresses.
Carried away by his successes, and by the extravagant adulation of a brilliant Court, Louis appears to
have thought that he was above criticism. During
this period of his career his political mistakes
(though often disastrous) were the natural result of
over-confidence or bad advice, and to some extent
could be excused on the ground of youth and inex-
perience.

The non-acceptance of the Dutch terms, followed
by the release of the Dutch prisoners, were blunders
which were redeemed by the brilliant campaigns of

Turenne, and the territorial acquisitions made at the peace of Nimeguen. The success which attended Louis' *Réunion* policy, and the preposterous claims with which he justified that policy, need not astonish a generation which has followed the policy of France in Africa and in the far East during the XIXth century. But the truce of Ratisbon was a most unfortunate blunder, and can with difficulty be explained. Louis was at that time intent on the construction of Versailles, he had acquired a brilliant European position, he was the most admired and envied monarch in Europe. He probably thought that the Netherlands were within his grasp, and that the hostility of the Emperor was of little account. Nevertheless the truce of Ratisbon was an error, the consequences of which were most serious.

The revocation of the Edict of Nantes, the attack on Philipsburg in 1688, and the devastation of the Palatinate in 1689 are the great blots in the reign to which most historians naturally turn. All of these have been fully discussed in previous chapters. Each brought its own retribution during the Spanish Succession war. France in her need sadly missed the men who would have been the flower of her troops, she realised what the revolution of 1688 had done for England, and she experienced the undying hostility of the Germans, anxious to avenge the devastated Rhineland.

When we approach the Spanish Succession war we are at once in a land where confusion worse confounded seems to reign. Most writers find that Louis' intention of placing Philip on the Spanish throne was in itself monstrous, and was the cause of the long war which proved so disastrous to France. In a previous chapter it has been sufficiently shown that the actual acceptance of the Will was not in itself a misfortune for the world, but that it probably offered to Europe the best solution of the difficult Spanish Succession question. The war was caused by Louis' extraordinary want of moderation in face of a highly excited state of feeling in Europe. If he had not reserved Philip's right to the French throne, if he had not seized the barrier towns, if in a word he had faithfully carried out the treaty of Ryswick and had not taken up an aggressive attitude, it is very probable that the war might have been averted. By bringing on his country through these ill-considered and rash acts a devastating war, Louis inflicted on France an injury almost comparable to that caused by the revocation of the Edict of Nantes, and in consequence on his death he left France unconquered indeed, but overwhelmed by the miseries entailed upon her by the long wars, and from which she did not recover before the Revolution. He left behind him, too, a legacy of discontent which proved in the end fatal to his family.

All these misfortunes might have been averted by a wise policy at the time of the acceptance of the Will. But the feeling of overweening pride and his exaggerated self-confidence, which in 1672 and in 1684 had been so strongly in evidence, seem again to have possessed Louis. No sooner did he win some great success than he appeared to lose all sense of moderation, and the power of seeing things as they were. Prosperity brought with it apparently an aggressive spirit and for the time eliminated all wise counsels. On the other hand, no sooner do danger and difficulties arise than the real heroism of the man appears, and we at once understand the influence that he wielded for so many years. The appointment of Chamillard was unpardonable and Louis' belief that he, at his age, could correct his minister's blunders, direct simultaneous operations with success in Flanders, on the Rhine, in Italy or in Spain, besides organising the whole of the Spanish government, fills us with wonder. All through his reign the feeling of admiration at his energy, his conscientiousness, his labours, his devotion to his country, his influence on men as widely different in their tastes and ability as were Bolingbroke and Villars, Saint-Simon and Bossuet, contend with the feeling of amazement at the pettiness of some of his acts, at his religious bigotry, at the influence of the Court over his choice of generals, at his preference for Villeroy to Villars, at his suspicions of Turenne.

Had Louis been content to devote his whole energies to the territorial extension of France, to the expansion of her colonies, and the increase of her trade, posterity might have accused him of ambition, and blamed him for his vast expenditure. Such a line of policy would, however, in his case have been excusable, for his interest in diplomacy was great, and his fondness of military operations excessive. He could, too, have found some justification in the similarity of his own views with those of most of his subjects, and he could always point out that in diplomacy and in war, France

held during his reign a leading position in Europe.
But from the date of his marriage with Madame de
Maintenon, his resolution to lead a sober and severe
life synchronises with a determination not to rest satisfied with a policy which had brought his country
glory and territory, but to plunge into the labyrinth
of religious controversies and to root out of France
all opinions which did not agree with those held by
himself and his spiritual advisers. Naturally ignorant, all his ignorance and all his intellectual defi-
ciences were at once revealed in a strong light as soon
as he allowed himself to be influenced by a number
of unstatesmanlike ecclesiastics, and encouraged by
a narrow-minded enthusiast like Madame de Maintenon.

There is not a touch of greatness in Louis' religious policy. That he was seriously religious there
is no reason to doubt. "Father," he once said to
Massillon after the termination of his first course at
Versailles, "I have listened in my chapel to many great
preachers, and I have been very well satisfied with
them ; but as often as I hear you, I am very ill satisfied with myself." But Louis' religious policy teems
with ignorance, vindictiveness, and short-sighted-
ness. After 1704 even Massillon was excluded from
Court favour, owing to his supposed inclination to
Jansenism. The interests of France were ignored,
measures utterly un-Christian and cruel were adopted,
and the country was left rent and torn by religious
divisions.

But in his attitude to Europe, Louis' greatness is
distinctly recognized. Though he left France at

war with herself over a religious question, he could at any rate rest satisfied that before he died western Europe was at peace. He was in all his political and diplomatic relations a great King. His designs were magnificent, and his appreciation of the true policy of France was, as a rule, correct. In his later years, during the Spanish Succession war, his greatness was more than ever apparent, and was acknowledged by English statesmen. The tragic incidents of his declining years only serve to bring out more distinctly his better and greater qualities.

Louis' mistakes, serious though they were, did not prevent his rule from conferring real benefits on France. The establishment of an orderly, well-organised government rescued the country from the chaos which characterised the Fronde period, and launched her on a career of prosperity which the long wars could only temporarily check. Throughout the length and breadth of the land the law reigned supreme. Feudal anarchy became impossible, and powerful nobles with great local influence ceased to exist in any part of France. The centralised administration which was established under the authority of the King worked its will unfettered by the States-General, the *Parlements*, the nobility, or any local bodies. At the Revolution this theory of a centralised administration was adopted by the Jacobins, and the system of Louis XIV. was not only adhered to but developed.

And this centralising tendency was only the natural outcome of the gradual development of France. She had been built up by the annexation

of outlying territories, each of which was allowed to
retain its privileges and customs. Thus Artois,
Brittany, Burgundy, Languedoc, and Provence retained their own provincial estates on Louis' accession, and not unfrequently by these estates a very
independent attitude was assumed. There seems
little doubt that it was for the benefit of France and
for the increase of her influence that the political
independence of these provincial estates should be
temporarily suspended by the growth of the King's
absolute authority. Union and centralisation were
demanded by the geographical position of France.
In a similar manner all independent life in the cities
disappeared. In most of the municipalities corruption was common and the government inefficient.
Louis' measures were, unfortunately more in the direction of abolition than of reform, and the net result
was that all interest felt by the citizens in the government of the towns was destroyed. But as a compensation, the system of guilds was broken down,
industries were organised, manufactures were encouraged, and France was prepared, at the beginning
of the eighteenth century, to take her part in the
coming industrial revolution.

The power of the monarchy, too, exercised a beneficial influence in the region of law. The political
powers claimed by the *Parlement* were set aside,
and they were bidden to limit themselves to their
judicial duties. Great improvements were also
effected in the legal system, and though much remained to be done, the code of Louis XIV. proved
of incalculable value. This centralised system was

then the outcome of the whole previous history of France; it conferred enormous benefits on the country, it was the only system fitted for the needs and aspirations of the French people, and as such has been adopted by all succeeding French governments.

The faults of the absolutism of Louis XIV. are obvious. With regard to the nobles the policy of the government did not go far enough. It has been very truly said by a modern writer that the absolute power of the King "was held in check by the innumerable usages and traditions of a highly civilised society." The existence of these traditions may have tended to incline the government to pursue a compromising policy with regard to the nobles, but whatever was the cause, the results of the policy adopted were most disastrous. The whole history of France in the seventeenth century proves conclusively that the nobles were unfit to be trusted with political power. In overthrowing their political influence, Louis' government had done well. But no attempt was made to destroy their privileges, and these remained to bring upon the nobles and with them the monarchy, revolution and ruin. The greatest mistake to be ascribed by Louis' government was that, in respect to the privileges of the nobles, it pursued an illadvised and fatal policy. Had Louis placed himself at the head of a social revolution and reduced the nobles to a condition similar to that enjoyed by the English peerage, the monarchy would probably have been saved, and France spared years of revolutionary trouble.

Much alleviation in taxation might have been given to France in the eighteenth century had Louis increased the powers of local assemblies over the collection of the *taille*. Louis' government like that of Justinian was costly, and its costliness was increased by the expense of collecting the taxes. The central administration was forced to employ an army of officials whose opportunities of profit were very considerable. Had the system of assessing and collecting the taxes by local assemblies been extended, a great saving would have been affected and taxation consequently diminished. It was a calamity for France that the results of the centralised system were not only the permanent impoverishment but also the destruction of much vitality in the provinces, and in the city governments, followed by the overwhelming increase of the influence of Paris. But the indirect results of the governmental system of France in the second half of the seventeenth century must not be entirely laid to the charge of Louis. In the social and political condition of France a strong centralised government was the necessity of the hour, and with the establishment of the unquestioned authority of the King, France enjoyed increased prosperity, while the sphere of her influence in Europe was widely extended. Had Louis destroyed the privileges of the nobles, had he entirely abolished the political functions of the *Parlements*, had he wisely given the local assemblies more power in the matter of taxation, France would have developed in the direction of a constitutional government. He had, however,

given France a definite form of government suitable
to the times in which he lived. The establishment of
a bureaucracy dependent on an absolutism did wonders for France in the seventeenth century. It is
much to be regretted that Louis' successors did not
introduce the modifications required by the existence
of new conditions and new ideas in the eighteenth
century. Their failure to adapt themselves to the
exigencies of the times cannot be laid to the charge
of the Grand Monarque.

Louis' latter days were clouded with grief. He had
witnessed the tragic death of the Duke of Burgundy
in 1712 at Marly " la funestre Marly," where one
of the best known and most pathetic scenes in his
life took place. Mary Beatrice, whom Louis had
always treated with the greatest respect and affection, had lost her daughter Louisa and in her grief
came to visit Louis still mourning over the sorrows
of his house. It is related that they laid aside all
court etiquette, weeping together in their common
grief because, as the Queen said, " We saw the aged
were left, and that death had swept away the young."
On August 10, 1715, Louis took his last walk in the
gardens at Marly, which is so closely associated with
Madame de Maintenon and so fully described by
Saint-Simon. To the last Madame de Maintenon
remained his watchful guardian and his intelligent
companion. Her devotion was unsurpassed, while
her virtuous existence at a Court distinguished, before her marriage to Louis, by frivolities and vice,
renders her worthy of much honour. " She never
did harm to a soul," was the verdict of the Regent

Orleans, " and she always tried to keep peace and harmony among all." Throughout her life she showed an unusual unity of purpose and ever conscientiously endeavoured to practise the doctrines which she had adopted. " Though her life was a romance, her character was prosaic. But her superiority consisted not in rare qualities, but in the possession of a high degree of those which are common to the majority of sensible persons." She was indeed worthy of being termed one of the most remarkable women in French history.

Louis' political interests remained as keen as ever, . and in one of his last letters he urged Philip V. to support the claims of the Pretender. With that chivalry which had led him to recognise the Pretender's claim to the English throne on James II.'s death, Louis again after the death of Anne seemed to be gradually preparing to re-assert by arms the claims of the Stuarts against the Hanoverian *régime*. But before steps could be taken which might have had momentous effects upon the fortunes of England, the aged King was no more. On August 11th he had written a letter to Philip, and after that day he never left his rooms. He met death with firmness and courage. His advice to his great-grandson showed an appreciation of his own errors. " Try," he said, " to keep peace with your neighbours : I have been too fond of war; do not imitate me in that, nor in my too great expenditure." He seemed conscious of the serious blunder made in the expulsion of the Huguenots, for he declared that the clergy were mainly responsible. On August 26th, addressing the Cardinals Berry, Rohan, and Le Tellier, he said that he died in the faith of the Church, then he added that he was grieved to leave the affairs of the Church in the condition in which they then stood, that they knew that he had only done what they wished, and that they had to answer before God for all that he had done. Madame de Maintenon was most constant, and sometimes nursed him for fourteen hours without a break. On August 26th, Louis himself begged her "to leave him and not to return, as her presence affected him too much." She remained almost all the 27th by the King's bedside. In the evening of the 28th she went to Saint-Cyr, but she spent most of the 29th with the King. On the 30th the King was worse, and bidding farewell to the Princesses and to Madame de Maintenon, he ordered the latter "to repair at once to Saint-Cyr." On September 1st the Great Monarch breathed his last.

In Spain the news of his death was received with more feeling than in France, where everyone was looking forward to a new *régime*. For fifteen years Louis had consistently supported Philip with counsel and with armies. It was to French assistance that Philip owed his throne and his ability to stand against a European coalition. It was due to Louis' advice and aid that Spain entered upon that new period of her existence, which culminated in the reign of perhaps Spain's greatest king, Charles III. Finally, it was under the influence of Louis that the system of political alliance between the two countries was inaugurated. It might be expected, then, that

28

Spain, which owed its regeneration to Louis, should receive the news of his death with some appearance of sorrow.

In France the event was marked by universal rejoicing. The absolute monarchy of France had already passed its zenith; with Louis' death it entered upon a period of steady decline. The central administration had indeed done much for France, but too high a price can be paid for uniformity and bureaucracy. The cries of joy which greeted the news of Louis' decease expressed perhaps unconsciously the general sentiment in favour of greater freedom of life and thought, and a widespread desire for some change. For the moment France was weary of military glory, she was suffering from the exhaustion produced by the late war, she was rent by religious divisions. Of Louis' great contemporary, the Emperor Aurungzib, who had lately died, it has been said: " Every plan that he formed came to little good; every enterprise failed." This *dictum* might accurately describe Louis' internal policy. In contrast to his foreign policy his home policy had been a grand failure. Painfully and methodically Louis had throughout his life done what he conceived to be his duty. " His ministers," says Michelet, " might change or die; he, always the same, went through his duties, ceremonies, royal fêtes, and the like with the regularity of the sun which he had chosen as his emblem." He had marked out for himself a path, and in the full belief that he was acting for the best interests of his country, had steadfastly pursued it. His scheme of government was an impracticable one for the France of the eighteenth century, and the universal gladness which welcomed the Regency showed that men recognised that absolutism was unsuitable for the new age. Louis made himself responsible for all the acts of his government. Though his successors—so unfit to rule—undoubtedly aggravated the existing evils in France, he must share with them the blame for the internal condition of his country during the greater part of the eighteenth century. When he died the principle of royalty had already received unconsciously a severe blow, and it would have required a very able succession of kings to restore that feeling towards the monarchy which had existed in France till within a few years of Louis' death. Still it would not have proved an insuperable task for an able and popular sovereign. The doctrine of the Divine Right of Kings remained unquestioned in France, the instinct of royalty was strong among the French people. The birth of the Duke of Burgundy had been the signal for the wildest rejoicing, and it was evident that the sentiment of loyalty was as yet little weakened. In spite of the disasters of the Spanish Succession war, and in spite of the King's age and the desire of the mass of the nation for a change, the reverence for the kingly office existed with almost unabated force.

Louis died convinced of the value of religion, and fully conscious of the sacred character and solemn responsibilities of royalty.

THE END.

INDEX.

Heroes of the Nations.

EDITED BY

EVELYN ABBOTT, M.A., FELLOW OF BALLIOL COLLEGE, OXFORD.

A SERIES of biographical studies of the lives and work of a number of representative historical characters about whom have gathered the great traditions of the Nations to which they belonged, and who have been accepted, in many instances, as types of the several National ideals. With the life of each typical character will be presented a picture of the National conditions surrounding him during his career.

The narratives are the work of writers who are recognized authorities on their several subjects, and, while thoroughly trustworthy as history, will present picturesque and dramatic "stories" of the Men and of the events connected with them.

To the Life of each "Hero" will be given one duodecimo volume, handsomely printed in large type, provided with maps and adequately illustrated according to the special requirements of the several subjects. The volumes will be sold separately as follows:

Cloth extra $1 50
Half morocco, uncut edges, gilt top . . . 1 75

The first group of the Series comprises the following volumes:

Nelson, and the Naval Supremacy of England. By W. CLARK RUSSELL, author of "The Wreck of the Grosvenor," etc.

Gustavus Adolphus, and the Struggle of Protestantism for Existence. By C. R. L. FLETCHER, M. A., late Fellow of All Souls College, Oxford.

Pericles, and the Golden Age of Athens. By Evelyn Abbott, M.A., Fellow of Balliol College, Oxford.

Theodoric the Goth, the Barbarian Champion of Civilisation. By THOMAS HODGKIN, author of "Italy and Her Invaders," etc.

Sir Philip Sidney, and the Chivalry of England. By H. R. FOX-BOURNE, author of "The Life of John Locke," etc.

Julius Cæsar, and the Organisation of the Roman Empire. By W. WARDE FOWLER, M.A., Fellow of Lincoln College, Oxford.

John Wyclif, Last of the Schoolmen and First of the English Reformers. By LEWIS SERGEANT, author of "New Greece," etc.

Napoleon, Warrior and Ruler, and the Military Supremacy of Revolutionary France. By W. O'CONNOR MORRIS, sometime Scholar of Oriel College, Oxford.

Henry of Navarre, and the Huguenots in France. By P. F. WILLERT, M.A., Fellow of Exeter College, Oxford.

Cicero, and the Fall of the Roman Republic. By J. L. STRACHAN DAVIDSON, M.A., Fellow of Balliol College, Oxford.

Abraham Lincoln, and the Downfall of American Slavery. By NOAH BROOKS.

Prince Henry (of Portugal) the Navigator, and the Age of Discovery. By C. R. BEAZLEY, Fellow of Merton College, Oxford.

Julian the Philosopher, and the Last Struggle of Paganism against Christianity. By ALICE GARDNER, Lecturer on Ancient History in Newnham College.

Louis XIV., and the Zenith of the French Monarchy. By ARTHUR HASSALL, M.A., Senior Student of Christ Church College, Oxford.

To be followed by:

Saladin, the Crescent and the Cross. By STANLEY LANE-POOLE.

Joan of Arc. By Mrs. OLIPHANT.

The Cid Campeador, and the Waning of the Crescent in the West. By H. BUTLER CLARKE, Wadham College, Oxford.

Charlemagne, the Reorganiser of Europe. By Prof. GEORGE L. BURR, Cornell University.

Moltke, and the Founding of the German Empire. By SPENSER WILKINSON.

Oliver Cromwell, and the Rule of the Puritans in England. By CHARLES FIRTH, Balliol College, Oxford.

Alfred the Great, and the First Kingdom in England. By F. YORK POWELL, M.A., Senior Student of Christ Church College, Oxford.

Marlborough, and England as a Military Power. By C. W. C. OMAN, A.M., Fellow of All Souls College, Oxford.

Frederic the Second, the Wonder of the World. By A. L. SMITH, of Balliol College, Oxford.

Charles the Bold, and the Attempt to Found a Middle Kingdom. By R. LODGE, M.A., Fellow of Brasenose College, Oxford.

Alexander the Great, and the Extension of Greek Rule and of Greek Ideas. By Prof. BENJAMIN I. WHEELER, Cornell University.

G. P. PUTNAM'S SONS

NEW YORK
27 WEST TWENTY-THIRD ST.

LONDON
24 BEDFORD ST., STRAND

The Story of the Nations.

MESSRS. G. P. PUTNAM'S SONS take pleasure in announcing that they have in course of publication, in co-operation with Mr. T. Fisher Unwin, of London, a series of historical studies, intended to present in a graphic manner the stories of the different nations that have attained prominence in history.

In the story form the current of each national life is distinctly indicated, and its picturesque and noteworthy periods and episodes are presented for the reader in their philosophical relation to each other as well as to universal history.

It is the plan of the writers of the different volumes to enter into the real life of the peoples, and to bring them before the reader as they actually lived, labored, and struggled—as they studied and wrote, and as they amused themselves. In carrying out this plan, the myths, with which the history of all lands begins, will not be overlooked, though these will be carefully distinguished from the actual history, so far as the labors of the accepted historical authorities have resulted in definite conclusions.

The subjects of the different volumes have been planned to cover connecting and, as far as possible, consecutive epochs or periods, so that the set when completed will present in a comprehensive narrative the chief events in the great STORY OF THE NATIONS; but it is, of course, not always practicable to issue the several volumes in their chronological order.

The "Stories" are printed in good readable type, and in handsome 12mo form. They are adequately illustrated and furnished with maps and indexes. Price, per vol., cloth, $1.50. Half morocco, gilt top, $1.75.

The following volumes are now ready (March, 1895):